Making Sense of Social Situations

How to Run a Group-Based Intervention Program for Children with Autism Spectrum Disorders

Albert J. Cotugno

Jessica Kingsley *Publishers*
London and Philadelphia

First published in 2011
by Jessica Kingsley Publishers
116 Pentonville Road
London N1 9JB, UK
and
400 Market Street, Suite 400
Philadelphia, PA 19106, USA

www.jkp.com

Library of Congress Cataloging in Publication Data
Cotugno, Albert J.
  Making sense of social situations : how to run a group-based intervention program for children with autism spectrum disorders / Albert J. Cotugno.
    p. cm.
  Includes bibliographical references and index.
  ISBN 978-1-84905-848-3 (alk. paper)
 1. Autism spectrum disorders--Patients--Rehabilitation. 2. Autism in children--Patients--Rehabilitation. 3. Group psychotherapy for children. I. Title.
  RJ506.A9C685 2011
  362.198'9289152--dc22
                              2010047565

British Library Cataloguing in Publication Data
A CIP catalogue record for this book is available from the British Library

ISBN 978 1 84905 848 3

Printed and bound in Great Britain

Contents

Part III The Use of Group Interventions in the Treatment of Individuals with Autism Spectrum Disorders (ASD): The Social Competence Enhancement Program (SCEP)   103

Part IV Social Competence Enhancement Program (SCEP) Tasks and Activities *with Cheryl Desautels*   187

List of Figures

List of Forms*

*Available for download at www.jkp.com/catalogue/book/9781849058483

Acknowledgements

If you can look into the seeds of time,
And say which grain will grow and which will not,
Speak then to me.

Macbeth, William Shakespeare, 1623

All those players who were instrumental in making my first book happen have similarly been there to support and encourage me through this second one. Many thanks again to Peter Szuch and Michael Cauley whose straightforward and practical advice and input kept me from getting too far off the mark, and to Scott McLeod, Director of MGH/YouthCare, where many of these thoughts took shape. Last and most important, this book is a tribute to my family, for no effort like this could proceed without the support of those we live with in our hearts every day; to my spouse, Debra Levine, and to my now-adult children who are doing great things of their own, Rebecca and David.

Also, I am most grateful to Cheryl Desautels who worked diligently on the development of the specific tasks and activities. Many more were developed, but only those considered most useful and critical were included here. Thanks also go to the staff of Jessica Kingsley Publishers who guided this project to completion and whose support was much appreciated.

In completing this second book, I came to understand the value of being surrounded by a dedicated, conscientious, intelligent, and highly ethical community of colleagues, friends, and family. I would therefore like to acknowledge all those who share a passion for helping and understanding others, especially children in need and especially individuals with ASD.

Preface

Autism Spectrum Disorders (ASD) are a cluster of developmental disorders referred to as Pervasive Developmental Disorders (PDD) that appear in children at or soon after birth and are characterized by significant and pervasive impairments in critical areas of development, including language and communication skills, typical behavioral skills and interactions, and social interactive abilities. While some children may be impaired in only a single area, others may exhibit problems across a broad range of development. Currently, the Centers for Disease Control and Prevention (2009) report that, in studies of broad cohorts of eight-year-old children across the United States, combined data indicate that 1 in 110 children is currently being diagnosed with some form of ASD, making ASD one of the most common disorders of childhood.

In a previous book (Cotugno 2009), a context and model for understanding ASD was presented together with a group-based approach to address and manage several prominent issues that interfere with social interactions and communications. This book further elaborates and details this approach and how to construct and implement a group-based intervention that focuses on social competence and social skills. In Part I, a review of the historical context and of diagnostic issues is provided, followed by a discussion and understanding of the social aspects of these disorders. Part II provides a review of the key components of the model with emphasis on core areas and core variables that must be addressed in ASD. Part III describes a model for group interventions for individuals with ASD which is referred to here as the Social Competence Enhancement Program (SCEP). This program is grounded within a stage-based, cognitive-developmental approach which makes maximum use of peer interactions, group therapeutic principles, cognitive-behavioral techniques, and direct skill instruction.

Part IV provides extensive examples of the group tasks and activities that make up SCEP. These tasks and activities address the specific stages of group development and the core areas and related deficits in ASD as they emerge in group work with children with ASD. Tasks and activities are also presented in the logical sequence in which they would be implemented in a group of children with ASD and in a format that makes for easy adjustment and accommodation based on the age, levels of functioning, and core variables needing to be addressed. The SCEP approach is a peer-group-based, interactive, therapeutic process aimed at developing and enhancing those social interactive and social communicative structures and skills of individuals with ASD believed necessary for growth and progress within a social world.

Part I
Autism Spectrum Disorders (ASD)

Part I provides an overview of issues timely and relevant to the study of Autism Spectrum Disorders (ASD). An historical perspective is presented to place ASD within the broader context of twentieth- and twenty-first-century thinking. This is followed by a review and history of definitions of ASD that have evolved. Finally, a theoretical and conceptual understanding of the use and integration of social competence and social skill development is provided within the context of understanding and managing ASD.

Chapter 1

ASD: A Brief History

Overview

Autism Spectrum Disorders (ASD) are a group of neurologically based disorders that significantly affect development in social, behavioral, and language/communication areas. ASD includes the diagnoses of Autistic Disorder (AuD), Asperger's Disorder (AD), and Pervasive Developmental Disorder–Not Otherwise Specified (PDD-NOS) which are considered to be part of the global category of Pervasive Developmental Disorders (PDD), due to their extensive, pervasive, and debilitating effects on the particular areas affected. At this time, the causes of these disorders are unknown and there are no known preventions or "cures." While ASD is believed to have neurobiological origins, its precise mechanisms are unknown and it is generally described and diagnosed based on behavioral and developmental features (National Research Council 2001). Although research into its origins and causes is ongoing, clear pathways to its understanding remain elusive.

Currently in most views, the set of ASD (AuD, AD, PDD-NOS) is conceptualized along a spectrum or continuum, regarding symptoms/characteristics, severity, and age of onset of symptoms/characteristics, for social, communicative, and behavioral issues. While there are clear common sets of symptoms and related behaviors, these may exist in a broad array of combinations, making diagnosis difficult.

Individuals with ASD exhibit a wide range of behaviors, often with significant variability from individual to individual. Although impairments in social interaction, communication, and repetitive and perseverative behaviors may be most obvious and prominent, other behaviors may be more subtle and variable. Individuals with ASD typically also have difficulties in one or more of the following areas: perseverative thoughts, persistent preoccupations; narrow, overfocused interests; high needs for routines and sameness; inflexibility and rigidity; poor anxiety management; poor perspective taking and theory of mind; clumsiness or poor fine or gross motor skills; sensory issues; attention problems; and inability to read or interpret nonverbal, social cues.

In this book, specific aspects of ASD are addressed, focusing primarily on significant impairments in social interaction, including an inability to understand and interpret nonverbal behaviors in others, a failure to develop age-appropriate peer relationships, a lack of interest or enjoyment in social interactions, and a lack of social or emotional reciprocity. In addition, there is also a focus on those concerns characterized by the presence of ongoing high levels of stress, tension, and anxiety and of repetitive and stereotypic patterns of behavior, interests, or activities, including intense and persistent preoccupations, a rigid or inflexible adherence to rituals or routines, and repetitive, stereotypic motor mannerisms.

This book focuses on individuals with ASD who function at the higher end of the ASD spectrum, which generally refers to those individuals with average or better cognitive abilities, no significant communication deficits, manageable behavior, and no significant mental illness. While this group is broad and diagnostically complex, these individuals share many characteristics and behaviors that can be addressed with the program and treatment interventions described here. The primary emphasis for this book is the basic inability of individuals with ASD to relate to and engage consistently in age-appropriate social interactions, particularly with peers. These individuals appear to lack the basic social competence necessary for the development of effective and successful interpersonal relationships with peers and significant adults.

For all individuals, the development of social competence depends on the interaction of inherent genetic and temperament characteristics, aspects of biological, physiological, cognitive, neurological, behavioral, and emotional development, and social experiences. In neurotypical development, social competence evolves from the development and interaction of several different aspects of social development, including the ability to recognize and understand a social situation, the ability to initiate a social interchange, the ability to understand its content and move it forward, and the ability to respond to the range of stimuli available from both other individuals involved and specific aspects of the situation or environment (i.e. engage in and follow a discussion or play activity in an appropriate setting). In essence, social competence consists of the capacity to engage in a reciprocal process of shared experience with another individual or individuals (Shores 1987) while communicating on many verbal and nonverbal levels and understanding context, situation, and environment. While extremely complex in nature, this process includes the capacity to attain and maintain developmentally appropriate levels of social recognition and awareness, social interest and motivation, social comprehension, memory, learning, social skill development, and social-emotional affective states (e.g. sympathy, empathy). Social competence is the result of ever-changing and evolving experiences across a wide range of development affecting one's capacities to understand and to interact with other human beings.

While social competence relates to the ability or capacity to engage successfully in social interaction, social skills, on the other hand, are the actual tools or skills that enable the social interaction itself to proceed and to work smoothly. Social skills are the tools an individual uses to initiate, to engage, to communicate, and to respond to others when involved in an interchange. In other words, social competence is the ability and capacity to engage in a reciprocal social interchange (consisting of the underlying structure necessary to recognize, acknowledge, engage, and follow through in the situation), while social skills provide the actual ways in which the individual performs in this situation (e.g. makes eye contact, says hello, asks a question, listens and formulates a response, arranges a subsequent meeting, says goodbye).

Some individuals with ASD lack many or all aspects of social competence, some possess few or no social skills, and many struggle with a variety and range of combinations of social competence and social skill deficits. The approach described here attempts to systematically assess the social abilities and skills of the individual with ASD and to place them thoughtfully in a social situation (i.e. small group, peer-based, structure-based, skill-focused, and adult-monitored situation) where the individual's social competence and social skill needs can be addressed. While individuals with ASD may benefit from a variety of different types of interventions (Klin and Volkmar 2000), it is believed that the core deficit in social interaction can be best addressed by focusing both on social competence and social skill development within a group setting with peers and monitored as needed by adults. This setting provides the environment for learning about and understanding the process of reciprocal social interchange and learning the skills needed to engage others successfully, while at the same time experiencing relationships, connections, and emotional experiences as part of a therapeutic group environment.

In this environment, related to both the individual within the group and the group as a whole, a cognitive-developmental model is adhered to at each point in this process. Development is viewed as experiencing and learning through stages and within each stage of development, building systematically an understanding of the individual's own and the group's capacities and abilities to engage, then teaching the relevant skills to interact effectively and in age-appropriate ways with peers in natural settings. This book will describe the group model developed which operates within a cognitive-developmental framework and which makes use of group therapy principles, peer-based interactions, structured cognitive-behavioral techniques, and skill-based instruction.

Definitions and diagnostic criteria related to ASD and PDD

Autism Spectrum Disorders (ASD) are considered to be neurologically based disorders of unknown origin that have gained increasing attention and interest of professionals recently. Particularly over the past decade, dramatic increases in the incidence and prevalence of ASD in the United States have been reported with most recent estimates ranging as high as 1 in 110 (Centers for Disease Control and Prevention 2009) and as high as 1 in 210 for children with Asperger's Disorder (AD) (Ehlers and Gillberg 1993; Kadesjo, Gillberg and Hagberg 1999). Overall, prevalence reports range from 0.3 to as high as 70 per 10,000 children (Fombonne 2003) and, on average, reflect a nearly 1300 percent increase over a ten-year span (1992–2002) of children classified with ASD who receive special education services (Center for Environmental Health, Environmental Epidemiology Program 2005).

Within the *Diagnostic and Statistical Manual of Mental Disorders*, Fourth Edition (DSM-IV) (American Psychiatric Association 1994), the most widely used manual for diagnostic classification, particularly within the United States, the diagnostic category of Pervasive Developmental Disorders (PDD) contains disorders characterized and defined by severe, serious, and pervasive impairments in several areas of development, including reciprocal social interaction skills, language and communication skills, or the presence of restricted, stereotypic, repetitive behavior, interests, or activities, providing sharp and marked contrast from the appropriate development in these areas by normally developing individuals. The DSM-IV category of PDD includes Autistic Disorder (AuD), Asperger's Disorder (AD), Pervasive Developmental Disorder–Not Otherwise Specified (PDD-NOS), Rett's Disorder, and Childhood Disintegrative Disorder (CDD).

Rett's Disorder and CDD, however, are both disorders associated with progressive loss of functioning and of skills that had previously been attained within the first few years of life as well as with severe mental disability. Both are low-incidence, rarely seen disorders, with Rett's Disorder known to occur only in females. Although both are of unknown origin, each appears to have strong neurological and genetic components, and the appropriateness of their placement within the PDD category remains controversial. While currently included as PDD, neither Rett's Disorder nor CDD is considered part of the autism spectrum.

ASD is considered a subcategory of PDD (see Figure 1.1) and includes AuD, AD, and PDD-NOS. These three diagnoses constitute the "autism spectrum" with AuD at one end, including lower-functioning individuals, and AD at the other end, including higher-functioning individuals. PDD-NOS appears to fall somewhere in the middle. In addition, each diagnosis itself also appears to operate on a continuum or range of functioning with lower-functioning individuals at one end and higher-functioning individuals at the other end.

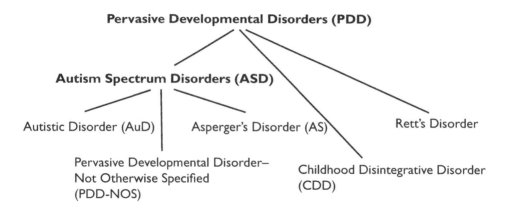

Figure 1.1 Pervasive Developmental Disorders (PDD) and Autism Spectrum Disorders (ASD)

Autistic Disorder (AuD)

AuD is a term used to describe individuals who demonstrate marked impairment or abnormal development in the three main areas of social interaction, communication (functional and/or pragmatic), and range of activities and interests (i.e. restrictive, stereotypical, repetitive, self-destructive). In DSM-IV, AuD is defined by 12 criteria, four each within the categories of social interaction, communication, and repetitive and stereotyped patterns of behavior, interests, and activities. To obtain a diagnosis of AuD, an individual must meet a total of at least six criteria. These six criteria must include at least two problems from the category of social impairment. Impairments in social interaction are defined by: difficulties with nonverbal behaviors such as eye-to-eye gaze, facial expression, body postures, and gestures to regulate social interaction; difficulties with developmentally appropriate peer relationships; an inability to spontaneously seek or share enjoyment, interests, or achievements with other people; and problems with social or emotional reciprocity.

The total of six criteria must include at least one deficiency from the category of communication. Deficits in communication are defined by: the absence or significant delay in the development of spoken language; significant difficulty in initiating or sustaining conversation; stereotypic, repetitive, or idiosyncratic language usage; and the absence of developmentally appropriate spontaneous pretend or social imitative play.

Finally, in meeting the minimum of six criteria necessary for a diagnosis of AuD, at least one deficiency must be present from the category of restricted, repetitive, and stereotyped patterns of behavior, interests, and activities. These deficiencies include: an intense and overwhelming focus or preoccupation with one or more stereotyped and restricted patterns of interest; an inflexible adherence to routines or rituals; stereotyped and repetitive motor mannerisms; and persistent focus or preoccupations with parts of objects. In addition, delayed or abnormal functioning must have been demonstrated by the individual in at least one of these three categories (social interaction, communication, or symbolic, imaginative play) prior to the age of three. Approximately 75 percent of AuD individuals appear to function in the range of mental disability, while 25 percent appear to be functioning at average or higher levels. Thus, at one end of the AuD continuum would be individuals with significant social interaction problems, significant communication or language delays, and restricted, repetitive, and stereotyped, even self-destructive, patterns of behavior and who may also experience significant, even profound, cognitive deficiencies. At the higher end of the AuD continuum would be individuals with less significant social interaction difficulties (e.g. possibly meeting only two of four DSM-IV social interaction criteria), less severe communication delays (e.g. possibly meeting only one of four communication criteria), and fewer or less intense restricted, repetitive, or stereotyped behaviors (e.g. possibly meeting only one of four behavioral criteria), and who may not possess any delays in cognitive functioning.

Those individuals diagnosed with AuD who are capable of functioning cognitively and intellectually at average or higher levels are often described with High-Functioning Autism (HFA) (DeMyer, Hingtgen and Jackson 1981). While HFA is not a diagnostic category in itself, it serves to help differentiate levels of functioning within AuD. However, the term also creates confusion in places where there appears to be overlap of HFA/AuD and AD.

Asperger's Disorder (AD)

AD is considered one of the ASD which involve individuals functioning at the higher end of the spectrum and generally with higher levels of competence in all of the key areas of functioning (social interaction, language/communication, patterns of behavior). While AD is considered a part of the autism spectrum, by definition it requires compliance in only two of three main categories required for AuD, those involving impairment in social interaction and the development of restrictive or repetitive patterns of behavior, interests, and activities. It is considered "milder" relative to AuD. In AD, there is typically no indication of functional language impairment (e.g. mechanics), although pragmatic language may be deficient, and there are no indications of significantly impaired intelligence or cognition. AD is thus considered to exist at the high end of the spectrum, including many individuals who are bright, verbal, and often high-achieving (Wing 1988). In DSM-IV, an AD diagnosis would apply only if the criteria of other PDD are not met. Most often this requires assessing the onset and presence of any specific communication or language deficits and whether this then requires consideration within the category of AuD. In DSM-IV, AD is defined by eight criteria, four each within the categories of social interaction and of restricted, repetitive, and stereotyped patterns of behavior, interests, and activities. To obtain a diagnosis of AD, an individual must meet at least six of the eight criteria. These six criteria must include at least two problems from the category of social impairment. Impairments in social interaction are defined by: difficulties with nonverbal behaviors such as eye-to-eye gaze, facial expression, body postures, and gestures to regulate social interaction; difficulties with developmentally appropriate peer relationships; an inability to spontaneously seek or share enjoyment, interests, or achievements with other people; and problems with social or emotional reciprocity.

In meeting the minimum of six criteria necessary for a diagnosis of AD, at least one deficiency must be present from the category of restricted, repetitive, and stereotyped patterns of behavior, interests, and activities. These deficiencies include: an intense and overwhelming focus or preoccupation with one or more stereotyped and restricted patterns of interest; an inflexible adherence to routines or rituals; stereotyped and repetitive motor mannerisms; and persistent focus or preoccupations with parts of objects. These must cause clinically significant impairment in social, occupational, or other important areas of functioning.

Pervasive Developmental Disorder–Not Otherwise Specified (PDD-NOS)

When full criteria are not met for one of the specific PDD (e.g. AuD, AD), but there is significant and pervasive impairment in one or more of the areas of social interaction, communication, or restrictive, stereotypic patterns of behavior, then a default category of PDD-NOS may be applied.

In DSM-IV, PDD-NOS is defined as severe and pervasive impairment in one or more of the three areas of social interaction, communication, and restricted, repetitive, and stereotyped patterns of behavior, interests, and activities. To obtain a diagnosis of PDD-NOS, an individual must meet criteria in one or more areas which include social interaction (at least two of the four criteria), communication (at least one of the four criteria), or restricted, repetitive, and stereotyped patterns of behavior, interests, and activities (at least one of the four criteria), but the individual must not meet criteria for another specific PDD (e.g. AuD, AD). PDD-NOS remains a somewhat ambiguous category used for individuals who do not clearly fit into any other PDD category. PDD-NOS symptom clusters are also more likely to include a mix of criteria that span the entire symptom continuum (e.g. profoundly impaired to high-functioning) and cover a broader range across the autism spectrum (e.g. autistic-like to Asperger-like), depending on the number and severity and extent of impairments.

Since the SCEP approach described in this book places primary emphasis on impairments in social interaction, individuals with PDD-NOS are included in the group interventions described only if there is significant impairment in social interaction or social interchange with generally adequate cognitive abilities. By definition, all AD individuals would be considered appropriate for this approach given the absence of language or communication deficits but the presence of impairments in social interaction with restricted, stereotypic, and repetitive thoughts or behaviors. Individuals with AuD would be included only if they have adequate communication skills and function at a high level, typically characterizing these AuD individuals as HFA. To best use this group-focused approach, basic functional language and communication skills are necessary and considered in the group placement process. Figures 1.2 and 1.3 provide descriptive ranges for the primary symptom clusters and for the related symptom clusters for ASD.

Communication	
Phonological/syntactic language	
Low/impaired	High/effective
Delayed, Absent	Well-developed speech
Not communicative	Effective communication
Pragmatic/semantic language	
Low/impaired	High/effective
Pedantic, verbose, literal	Abstract/complex language
Does not understand nonverbal communication	Understands/uses nonverbal communication
Social	
Lack of responsiveness	Appropriate social skills
Unusual social patterns	Social reciprocity
Social isolation, no friends	Friends and social networks
Behavior	
Rigid/inflexible	Flexible/makes transitions
Prefers objects to people	Approaches peers to play/engage
Circumscribed interests	Varied and broad interests
Highly repetitive behaviors	Flexible/frequent shifting

Figure 1.2 Primary symptom clusters for ASD

Cognitive-intellectual abilities				
Profound/severe impairment	Mild/moderate	Low Average	Above average	Superior
Attention				
(Focused, sustained, selective, flexible)				
Inattentive				Very attentive
Joint attention				
Inattentive				Very attentive
No eye contact				Consistent eye contact
Motor				
Motor integration deficits	Clumsy			On-target motor skills
Emotional				
Highly anxious/very stressed				Manages stress/tension effectively
Dysregulated				Well adjusted, regulates effectively
Sensory				
Sensory overload				Experiences flexibly/effectively
High thresholds/sensitivities				Normal thresholds
Onset of possible PDD				
Within first year	Three years	Six years		Eight years +

Figure 1.3 Related symptom and behavior clusters for ASD

While there is general consensus around the definition of AuD, there is more confusion and controversy around other ASD, such as AD and PDD-NOS, as well as the gray areas where the PDD overlap. For example, several definitions have been developed and used by different researchers in the study of AD. Volkmar *et al.* (2004) identified at least five different definitions for AD currently in use. Nevertheless, the most widely used criteria continue to be the DSM-IV and the *International Classification of Diseases*, Tenth Edition (ICD-10) (World Health Organization 1993). However, since multiple definitions have remained in use, this confusion and controversy remains centered upon the most appropriate diagnostic criteria and where these criteria overlap and intersect with AuD. Most importantly, this in turn has made it difficult and confusing to understand previously completed and current research and outcomes where different diagnostic criteria have been applied.

Brief historical background of ASD
Early developments

In 1908, a Swiss psychiatrist, Eugen Bleuler, introduced the term "schizophrenia" into the psychiatric/psychological nomenclature and two additional concepts to explain it: ambivalence—the ability for mutually exclusive contradictions to exist side by side within the psyche—and autism—a detachment and loss of contact with reality, "a withdrawal of the patient to his fantasies, against which any influence from outside becomes an intolerable disturbance" (Bleuler 1951, first published 1916). Bleuler used the term "autism" as a way of describing a specific type of social withdrawal that he observed in schizophrenia—that is, a near complete withdrawal from social interaction and relationships and a turning in to oneself to the exclusion of the world around oneself.

Although Bleuler worked primarily with adults, his descriptions of schizophrenic disorders were also applied to children by others (Bender 1952; Caplan 1955; Mahler 1952). At that time, the term "autism" was being used primarily to describe the process of withdrawal and detachment observed and a collection of symptoms related to it, specific to particular types of serious mental disorders. For a significant amount of time, the terms "childhood schizophrenia" and "early infantile autism" were used interchangeably, as it was the appearance of significant withdrawal and detachment from the real world that was viewed as the hallmark of serious infantile and childhood disturbance. This was seen primarily as a function of a mental (i.e. emotional) disorder which at the time was considered to have its origins in factors related to constitutional, familial, and environmental breakdowns.

At that time, there were few organized systems of diagnostic classification for children (Rie 1971). The earliest systems did not differentiate schizophrenia or psychosis from autism, and severe disorders of childhood were limited to infantile psychosis or childhood schizophrenia (Santangelo and Tsatanis 2005). Leo Kanner (1957), who wrote the first textbook in English on child psychiatry in 1937, considered autism an early form of childhood schizophrenia traceable to maternal influence (Alexander and Selesnick 1966). As research and theories expanded the understanding of the role of mother–child relationships (Bender 1952; Bowlby 1952; Klein 1954; Mahler 1968) and considered biological, physiological, and genetic factors as well as social, cultural, and emotional connections, Kanner shifted his views of autism toward an understanding of it as a genetic and organic disorder (Kanner 1957, 1958). It was in this context that Kanner, while working at Johns Hopkins Hospital in Baltimore, reported detailed descriptions of children he was observing and working with who presented with problems and disturbance from birth. These problems resulted in a particular and clearly observable constellation of symptoms, different from those of childhood schizophrenia, including unusual, detached, withdrawn, unpredictable, often uncontrollable behaviors. Kanner's description of 11 children focused on the core issues he described as autistic aloneness, an insistence on sameness, and islets of ability. He introduced the label "early infantile autism" or "childhood autism" to describe these children and to separate this category diagnostically from childhood schizophrenia (Kanner 1973, first published 1943).

The autistic aloneness that Kanner described included what appeared to be a total shutdown from outside stimulation that was characteristic of these children, apparently replaced by versions of their own internal world, presumably safer and better fitted to the child's needs and less psychologically demanding. The insistence on sameness that Kanner described was reflected in the repetitive and stereotypic movements, behaviors, verbalizations, and preoccupations that often dominated these children's interactions with the world. Kanner's reference to islets of ability provided descriptions of children with a range of abilities that included many with profound cognitive deficiencies to those with average or higher intelligence, advanced vocabulary, and excellent memory. He observed this range as occurring within several different areas of cognitive functioning.

Following Kanner's description, other views began to emerge and to consider broader, non-emotional considerations and causes, including the view that organicity and genetics may play a dominant role in the development of Kanner's autism. Overall, Kanner's work formed the basis for our current understanding of autism and the subsequent use of the term "autism" in its modern sense. His description of children with early infantile autism emphasized the self-absorption, withdrawal, and social detachment that he observed, yet disagreed with the view of many at the time that these children were demonstrating a psychotic or schizophrenic reaction or disorder or that they were reacting primarily as a result of emotional, familial, or environmental factors.

Kanner's 1943 article, entitled "Autistic Disturbance of Affective Contact," published in the now-defunct journal *Nervous Child*, defined early childhood autism as consisting of:

1. "an extreme autistic aloneness that, wherever possible, disregards, ignores, shuts out anything that comes to the child from outside and includes a profound lack of affective contact with other people"

2. "anxiously obsessive desire for the preservation of sameness"

3. "a fascination for objects," but used only for repetitive activities

4. unusual, repetitive, pedantic language "not intended to serve interpersonal communication"

5. "islets (islands) of ability" (e.g. special skills, such as pensiveness, memory, motor skills, music, math).

Kanner's original diagnostic criteria for autism (1943) were modified in 1956 (Kanner and Eisenberg), noting several additional features apparent in many but not all of these children, which he considered important to the diagnosis but not of primary importance. These additional features included:

6. impairment in nonverbal and social communication

7. a lack of coordinated motor movements (gross and/or fine motor) and a sense of clumsiness

8. repetitive, stereotypic movements

9. a range of unusual sensory experiences and needs

10. mimicking of others in non-deliberate and non-malicious ways

11. poor behavioral regulation, often in response to disruption of routine or fixed patterns or to unusual arousal levels.

In discussing the 11 children he included in his article, Kanner described these children as having "come into the world with innate inability to form the usual biologically provided affective contact with people" (Kanner 1973).

At essentially the same time, Hans Asperger, a pediatrician at the children's clinic of the University of Vienna, published a paper describing similar types of children as Kanner. His sample of four boys, taken from a representative group of 200 children he had worked with, described children who were unable to interact socially and exhibited repetitive and stereotypic behavior, but were capable of astounding achievements outside of their social inadequacies. He (as Kanner had done) used the term "autistic" to describe these boys' inabilities to connect and relate to the social world around them.

Asperger's paper, entitled "Autistic Psychopathy of Childhood," was published in German in 1944, but was known to few outside the German-speaking world until Lorna Wing referred to it in her research on autism in the late 1970s. It was subsequently translated and published in English (Asperger 1991) in Uta Frith's book on Asperger's Syndrome (Frith 1991). Asperger described "autistic psychopathy" as consisting of:

1. a "disturbance in social integration"

2. pedantic, peculiar language and the absence of reciprocity

3. impaired nonverbal and social communication

4. repetitive, stereotypic patterns of activities and play

5. isolated areas of special skills and interests.

Asperger also made mention of several additional areas of concern, including:

6. good vocabulary and excellent logical thinking

7. unusual sensory responses and experiences

8. poorly coordinated movements and clumsiness

9. poor behavioral self-regulation.

Asperger described these children he studied as having "a common fundamental disturbance...of contact" with other individuals with whom they came in contact (Asperger 1979, 1991). Asperger's paper is strikingly similar to Kanner's in many ways. They both described children who were unable to integrate themselves socially or to form appropriate social relationships with others, and who demonstrated unusual repetitive and stereotypic patterns of language, behavior, and movement.

> Both [Kanner and Asperger] recognized as prominent features in autism the poverty of social interaction and the failure of communication; highlighted stereotypic behavior, isolated special

interests, outstanding skills and resistance to change; insisted on a clear separation from childhood schizophrenia;… On all the major features of autism Kanner and Asperger are in agreement. (Frith 1991, p.10)

By the 1960s, autism was being viewed primarily as a completely separate syndrome from other childhood mental disorders, likely with genetic rather than emotional origins, demonstrated by significant impairments in several areas, including language and communication, social interaction, imagination, reality responses, and motor movements. Following renewed interest in ASD in the late 1970s and 1980s, multiple sets of criteria for ASD were published (Frith 1991; Gillberg 1983; Szatmari, Bremner and Nagy 1989; Wing 1981), including Kanner's (Kanner and Eisenberg 1956) and Asperger's (Asperger 1979) own modifications.

Later developments

In 1981, Lorna Wing, working in Great Britain, described 34 cases of children and adults with autism whose profiles of abilities appeared to have great resemblance to those described by Asperger (1991). Wing subsequently used the term "Asperger's Syndrome" to describe a new diagnostic category (Wing 1981). Wing observed many children who did not fit current descriptions of the autistic child, but who still appeared to fit within the broadest definitions of autism. For these children, she used the term "autistic continuum" which later she adjusted to "autistic spectrum." This allowed for a wide range of descriptions and symptoms related to autism to be included, based on where on the continuum the individual was considered to exist, using nine different criteria, each ranging from profound to mild (Wing 1991). Thus, at the lower end of the spectrum were the severely autistic individuals with profound disability, no or quite poor language or communication, very limited capacity to interact or engage with others, repetitive, ritualistic, or stereotypic behaviors and verbalizations, and the absence of imaginative, flexible, symbolic play and thinking. At the other, higher end of the spectrum were those considered as high-functioning autistic individuals (HFA), with average to superior intelligence, appropriate and often advanced language development, but with peculiar, pedantic, and odd usage of language, very limited to quite variable capacity to interact or engage others in appropriate social interactions, and generally some form of repetitive, stereotypic, or ritualized behavior or area of interest.

1908	Eugen Bleuler	Introduces the term "schizophrenia", which he describes using the concepts of ambivalence and autism.
1938	Hans Asperger	Publishes first paper describing "autistic psychopathy" observed at Children's Hospital in Vienna.
1943	Leo Kanner	Publishes paper describing 11 boys with "disturbances of affective contact" at Johns Hopkins in Baltimore.
1944	Hans Asperger	Publishes paper extensively describing "autistic psychopathy" in four boys observed at children's clinic at the University of Vienna.
1978	ICD-9	World Health Organization officially lists Infantile Autism as a diagnosis in the *International Classification of Diseases*, Ninth Edition.
1980	Hans Asperger	Dies on October 21.
1980	DSM-III	Infantile Autism included for first time in the *Diagnostic and Statistical Manual of Mental Health Disorders* within a new category of Pervasive Developmental Disorders, distinct from psychotic disorders.
1981	Leo Kanner	Dies on April 4.
1981	Lorna Wing	Uses the term "Asperger's Syndrome" for first time, considering it one of several entities within ASD.
1981	DeMyer, Hingtgen and Jackson	Use of the term "High-Functioning Autism" for the first time.
1987	DSM-III-R	Infantile Autism diagnostic label changed to Autistic Disorder.
1988	London	First international conference on Asperger Syndrome.
1988	Lorna Wing	Uses the term "autistic continuum" to define the range of possible autism disorders, ranging from profound to mild.
1989	Christopher Gillberg	Publishes a set of diagnostic criteria for AD which emphasize obsessional and narrow patterns of interest; revises these criteria in 1991.
1989	Peter Szatmari	Proposes diagnostic criteria for AD which emphasize social isolation.
1991	Hans Asperger	1944 paper is translated into English for the first time and published in Uta Frith's edited book, *Autism and Asperger Syndrome*.
1993	ICD-10	Diagnostic category for PDD expanded from two diagnoses (AuD, PDD-NOS) to five, adding Rett's, CDD, and, for the first time in DSM, AD.
1994	DSM-IV	Follows ICD-10 in expanding PDD category to five diagnoses, including AuD, AD, and PDD-NOS.
2013	DSM-V	Planned revision of DSM with significant changes to PDD category discussed.
2015	ICD-11	Planned revision of ICD-10.

Figure 1.4 Significant developments in the history of ASD

Wing used the term "Asperger's Syndrome" to identify this high-functioning group of individuals with ASD who demonstrated the "triad of social impairments" Wing had observed—impairments in social relationships, communication, and make-believe play—differentiating this group from the traditional autistic and HFA groups, but acknowledging that AD was still likely one of several categories within the "autistic continuum" (Wing 1988). Wing's (1981) descriptions of individuals along the autism spectrum are the most detailed. As a result of her own research and review of the available autism and AD literature, she initially provided a triad of behavioral symptom manifestations necessary for an ASD diagnosis, requiring:

1. impaired social relationships

2. impaired communication

3. impaired make-believe play.

These criteria were later modified (Wing 1991) to include:

1. impairment in social reciprocity

2. unusual, odd, pedantic, and stereotypic speech

3. poor nonverbal and facial communication

4. insistence on repetition and sameness

5. specific, often highly narrow, interests

6. poor motor coordination.

And modified further with the addition of impairments in:

7. social imagination

8. sensory inputs

9. repetitive, stereotypic movements.

In addressing broader ASD issues, Wing expanded her list to include criteria typically seen in varying degrees in individuals falling on the autistic continuum. Each criterion exists within a range from profound impairment to no impairment. Although she places primary emphasis on the triad of social impairments, she asserts the importance of understanding other variables, including their severity, in understanding these individuals and in making proper and appropriate diagnosis.

Interest in autism research and what came to be known as "autism spectrum disorders" moved rapidly forward through the latter part of the twentieth century, focusing primarily on diagnostic issues, causal factors, subtypes and classification, and treatment and intervention models. Works by Michael Rutter, Eric Schopler, Leo Kanner, Uta Frith, Christopher Gillberg, Fred Volkmer, and Lorna Wing were particularly influential during this time.

Later diagnostic issues

Infantile autism was officially recognized and adopted by the World Health Organization in 1978 in the *International Classification of Disease*, Ninth Edition (ICD-9) manual (World Health Organization 1978) and by the American Psychiatric Association in 1980 in the *Diagnostic and Statistical Manual of Mental Disorders*, Third Edition (DSM-III) (American Psychiatric Association 1980) with later modifications in DSM-III-R (American Psychiatric Association 1987). At that time, DSM-III, DSM-III-R, and ICD-9 contained a main category of Pervasive Developmental Disorders (PDD) with two subcategories of Infantile Autism (the term used in DSM-III)/Autistic Disorder (AuD) (the modified term used in DSM-III-R) and Pervasive Developmental Disorder–Not Otherwise Specified (PDD-NOS). PDD-NOS was a category used for any individuals who did not meet full criteria for AuD but were still considered to have a PDD.

At the first international conference on Asperger's Syndrome held in 1988 in London, a group of key figures in the autism/Asperger's field were unable to reach consensus on diagnostic criteria (Szatmari 1991) and, alternatively, several proposed their own diagnostic criteria applying to ASD (Gillberg 1991; Gillberg and Gillberg 1989; Szatmari *et. al* 1989; Wing 1991).

In revisions of ICD-10 in 1993 and DSM-IV in 1994, both manuals adopted a broader categorization of PDD, continuing to highlight AuD's central place, but including an additional four diagnostic categories, Asperger's Disorder (AD), PDD-NOS, Rett's Disorder, and Childhood Disintegrative Disorder (CDD). The publication of ICD-10 and DSM-IV also marked the initial inclusion of AD in a published diagnostic manual.

Despite the inclusion of AD in DSM-IV as a PDD distinct from AuD and PDD-NOS, a consensus has never been reached regarding the criteria used to classify or differentiate AD from higher-functioning forms of autism (e.g. HFA). Many clinicians have continued to conceptualize AD as a mild variant of autism (Ghaziuddin, Leininger and Tsai 1995) and to continue to view AD as a spectrum disorder rather than to view it from a categorical perspective (Attwood 2007; Leekham *et al.* 2000) as found in DSM-IV.

In summary, definitions for ASD include a varying combination of criteria but always address impairments in social interaction, communication (verbal and nonverbal), and behavioral issues (e.g. restricted, repetitive, stereotypic behavior; rigid adherence to routines; restrictive, narrow interests). Impairments in motor issues, sensory inputs, or imaginative/pretend play are included in some but not all criteria sets. Questions regarding diagnostic categorization and nomenclature and diagnostic distinctions have yet to be answered satisfactorily and further research and study must continue to address and clarify these issues. Future revisions of DSM (i.e. DSM-V, scheduled for release in 2013) may provide some clarification of these issues.

Chapter 2

Socialization, Social Competence, and Social Skills

Individuals with ASD are described by a range of difficulties and problems relating to social interactions. They may appear aloof and disconnected, they may ignore others, they may be unaware of physical boundaries and invade the space of others, they may be annoying, confrontative, even aggressive, with others. The list of potential social interactive difficulties and problems for the individual with ASD is long. From the perspective of individuals with ASD, they may feel misunderstood, constantly criticized, isolated, alienated, ignored and left out of group activities, scapegoated and targeted, and frequently frustrated and discouraged. They are reported to experience more social isolation and loneliness (Bauminger, Schulman and Agam 2003), higher sensitivity to criticism (Wing 1981), and a greater risk for dysthymia and depression (Ghaziuddin, Ghaziuddin and Greden 2002; Szatmari 1991).

Overview

Socialization is a critical process in human development, but in the individual with ASD it presents as a significant and problematic core deficit in ASD. In neurotypical development, the socialization process includes two interrelated concepts of development:

1. social competence: the capacities and abilities to recognize, understand, and engage in appropriate reciprocal interchange with one or more individuals

2. social skills: the actual tools or learned skills for appropriate social interactions and social communication.

Social competence relies on innate capacities and acquired abilities, and relates to the underlying structures and processes present in the individual and necessary for subsequent development. Social competence provides the foundation on which further development can proceed. Social skills are the mechanisms through which individuals actually carry out a reciprocal social interchange. They are specific tools or skills needed for the socialization process to move forward and for meaningful relationships to be attempted and to succeed. For human beings, social competence provides the capacity to learn socialization skills—that is, the "legs" on which individuals can move forward—while social skills are the tools and techniques—the actual process of "learning to walk."

Early development

Most children with ASD suffer from some degree of impairment in social interaction. This may involve impairment in social competence—the underlying processes necessary for further development—in social skills—the tools necessary for the social interchange to actually occur—or the combined effects of the impairments in both social competence and social skill development. Because children with ASD will differ, often dramatically, from one child to the next in the degree and extent of their social impairments, there is no "typical child with ASD." In terms of social impairments, children with higher levels of severity and lower levels of functioning will be more noticeable at an early age, often during the first year of life. This may include the child's inability or unwillingness to make appropriate eye contact, to respond to a parent's smile or facial expressions, to track interesting objects or loud sounds in his environment, to seek physical contact or cuddling, or to initiate interactions with the world outside of himself. He may appear distant, disinterested, or disengaged in the social contacts that most other children thrive on.

However, it is not uncommon for children who are higher-functioning on the autism spectrum (i.e. HFA, AD, some PDD-NOS) to appear quite typical in their interactions during infancy and early childhood. This may relate to the low severity, low frequency, or reduced need for expression of the behavior. It may appear as if the child is choosing not to respond (i.e. has the ability, but "chooses" not to implement), is not sufficiently motivated to respond (i.e. another sibling readily initiates for the child), has few opportunities to respond (i.e. limited number of individuals involved in his day-to-day activities), or the child's responses may be considered within the range of normal functioning for that age (i.e. "he will play with legos all day if you let him").

With children on the higher end of the autism spectrum, language development may occur early and is often advanced, making these children appear more "mature" at young ages, when, in fact, social competencies and/or social skills may be quite limited, overshadowed by their competencies in language usage and vocabulary skills. By preschool, unusual or deficient social interactions are typically noticed in broader, peer-based environments and brought to parents' attention. This may include a range of possible behaviors, including stilted, pedantic, or idiosyncratic language, solitary play, a lack of understanding or empathy for others, or an inability to make or maintain friendships.

With the highest-functioning individuals with ASD, it is not unusual for social problems to go undetected until entering elementary school settings. Given the range of differences between ASD children, they may be considered only as quirky, a bit odd or unusual, as loners, or just as socially inept. With the more recent increased interest and attention and emphasis on early screening, the average age of diagnosis of ASD has dropped considerably to approximately four and a half years old (National Foundation for Autism Research 2010), although for individuals on the higher end (e.g. AD), it continues to be later (Attwood 2007).

Common social concerns reported by parents/caretakers during the early stages of the social developmental process and by school personnel of children ultimately diagnosed with ASD often include:

1. lack of attachment and "bonding"

2. poor eye contact or an eye gaze that fails to follow the parent/caretaker

3. failure to greet or respond to the parent/caretaker spontaneously

4. failure to seek out parent or others for comfort

5. little or no expression of emotion or inappropriate expression of emotion

6. failure to understand "personal space."

Later in development, other behaviors reported by parents/caretakers and school personnel of children ultimately diagnosed with ASD include:

7. failure to attend or to "connect" in social relationships

8. aloofness from or disinterest in social relationships

9. lack of empathy or concern for others' feelings or emotions

10. lack of social reciprocity

11. lack of social imagination

12. dislike of team sports or activities.

In addition, parents of children with ASD generally report a range of behaviors quite different from those normally reported by parents/caretakers of neurotypically developing children, including:

13. child does not seek out parent/caretaker to engage in play

14. bedtime routines become highly ritualized and lack comfort and nurturance

15. child gets "stuck" on tasks or activities and cannot let go

16. child blurts out whatever he may be thinking

17. child is frequently taken advantage of, teased, bullied, or victimized.

While there is growing research in many of the areas that contribute to successful social interaction (e.g. facial recognition, joint attention, empathy, theory of mind, imagination), there is no clear understanding why these impairments in social interactions occur in children with ASD. Nevertheless, they clearly present significant barriers for children with ASD in managing and coping with the social world they must exist within. Helping children with ASD to understand their own profile of strengths and limitations, to understand the world around them, and to manage social interaction and social interchange effectively are the primary goals of the interventions described in this book. In this context, social development from the perspective of normal development and from the perspective of the individual with ASD is described.

Social cognition
Normal social development follows a generally consistent and systematic path beginning at birth. Much attention, particularly over the past 50 years, has been paid to the origins and developmental pathways of social development and social competence. There is strong emerging data supporting the view that newborn infants demonstrate significant capacities for the perception,

initiation, and direction of early physical and social interactions, and from birth are processing and responsive to significant amounts of sensory (visual, auditory, etc.) information. These newborn behaviors include facial expressions, imitations, and behaviors which initiate, encourage, and reinforce social interactions with their surroundings. Evident within the first year of life, the child is capable of performing an ever-increasing series of necessary developmental tasks (e.g. exploration, sharing, fantasy), influenced by parental, familial, and environmental reactions and responses (Bowlby 1952). In this way, many of the child's innate social abilities and social-emotional response patterns are shaped by these interactions of the child's personality and temperament with caretakers, family members, peers, and other environmental influences.

It is this process of normal social development that results in increasing social and reciprocal interactions, which meet the needs of both the child and his caretakers and which appears to be absent or derailed for the individual with ASD. In contrast to the neurotypical child, the child with ASD may lack the capacity to establish and sustain eye contact, may not be capable of using facial expressions to convey feelings and emotions, may not be able to create verbalizations that appropriately match or fit with the social situation, and may not accurately interpret or understand the nature and meaning of interactional cues given to them by others. Many of these factors, such as the absence of eye contact/eye gaze, facial misperception (Klin *et al.* 2002), inattention, inappropriate verbalizations, misinterpretation of verbal and nonverbal cuing, and other social interactional breakdowns (Barry *et al.* 2003; Klin *et al.* 2002) have been reported as core deficits in ASD contributing directly to the social impairments seen in individuals with ASD.

It is clear from birth that social development requires experience with consistent and ongoing two-way reciprocal interactions, with the ways each individual in the interaction responds to the other determining the depth and quality of the interchange. With repetition, maturity, and development, the interactions should become more detailed, complex, and sophisticated. While the child with ASD may be capable of perceiving and processing the requests for socially appropriate interchanges (e.g. "Mother is smiling at me"), he may lack the capacity to respond spontaneously in kind (e.g. look when his name is called, smile when someone smiles at him) (Dawson *et al.* 1998), or be delayed in his responding (possibly a cognitive processing problem), thus altering the social interchange (i.e. the other individual does not receive the expected and socially appropriate response), derailing the reciprocal process. When this aspect of social development (i.e. social reciprocity) is derailed from an early age, the individual's ability to learn and benefit from all the social interactions and interchanges that will subsequently occur will be severely limited.

As children grow and these social exchanges and social interactions increase, evolve developmentally, and are reinforced, they are increasingly employed and more selectively used, as they are fine-tuned to fit the individual's needs and environment. Providing a foundation on which subsequent language and cognitive-development can grow, social interaction takes its prominent place as a necessary and critical piece of developmental growth and maturity.

It appears that children with ASD may follow a different developmental path from neurotypical, non-ASD children (Barry *et al.* 2003), although current research is not yet clear on this issue, partly due to the significant variability from individual child to child with ASD and the ongoing controversy over diagnostic differentiation and categorization. This path for many children with ASD begins with what appears to be normal social development, usually for the first year or two of life, then abruptly stalls, usually within the second or third year of life. However, for others, development may appear derailed from birth.

The developmental path for both the neurotypical child and the child with ASD, however, is dependent upon the innate capacities for socialization that the child is born with (i.e. the underlying structures or processes), enabling development to move forward through a consistent and relatively predictable series of stages which include the acquisition of social skills appropriate to the child's age and stage. If the innate developmental capacities of a child are derailed, either prior to birth, at birth, or in the first years of life, then the developmental path will be altered and changed, dependent upon the specific capacities the child does possess to progress through developmental stages as they are confronted. When one considers the population of individuals with ASD as a whole, there is no specific developmental path that emerges as fixed or consistent, and wide variation within this group and between individuals occurs.

Nevertheless, for both the neurotypical child with adequate innate developmental capacities and the child with derailed or deficient aspects of social development, subsequent social competence will depend on the child's abilities (or inabilities) to learn and develop the necessary social skills and tools for effective social interaction and social communication. Clearly, for the child with ASD, who may possess limited innate developmental capacities, the socialization and social learning process will be extremely difficult.

Stages of the socialization process

Normal socialization in most individuals follows a predictable pattern of development that includes a fixed set of stages beginning at birth. Each stage consists of a series or cluster of learning experiences and interactions with objects, individuals, and groups, providing a foundation for subsequent experiences and interactions to take place. While the experiences and interactions within each stage are qualitatively different from one stage to the next, they are reliant on the development that occurs in previous stages. Thus, both development and progress or deficits and derailment at one stage will affect all subsequent experiences and interactions occurring at later stages. Understanding the socialization process, its developmental flow, and its movement through stages provides a basis for understanding and treating issues that arise with children with ASD within a group-based setting.

Stage 1

In the first days and months following birth, infants respond and react to both internal and external stimuli in their environment with the sole purpose of getting their basic needs met. As they grow and develop and as their basic needs are met in a consistent and predictable manner, they respond more actively to an ever-growing range of sensory and social stimuli. They learn to attend to and progressively differentiate sounds, faces, and types of interactions (e.g. friendly vs. hostile). The beginnings of basic trust in others, particularly caretakers who respond to their needs, develop during this stage.

Stage 2

By the second half of the first year of life, infants have begun a sophisticated process of imitation of sounds, simple acts, and gestures, as a form of engaging and connecting with others. This process takes on an increasingly more active function as the child is no longer responding passively to another's initiations but actively soliciting the attention and involvement of others through his own actions and behavior. The beginnings of solitary play as a means of learning about the world can also be seen emerging as another way of learning about and exploring one's environment. The beginnings of an individuation process take hold and solidify during this stage.

Stage 3

By the second year of life, toddlers now become mobile *and* active in seeking out increasing amounts of external stimulation and social contact. They begin to actively respond and adapt to others' needs and to cooperate in joint tasks and activities. Solitary play no longer appears completely satisfactory as engaging others in parallel play begins to take precedence, and being with others and seeking their attention become paramount. During this stage, the child's sense of autonomy increases and differentiates from the control imposed solely by others.

Stage 4

By early childhood, social interactions increase at a dramatic rate as connections begin to extend beyond the family to self-initiated social contacts and interactions with others. Children begin to seek out groups of other children, particularly similar-age peers, as a preferred social situation to solitary play, and primitive friendships begin to develop and take root. Adults are seen in the role of authority, as providers and as protectors, but also as those from whom the child seeks independence in early stages of autonomy. Self-initiative, more complete autonomy and sense of self, and imagination develop rapidly during this stage.

Stage 5

By later childhood, self-control, independence, autonomy, and social networks become the central forces of social interactions. Social acceptance, particularly within groups, is highly valued and sought after and becomes a necessity for further social maturity and development to take place. Recognizing and understanding one's strengths and weaknesses occurs in increasingly more realistic ways and influences development and interactions during this stage.

Stage 6

By adolescence, the capacity for true friendships, meaningful interactions, mutual reciprocal interchanges, social intimacy, and empathy has evolved. While there may emerge an increased interest in independence and solitude, there is also an increased interest in the development of a set of individual and group values and standards apart from parental and adult authority, at times triggering a rejection of adult value systems. Developing a true sense of one's personal identity, both as an individual and as part of groups, emerges during this stage.

Stage 7
Entering adulthood brings a level of maturity and intimacy to relationships and the capacity for long-term meaningful connections with others. These are highly valued and cherished and seen as goals as they provide a springboard further into mature phases of adulthood (e.g. marriage, career, parenthood).

Social competence
In neurotypical development, as the individual progresses through stages, he experiences varied and multiple levels of complexity in interactions, learns in a variety of different environments and situations, learns to understand and integrate emotional reactions within a social context, and, with learning and experience, makes decisions and choices regarding specific responses (i.e. behaviors, language, thoughts, sensory reactions, etc.) dependent on the individual's knowledge and understanding of what is occurring in a specific interaction, exchange, or situation. The level of social competence attained is dependent on the individual's ability to progress through these social developmental stages, making use of the range of experiences and interactions that occur within each stage as he progresses forward. Within the process of attaining social competence, an individual acquires the ability to recognize situations that involve social interaction, the ability to initiate a social interchange, the ability to understand its content and meaning so that it is able to progress and move forward, and the ability to respond selectively and appropriately to the situation based on what is observed, processed, experienced, and understood (i.e. engage in and follow a discussion or play activity). In summary, social competence is the capacity to engage in a reciprocal process of shared experience and interaction with another individual or individuals (Shores 1987). Although extremely complex in nature, this process includes the capacity to move through stages of socialization while learning, refining, and mastering a broad range of social interactions, and to attain and maintain developmentally appropriate levels of social recognition and awareness, social interest and motivation, social comprehension, memory, learning, social skill development, and social-emotional affective states (e.g. sympathy, empathy). Social competence provides the foundation and capacities to learn and make use of specific social skills.

In essence, the development of social competence is embedded within the progression through stages of socialization. It involves the presence of innate capacities for socialization, the developmental thrust pushing for increased social contact, adequate and sustaining parental, familial, caretaker, and environmental experiences matching stage-based social needs, and the capacities to learn and retain needed skills. In a group-based approach, each of these issues must be considered and addressed as the group is constructed, as individual and group goals are formulated, and as tasks and activities are planned, and modified on a regular basis.

Social skills

Social skills are defined as complex sets of behaviors that allow an individual to engage in positive, mutually reciprocal, and beneficial social interactions (Gumpel 1994). Possessing a range of social skills may allow the individual to initiate, maintain, manipulate, or solidify a social interaction, thereby creating a "social relationship." This may also have secondary gains of improving social status (Odem and McConnell 1985).

As one traverses the developmental path toward social competence, skills specific to each stage are learned (e.g. effective skills are retained, ineffective skills are discarded), then modified and integrated as the individual moves on to the next stage and the next and so forth. Social skills are the learned behaviors an individual uses to initiate, to engage, to communicate, and to respond to others when involved in a social interaction. The socially competent individual is aware of the existence of a social situation or impending social interaction and recognizes the level of the need and has the ability to engage in a reciprocal social interchange (the underlying structure necessary to recognize, acknowledge, and implement in a social situation). Possessing and using the appropriate social skills to follow through successfully with a social interaction (e.g. make eye contact, say hello, ask a question, listen and formulate a response, arrange a subsequent meeting, say goodbye) is the final step in the development of social competence.

Individuals with ASD all appear quite unique with social capacities that extend across a broad range of social competence and social skill strengths and deficits. In general, however, most individuals with ASD suffer from a significant degree of social impairment that may include some combinations of significant social competence deficits and social skill deficiencies. With an understanding of this process, assessment of the skill deficits of the individual with ASD can proceed in order to construct an adequate intervention plan.

While some individuals with ASD lack many or all aspects of social competence, and thus social skills will be unable to develop appropriately, some possess sufficient social competence for the acquisition of some limited skills. However, many struggle with a broad range and variety of social competence and social skill deficits. The approach described here attempts to systematically assess the social abilities and skills of the individual with ASD and to place them thoughtfully in a social situation (i.e. small group, peer-based, structure-based, skill-focused, and adult-monitored situation) where the individual's needs can be addressed. Although individuals with ASD benefit from a variety of different types of interventions, it is believed that the core deficit in social interaction can be best addressed by focusing on social competence and social skills development within a group setting with peers, monitored by adults. This setting provides the environment for learning about and understanding reciprocal social interchange and learning the skills needed to engage others successfully, while at the same time experiencing relationships, connections, and emotional experiences as part of a group.

Specific social competencies and social skills targeted will relate to the individual's specific needs which are assessed and considered during initial assessment described in Chapter 14 and elaborated in the goal-setting process described in Chapters 13 and 14.

Social competencies viewed as essential for appropriate social development and which appear necessary in order to build adequate social skills include:

1. recognition and understanding of the need for social interchange and the inherent complexity of social interchange

2. acknowledgement of the need and importance of experiencing and understanding what it means to be part of a group

3. development and enhancement of the capacity to create and sustain meaningful interpersonal relationships with others, especially peers

4. effective employment of the range of self-based functions, such as self-awareness, self-management, self-regulation, self-control, and insight

5. management and control of the stress and tension involved in approaching and interacting with others in social situations

6. sufficient development and functioning of attentional capacities, particularly those required for appropriate social interaction, such as joint attention

7. the capacity to consider and tolerate thoughts, behaviors, and emotions of others so as to remain open and flexible in interactions with others

8. the capacity to be open and flexible in our thinking, behaviors, and emotions so as to allow others to join us in social interchange

9. the capacity to move smoothly from one thought, issue, topic, action, or emotion to another without difficulty (i.e. rigid adherence, undue stress or tension, distractibility, disturbance of emotions)

10. recognition of sensory experiences when they occur and understanding how they impact and influence social interactions

11. the capacity to understand and appreciate the thoughts, behaviors, and emotions of others as they occur in a range of personal and interpersonal situations (also described as having *theory of mind*)

12. recognition and management of emotions that arise in social interactions and understanding how they impact the social relationship.

Focusing on the building and enhancement of social competence as the foundation for social skill development provides an approach for the explicit teaching of necessary social skills. With an emphasis on group-based approaches that stress the development of the underlying social competence abilities, methods that teach the necessary social skills must include aspects of the following:

1. The social skills to be taught must be defined and connected to overall social competence.

2. The social skill must be broken down into simple steps that can be easily learned, practiced, and repeated in different situations.

3. Each skill or set of skills must be directly connected to individual and group goals as constructed within the group.

4. There must be adequate opportunity for modeling by peers to enhance learning and reinforcement.

5. Mastery and success of the social skill must be adequately understood, integrated with other behaviors and interactions, and reinforced.

6. Behaviors which inhibit social interaction must be targeted for reduction and extinction.

7. Multiple strategies to complete a social skill interaction must be developed and implemented.

8. Skill instruction is considered dynamic, ready to be changed or modified at any point, to meet the needs and goals of the group.

9. Individual and group goals which focus on specific social skill development are evaluated systematically and progress assessed.

10. Those social skills selected and taught must emphasize carryover and generalization to real-life situations outside the group.

With the development of appropriate social competence, the list of social skills contained in Figure 2.1 is viewed as only a small sample of the range of skills that may be targeted as essential for appropriate social development.

Entering a group
  introductions of self
  initiating a conversation
  maintaining a conversation (conversational skills)
  expressing interest in others
  following directions
Initiating and expanding discussions using personal information and preferences
  soliciting personal information from others
  sharing personal information relevant to the topic or discussion
  taking turns in conversation, activities, tasks, or games
  acknowledging points/information that others contribute
  following changes in topic
  offering an opinion or suggestion
Playing by the rules
Asking for help
Regulating the intensity and quality of one's interactions
  voice tone/voice volume
  facial expressions
Understanding and respecting body space
Cooperation
  sharing (of things that matter to the individual)
  compromise
  being a good sport
  apologizing
Giving and receiving compliments and encouragement
  giving and receiving criticism

Recognizing and using emotions in interactions
>   expressing feelings
>   assertiveness
>   disagreeing

Friendship
>   discussing and understanding what is a friend
>   discussing and understanding what is a friendship

Managing conflict and confrontation
>   confronting teasing, putdowns, or bullying in a group

Recognizing and interpreting verbal, nonverbal, and conceptual cues
>   understanding and using verbal interchanges
>   reading verbal signals
>   reading nonverbal signals

Using humor

Perspective taking
>   sympathy and empathy

Discussing and resolving decision-making issues

Discussing and resolving problem-solving issues

Exiting a group
>   ending a conversation

Dealing with loss, terminations, and goodbyes
>   recognizing the loss associated with goodbyes
>   expressing the loss associated with goodbyes
>   recognizing the feelings and emotions associated with goodbyes
>   creating memories to preserve the relationships
>   celebrating the loss, termination, or goodbyes
>   saving the loss, termination, or goodbyes
>   saying goodbyes

Figure 2.1 Selected social skills to be addressed

Part II
Understanding Individuals with Autism Spectrum Disorders (ASD)

Part II focuses on how to understand and address several key components that emerge in group interventions with individuals with ASD. First, general areas of functioning important for every individual's development are considered, but from the perspective of the individual with ASD. The focus here is on seven main areas of functioning, referred to as core areas. Each is described briefly. Specific core variables (often referred to in the ASD literature as core deficits) within each core area that relate specifically to the individual with ASD and appear most important are then defined and discussed.

Each of the core variables emphasized in this approach (self-regulation; emotion competence; stress and anxiety control and management; attention; joint attention; flexibility, change, and transition; perspective taking; and relatedness/empathy) is highlighted and described. While this is not assumed or intended to be an exhaustive list of possible variables that could be addressed, these variables in particular are considered of primary importance to address and manage if appropriate group and social interactions, social competencies, and social skills are to be acquired.

Each core variable is initially considered separately as it applies to individuals with ASD through a cognitive-developmental perspective. Issues of management and treatment are then considered and how they apply to the group-focused, peer-based, cognitive-developmental stage model that will be described in later chapters.

Chapter 3

The Core Areas of Development and Related Deficits of ASD

With its beginnings in gestation, human development is a complex process of interrelated functions that develop, change, and evolve, continuously moving toward increased differentiation and complexity and affected by genetic, familial, social, environmental, and behavioral factors. There are seven main areas of development that individuals proceed through from birth through the lifespan. Each of these areas may be discussed as if they proceed through their own individual path of development; however, most are reliant and dependent on several other areas for their capacity to proceed forward.

An understanding of the divergent pathways in development that often occur in ASD has not yet emerged, but advances in individual and in intersecting areas of development continue at a rapid pace. Within the SCEP model, fundamental areas of development, called core areas, are addressed as they relate to individuals with ASD, and an attempt is made to highlight key issues within each area that affect overall functioning.

Core areas are considered to be broad psychological-neurological domains that include within them many specific aspects of individual functioning. Core areas are not considered as separate or independent from one another, but rather as related and overlapping with one another. Within each of the seven core areas described here, several core variables are specifically addressed within each area and these are described and discussed later in Chapters 4–10.

In this stage-based cognitive-developmental model, the seven core areas of ASD considered are:

1. the social area

2. the emotion area

3. the cognitive/executive function area

4. the communication area

5. the behavior area

6. the sensory area

7. the motor area.

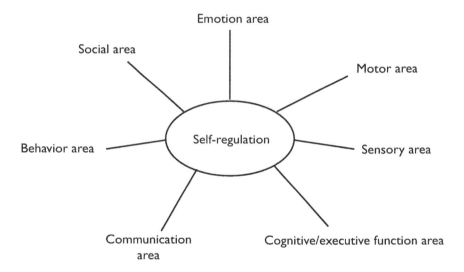

Figure 3.1 Core areas of development

The social area

Social development has been described and considered in detail, particularly as it relates to ASD, in Chapter 2. In that context, the development of social competence and the acquisition of social skills are addressed.

Social competence

The ability to recognize and respond appropriately to a social situation defines human interaction. For individuals with ASD, it is this core deficit in social interaction that undermines the ability to understand and to relate to others in appropriate and expected ways. In this approach, social competence is defined as a complex combination of cognitive, social, and emotional abilities which come together as a social situation or social interaction arises. It consists of the sets of abilities that make up an individual's "social intelligence" and that allow an individual to learn and acquire sets of social skills to use in social interactions.

For example, when an individual walking down the street is approached and addressed by another individual, a social situation has emerged and presented itself, calling upon the social competence of both individuals. How do they each assess and view the situation (positive/negative)? Do they know or recognize each other? Is there history to the interaction? What social skills does each possess? Are they lonely, busy/rushed, preoccupied, overwhelmed, upset/angry, etc.? The social competence or social abilities of each individual will provide him with the capacity to recognize and understand the nature of the situation. The social skills possessed by each individual will allow him to consider and formulate responses to the complex set of interactions (verbal and nonverbal) that may follow.

Key underlying capacities or variables determine the level of social competence attained by each individual and will become factors in how this situation is experienced and understood by each individual. Will one or both individuals be stressed or anxious about the interaction (emotional variables)? Will one or both be able to recall important information about a previous interaction (e.g. name, last time seen) (cognitive variables)? And will one or both engage in the proper or polite greeting (social variables)?

In this situation, it can be seen how social competence is a function of the combined cognitive, social, emotional, and communication capacities to adapt and engage in a spontaneous, socially acceptable, and mutually satisfying social interaction. In this way, social competence consists of the abilities to recognize, understand, and engage in a social interchange. The elements of social competence also provide an individual with sufficient capacities to acquire, learn, and implement sets of social skills necessary for successful and mutually rewarding, reciprocal social interchanges. Social competencies may include broad areas of functioning or they may be defined quite narrowly. Examples of broad social competencies (or structure or process) include stress and anxiety control and management, attention, flexibility, relatedness, self-control/

self-management, and perspective taking. Examples of narrowly defined social competencies include anxiety when meeting unfamiliar individuals, attention in a specific type of situation, joint attention only to certain individuals, memory for faces, and eye contact.

Social skills

While social competence relates to the underlying abilities or capacities for social interchange (e.g. attention to another individual, anxiety management), social skills are the sets of learned and acquired behaviors that allow individuals to "complete" a social interaction successfully. The implementation of social skills follows from the level of social competence the individual has attained. In the socially competent individual, the social interaction is perceived and understood accurately. In the socially competent individual, specific learned and acquired skills are employed in the social interchange, based on the individual's competence to read and "understand" the situation and on the individual's possession and availability of a range of social skills to be employed in any given situation.

Social skills may also refer to a broadly defined set of general skills or may be more narrowly and precisely defined. Examples of broadly defined social skills (more often sets of skills) include conversational skills, listening skills, attending to verbal and nonverbal signals, and using facial expressions. Examples of more narrowly defined social skills include saying hello, shaking hands, asking permission, waiting your turn, and acknowledging another's feelings.

The socially competent individual possesses:

1. the abilities to recognize, understand, and engage in a social interaction

2. sufficient learned and acquired social skills to engage another individual successfully and to "complete" a mutually reciprocal, mutually gratifying interaction with that individual.

The social area includes capacities for social competence and the acquisition of social skills, the ability to engage in and to conduct personal and interpersonal interactions appropriately and effectively, the ability to attract, develop, and maintain relationships and friendships, the ability to engage in appropriate behavior for a range of different types of social interactions and situations, and the ability to experience and express social emotions, including sympathy and empathy.

Impairment in social functioning is considered a core deficit in ASD and in many cases may be the most critical and debilitating area of concern for this group. While this area consists of numerous components directly related to and necessary for social interaction and functioning (e.g. listening skills, conversation skills, social comprehension), these components also overlap with other areas occurring alongside the social domain (i.e. initiating conversation—anxiety, an emotion component; listening skills—joint attention, a cognitive/executive functioning component). When considering the social area within this model, a focus is placed on key aspects of social competence, including the situation, the interchange, and the response, and the acquisition and development of related social skills. This requires recognition and understanding of the interrelated nature of the core areas and how an individual is constantly drawing upon competencies and skills from multiple core areas of functioning. The comprehension and understanding of social interactions and social situations requires a complex set of interrelated functions that must operate efficiently and in age-appropriate and developmentally appropriate ways. The social area is not an area that can be described simply by singling out one or two components, and in all situations components from other core areas will be involved, such as the cognitive/executive function area (e.g. processing information and formulating responses), the emotion area (e.g. emotion recognition, labeling, understanding, and regulation), and the sensory area (e.g. sensory and physiological feedback experienced in a pleasant or stressful interaction).

Relative to the social area and group functioning, two specific core aspects of social functioning and interaction (referred to here as core variables) were selected because of their importance in the process of recognizing, understanding, engaging in, and successfully negotiating the social interactive process. They are joint attention—the process of recognition, awareness, and connection with another individual or group—and relatedness—the process of "connecting" with others in an interaction or communication. While each of these core variables overlaps with other core areas, they are placed within the social area because they are considered primary, essential, and critical for social interactions to proceed effectively and successfully.

As with each core area, it is critical to review the parent, teacher, and professional information that is collected together with all interview data to obtain a comprehensive understanding of the nature and extent of any social impairment that may exist and how it affects functioning. This process is discussed in Chapter 14. Following this review, completion of the SCEP Individual Profile: Social Interaction Assessment (see Form 14.9) provides additional information to be considered, as necessary, in individual and group goal construction.

The emotion area

"It is impossible to separate the topics of social and emotional development as, for its very existence, the former depends on the latter" (McCandless 1967, p.436).

Most descriptions of early emotional development parallel those of social development (see Chapter 2). Earliest emotions are typically described as occurring within a social-interactive context (smiling, cooing, baby talk at 6–10 weeks; laughter at 3–4 months; separation anxiety at 7–12 months, etc.), and it is clear that emotional and social developments are intertwined. Early caregiver interactions provide cues regarding the type and quality of both emotional and social experiences that will influence the experience for the individual. These earliest caregiver–infant interactions demonstrate and model emotions and emotional displays, reinforce or extinguish certain emotional experiences and reactions, and encourage or discourage the expression or display of particular emotions.

By the end of the second year, emotions evolve in more developed and less primitive forms, and become more involved and intertwined in social experiences, particularly those outside of the caregiver–infant/toddler relationship. As language develops during the second year, communication (i.e. the labeling and expressing of emotions) becomes a significant aspect in the process of learning about and expressing emotions. As social interactions become more complex and sophisticated, they exert a strong influence on the development of emotions, particularly whether and how they are acknowledged, how they are expressed, and how they are managed and regulated.

By the third year of life, children are capable of recognizing and labeling a variety of different emotions, and this capacity grows significantly in the ensuing years. At the same time, the ability to understand and regulate emotions begins to develop and differentiate from other aspects of development. Ultimately within this social context, individuals proceed toward mature emotional development, involving the recognition and awareness, labeling and expressing, understanding, regulating, and integrating of emotional processes (Denham 1998). However, while emotional and social development are highly related areas and must be viewed as intertwined, they are still considered and in many ways operate as separate and distinct constructs (Denham *et al.* 2003; Rose-Krasnor 1997).

Within the SCEP model, the emotion area is considered to include capacities for recognizing, labeling and expressing, and understanding emotions in oneself and in others, for knowing how to respond to these emotions whether in oneself or in others, for assuming personal responsibility and self-control of one's emotions and related behaviors in individual or group situations, and for understanding the connections between emotions, self-control, and the specific situation one is in.

In its most basic way, emotional development relates to the experience, recognition, acknowledgement, labeling, understanding, and regulation of emotions (Denham *et al.* 2003). Typically, emotions are viewed as an internal state, generally abstract and not easily defined, but clearly experienced by individuals in unique ways and influenced by their genetic makeup, temperament, and experiences. The range of emotions capable of being experienced tends to increase and expand with age, development, and experiences. While emotions can be experienced by individuals when alone or isolated, emotions tend to be much more commonly and directly linked to social experiences and social interactions and, ultimately, to an individual's level of social competence (Rose-Krasnor 1997; Saarni 1990). It is in this intersection of emotions and social interactions that we address those emotional experiences necessary for group-based, social-interpersonal interactions to take place.

Although there are many theories about how emotions develop in humans, there is little understanding of how or why they become derailed in individuals with ASD. Certainly, that there is such variation in the emotional development of individuals with ASD (as well as in social, cognitive/executive function, and behavior areas) further complicates an understanding of this issue. While DSM-IV describes the absence of social reciprocity as diagnostic criteria for PDD/ASD, there is limited description of how to interpret or use this description. Otherwise, DSM-IV uses no specific emotional criteria to establish the presence or absence of a PDD/ASD diagnosis. Nevertheless, the issue of management and regulation of emotions is an important aspect to address, particularly given the high likelihood of comorbidity of mental health issues, such as anxiety and depression, for the PDD population (Leyfer *et al.* 2006; Tonge and Einfeld 2003). Numerous reports describe individuals with ASD as having difficulty accurately identifying emotions, particularly when multiple emotions are involved (Kuusikko *et al.* 2009), as more likely to perceive ambiguous emotional situations as negative (Kuusikko *et al.* 2009), as unable to express emotions clearly (Frith 1989), and as having difficulty recognizing and understanding emotions in peers (Ritvo 2006).

In the SCEP model, issues relating to the emotion area as they relate to social-interpersonal functioning and their fit within a developmental continuum are considered. Thus, basic emotional functions necessary for usual and typical interactions within a group setting or interpersonal interaction are addressed. In the intersection of emotional and social development, where emotions meet social interactions, two particular core variables are highlighted and focused upon: emotion competence, involving the recognition, labeling and expressing, understanding, and regulation of emotions, and stress and anxiety control and management, involving the ability to recognize and acknowledge, manage and cope with, and understand the effects of stress and anxiety on group and social-interpersonal interactions. These two variables were selected and are addressed because they appear early in emotional development and because they are regulators (i.e. controllers) of emotional and stress and anxiety experiences. The capacities to regulate, control, and manage self issues and emotions will very strongly influence and predict the nature and quality of the individual's social interactions. In the individual with ASD, these issues are frequently underdeveloped, poorly developed, or delayed, undermining the possibility of successful social interactions. As such, groups within the SCEP model are constructed so as to manage or address emotions and related issues as they affect ongoing functioning and development. They are not constructed to manage or address serious emotional issues or disturbance which would require separate comprehensive assessment, diagnosis, and intervention (e.g. neurodevelopmental evaluation, directed psychotherapy).

Within the SCEP model, emotion competence is defined as the ability to recognize, label, express, understand, and regulate the range of emotions experienced across a variety of situations and experiences in which they arise. Emotion competence additionally entails the need to conform with cultural, social, and personal expectations, employing a range of self-regulatory functions. Self-regulation within this model is defined as the ability to regulate, control, and manage the variety of one's experiences as they range from personal to interpersonal, concrete and specific to abstract, internal to external, and genetic to environmental. Self-regulation encompasses self-control, self-awareness, insight, and self-monitoring.

As with each core area, it is critical to review the parent, teacher, and professional information that is collected together with all interview data to obtain a comprehensive understanding of the nature and extent of any emotion impairment that may exist and how it affects functioning. This process is discussed in Chapter 14. Following this review, completion of the SCEP Individual Profile: Emotion Competence Assessment (see Form 14.4) provides additional information to be considered, as necessary, in individual and group goal construction.

The cognitive/executive function area

The cognitive/executive function area involves a range of cognitive capacities, necessary to engage in effective social-interpersonal interactions. These include attention (focused, sustained, selective, flexible, and joint), thinking, planning, memory, organization, decision making, problem solving, and self-monitoring/self-regulating. Elements of cognitive/executive functioning relate to an individual's ability to plan, organize, access memory, stay focused, think clearly, integrate, self-monitor, and follow through on informational demands in order to produce a final desired product (i.e. read, study, have a conversation, etc.). These aspects of cognitive/executive functioning focus primarily on process rather than skill functions. This area significantly overlaps with social, emotional, and communication elements in the management of social interactions, of emotions, of behavior, and of verbal and nonverbal responses.

In the area of cognitive/executive functioning, children with ASD are consistently reported to demonstrate a range of "splinter skills"—that is, relative strengths in the context of other weaker abilities (National Research Council 2001). A clear understanding of the cognitive strengths and weaknesses of the individual with ASD is necessary in order to specify core variables to focus upon. Information is obtained from a review of previous and current evaluations, clinical interview, and parent, teacher, and interviewer observations, and provides a profile that includes information from the following areas:

- verbal/language functioning
- nonverbal reasoning
- perceptual-spatial functioning
- visual discrimination/visual processing
- abstract and conceptual thinking
- attention
- memory
- speed of verbal and visual processing.

The obtained cognitive profiles (see Forms 14.14, 14.15, 14.16) should provide the group leader with a deeper and clearer picture of the individual's strengths and weaknesses and of how and where to address important issues as they arise in group-based situations (i.e. does the individual express himself clearly?, does the individual demonstrate adequate attention?, can directions be remembered?, are visuals and verbals required?, etc.).

One component within the area of cognitive/executive functioning consistently found to be of concern relates to the core variable of attention and its components. To assess thoroughly, it is necessary to obtain information on each aspect of attention—focused, sustained, selective, flexible, and joint attention—and to consider the role of each in the individual's overall functioning as it relates to group and interpersonal interactions.

Within group and interpersonal interactions, the abilities to focus, sustain, direct selectively, and shift attention flexibly are constantly called upon in the processing and management of relevant information. Successful and meaningful group and social interactions require the involvement and coordination of multiple aspects of attention working in synchrony.

Joint attention is considered in this model as a closely related but conceptually separate component of attention. While it is viewed as a developmental endpoint (see Figure 7.1) requiring elements of focused, sustained, selective, and flexible attention, it also occurs primarily within the context of social and interpersonal interactions. It is therefore considered primarily related to the social area of functioning, but with a clear and obvious grounding in the cognitive/executive functioning area.

Self-regulation within the context of cognitive/executive functioning is considered and addressed because of its importance in group social situations. As within other core areas, it is defined as the ability to manage, control, adjust, and regulate one's thinking, feelings, behavior, or interactions, and is considered as directly related to information processing; however, that information can arise from any one or combination of different areas, including cognitive, emotional, social, sensory, or motor areas, and thus requires integration and coordination, generally a cognitive/executive function task. As mentioned within the SCEP model, it is recognized that self-regulation occurs within each core area (see Figure 3.1), but, for purposes here, it is most important to address self-regulation as it occurs within and affects the cognitive area (thinking/behavior), the emotional area (feelings/behavior), and the social area (thinking/feelings/interactions).

As with each core area, it is critical to review the parent, teacher, and professional information that is collected together with all interview data to obtain a comprehensive understanding of the nature and extent of any cognitive/executive functioning impairment that may exist and how it affects functioning. This process is discussed in Chapter 14. Following this review, completion of the SCEP Individual Profile: Cognitive/Executive Function Assessment (see Form 14.10) provides additional information to be considered, as necessary, in individual and group goal construction.

The communication area

The communication area includes capacities for language acquisition and usage, such as verbal/nonverbal, expressive/receptive, and semantic/pragmatic. This includes: the ability to adequately and correctly use and understand structural and mechanical aspects of language, such as grammar, vocabulary, and articulation; to initiate, maintain, take turns in, and close a discussion; to select appropriate topics; to ask, listen, and respond to questions; to understand and interpret abstract, figurative, and literal language; to use appropriate tone and volume; and to understand and use different styles of speech appropriate to the situation.

The SCEP model typically deals with individuals with ASD who have acquired at least the basic mechanisms of language and who can engage in basic communication and conversation with others. However, it is the nature of that communication rather than the fundamental structural use of language that is considered most important here. Thus, the focus within the SCEP approach is not on the phonology (speech sounds) or syntax (rules of grammar) of an individual's language use; rather it is on an individual's semantic (understanding and creating meaning) and pragmatic (using language to communicate intent, purpose, and meaning) use of language. It is the semantic and pragmatic communications that are of constant and primary importance in peer-focused, group-based situations and interactions.

In group situations, the semantic and pragmatic language communications embedded within social interactions are particularly important and necessary to understand in order to respond appropriately to them. Therefore, a goal of this approach is to understand and assess the individual's semantic and pragmatic expressive and receptive language capacities as related to group and interpersonal interactions. Also within this cognitive-developmental model, the focus of groups with younger children emphasizes more interactive, nonverbal types of tasks/activities, while with groups of older children and adolescents primarily verbal-language forms of communication in tasks and activities are emphasized.

Communication difficulties have been consistently noted as primary impairments in many forms of ASD. Kanner (1973) and Asperger (1991) both emphasized these in their original papers and they remain a core feature of autism and to a lesser extent of any other PDD. The expressive and receptive language capabilities of individuals with ASD cover a broad range from a lack of basic language capacities to high-functioning language capabilities. The SCEP model described here is most appropriate for individuals with ASD who have acquired basic language skills (phonological and syntactic), but may have ongoing difficulties with semantic and pragmatic aspects of language involving understanding of meaning and intent of both language-based and nonverbal communications.

Paul and Wilson (2009) provide a useful description of communication as consisting of three domains: speech, language, and communication. Speech is considered "the expression of language through the use of sounds produced by oral gestures" (p.172), while language is considered "the formulation of ideas and messages through rule-based combinations of words" (p.172), and communication is considered to be the "forms of sending and receiving messages whether through use of spoken language, gestures, body language, written language, or sign language" (p.172). In this model and within the core area of communication, no particular core variables are targeted or specified. However, issues related to the domains of pragmatic and semantic communication are recognized and addressed. The assumption is made that phonological and syntactic communication (speech and language mechanics), if a serious concern for the individual, will significantly limit progress in a group-based intervention and must be specifically addressed elsewhere (e.g. speech and language therapy), prior to engaging in a language-emphasized group situation.

As with each core area, it is critical to review the parent, teacher, and professional information that is collected together with all interview data to obtain a comprehensive understanding of the nature and extent of any language impairment that may exist and how it affects functioning. This process is discussed in Chapter 14. Following this review, completion of the SCEP Individual Profile: Pragmatic Language Assessment (see Form 14.11) provides additional information to be considered, as necessary, in individual and group goal construction.

The behavior area

The behavior area as defined here includes the ability to recognize, manage, and control impulses and behaviors arising from an awareness and/or enforcement of demands and expectations in specific situations (i.e. in a group interchange, in a classroom discussion, on the playground). This ability to recognize, manage, and control behavior relates directly to the ability to recognize, label, and understand emotions, to the ability to communicate one's needs clearly and in comprehensive ways in these situations, and to the ability to recognize and understand the implications of responding to or acting out these behaviors upon others who may be directly affected. Thus, the control, regulation, and management of behaviors intersects with and requires the involvement of other core areas, such as cognitive/executive functioning (recognizing, understanding), social (in keeping with social, group, and interpersonal expectations), communication (expression), emotion (awareness of the "emotions" in the interaction), sensory (physiological and physical experiences), and motor (action/reaction, control/management, redirection/diffusion).

Within the behavior area, it is believed critical to possess the capacity to be aware of and to recognize a behavior as it emerges, to label it, to understand where it comes from (i.e. personal, interpersonal, or situational source), and to manage it appropriately given the situation. For the individual with ASD, this area encompasses behavior and functioning related to personal experiences and to interactions with the world as they fall within a range from developmentally immature and problematic to developmentally mature/age-appropriate and effective behavioral management. The main purpose here is to focus on behaviors related to ASD when they fall within the range of concern (i.e. problematic)—that is, to focus on behaviors that overlap, affect, and potentially interfere with effective peer, group-based interactions. It is believed that any behavior which negatively affects or interferes with positive peer interactions increases a child's risk for exclusion and isolation from social, educational, family, and community services (National Research Council 2001).

Within the SCEP group model, behaviors are recognized and labeled, then strategies are learned and practiced in the service of fostering control, management, and redirection/diffusion. Sets of tasks and activities are constructed so the child can recognize a behavior, develop an understanding of what is happening, and learn strategies to cope and respond, while developing his ability to self-regulate in group, interpersonal situations and experiences.

The primary core variable included within the behavioral area relates to self-regulation, the ability to slow down or stop one's immediate reaction in order to process (recognize, label, decide/problem-solve) available information, then to engage in a response (action) which appropriately meets the personal, interpersonal, and environmental demands of the situation. As said before, the core variable of self-regulation resides within each area, including the behavioral area, while at the same time it also significantly overlaps and intersects all other core areas.

As with each core area, it is critical to review the parent, teacher, and professional information that is collected together with all interview data to obtain a comprehensive understanding of the nature and extent of any behavior impairment that may exist and how it affects functioning. This process is discussed in Chapter 14.

The sensory area

Although individuals with ASD frequently present with sensory issues, these have not been clearly defined within this population and, as a result, they have not been specifically included as diagnostic criteria in DSM-IV (American Psychiatric Association 1994) or ICD-10 (World Health Organization 1993). While sensory issues are generally not included in diagnostic criteria of ASD, sensory experiences are recognized and acknowledged as playing a significant and often complicating role in the life of the child with ASD. Both Kanner (1973) and Asperger (1991) reported observing problems related to sensory processing in the children they studied and several others since then (Attwood 2007; Wing 1991) have included sensory issues in their diagnostic criteria as significant issues related to ASD. While it is well documented that unusual sensory reactions are common in individuals with ASD, the extent to which these are specific to ASD is not clear. Nevertheless, since sensory issues are common in ASD, and although they may not be clearly understood from a diagnostic perspective, it is important to consider their role in the overall functioning of the individual with ASD. While there are many individuals with ASD who process and experience sensory information accurately and effectively, there are also many other individuals with ASD with serious sensory concerns. For these individuals, their sensory experiences are likely to significantly affect and influence their ability to manage and function effectively in many core areas. In the consideration of sensory experiences, the key factor here would relate to whether these issues affect the individual's social and group interactions and how the individual can learn to recognize and manage them within the peer group situation.

The sensory area includes awareness, regulation, and management of a range of levels of sensitivity (physical, emotional, environmental, etc.), including the seven primary senses (tactile, visual, auditory, gustatory, olfactory, vestibular, and proprioceptive). Sensory processing allows the individual to experience, evaluate, and respond to information which enters through seven basic sensory systems: vision (visual), sound (auditory), touch (tactile), taste (gustatory), smell (olfactory), body awareness (proprioceptive), and balance (vestibular).

While sensory concerns are common with ASD, there is no specific pattern to which specific sensory systems may be dysfunctional. In general, reactions to sensory stimuli appear to be more intense at the most severe end of the autism spectrum and least intense, even absent, at the less severe end of the spectrum. Nevertheless, consideration of all systems with a focus on those which specifically influence and interfere with social and group interactions is recommended.

As with each core area, it is critical to review the parent, teacher, and professional information that is collected together with all interview data to obtain a comprehensive understanding of the nature and extent of any sensory impairment that may exist and how it affects functioning. This process is discussed in Chapter 14. Following this review, completion of the SCEP Individual Profile: Sensory Assessment (see Form 14.12) provides additional information to be considered, as necessary, in individual and group goal construction.

The motor area

The motor area includes large and small body and fine-motor capacities and includes coordination and integration of all motor skills. Individuals with ASD often exhibit motor issues and concerns, although, most commonly, they are generally described as subtle and not related to a primary motor deficit. These individuals are often described as clumsy, poorly coordinated, lacking good eye–hand coordination, poor in sports, or unable to learn to ride a bike, dribble a basketball, bat a ball, run and kick, etc. Individuals with ASD have been reported to demonstrate significant deficits in general gross-motor functioning (Provost, Lopez and Heimerl 2007), in running and walking gait (Vilensky, Damasio and Maurer 1981), in running speed, agility, balance, and bilateral coordination (Ghaziuddin *et al.* 1994), and unusual posture (Adrien *et al.* 1993). Some of these children may require evaluation and implementation of intensive interventions (e.g. physical therapy, adaptive education).

As with each core area, it is critical to review the parent, teacher, and professional information that is collected together with all interview data to obtain a comprehensive understanding of the nature and extent of any motor impairment that may exist and how it affects functioning. This process is discussed in Chapter 14. Following this review, completion of the SCEP Individual Profile: Motor Assessment (see Form 14.13) provides additional information to be considered, as necessary, in individual and group goal construction.

Chapter 4

Self-Regulation: A Core Variable

Self-regulation refers to the ability to manage, control, adjust, regulate, and direct one's thinking, feelings, behavior, or interactions in both a self-focused and an interpersonal process. The term "self-regulation" is used here to encompass the total process of management, control, adjustment/adaptation, regulation, direction, and monitoring. This process can relate to single areas of thinking (cognition), feelings (emotion), actions (motor), sensations (sensory), or interactions (social), or, as in most situations, relate to combinations of areas (e.g. using thinking to control feelings, when peer (social) pressure influences behavior, when sensations trigger associations, when fear triggers flight) operating in some sequential pattern or operating simultaneously to affect outcomes.

In simpler terms, self-regulation has two parts: an internal process—what the individual experiences (thinks, feels, senses, etc.)—and an external process—the individual's responses or actions that intersect with the world outside of oneself (i.e. controlling behaviors or words when thinking angry thoughts, waiting one's turn, formulating and expressing a good response, etc.). When an individual self-regulates, he is responding and accommodating to complex sets of interacting variables, each of which may involve the processing of its own sets and sources of data and each of which may require multiple steps. In the SCEP model, the focus is placed on understanding and learning how to address each of these steps in the process and how to foster ongoing and consistent self-regulation of thoughts, feelings, behaviors, and interactions. However, the major emphasis here is on self-regulation as it occurs within group-based, social interactive processes and how it affects their outcomes.

It is recognized that, while this addresses social interactions primarily, it also addresses thoughts, emotions, and behaviors as interwoven within (and often inseparable from) group-based, social interactions.

Rarely does one assess self-regulation itself; rather it is viewed as embedded within many areas of functioning, such as self-control (management of impulses and behavior), emotion regulation (management of feelings and emotions), social regulation (management of interactions and social-interpersonal situations), cognitive control (management of information and thoughts), sensory regulation (management of sensory and physiological feedback), and motor control (management of movements). The overlap between all core areas is substantial, and individuals with ASD often experience age-appropriate self-regulation in some areas, while exhibiting poor self-regulation in others. Of concern here, relative to social-interpersonal and group interactions, is an understanding of the individual's strengths and limitations in self-regulation in areas that impact the quality of peer-group interactions. Self-regulation is not considered as an independent, separate, or distinct core variable, but as one that is embedded within each core area and related to it in specific ways (see Figure 3.1).

The assessment of self-regulatory capacities is generally made within one or more of the specific core areas of functioning, while considering self-regulation as a central and critical component necessary for effective functioning within those core areas. The SCEP Individual Profile: Self-Regulation Assessment (Form 14.3) is a general assessment of self-regulation which includes a summary aspect (or average score). Each individual item within the Self-Regulation Assessment relates to a specific core area and provides information on the degree of dysregulation that may occur within the individual and which areas may be most affected. This data will be critical for placement decisions and for the construction of "best fit" groups, for constructing individual and group goals, and for the construction and use of particular tasks and activities within any given group.

At the outset of group, individual goals must address the individual's strengths and limitations in self-regulation so as to bring these in line with the needs of the group. This requires consideration of self-regulation within each core area of functioning with individual goals that provide a developmental progression toward competence and mastery. Later, at each stage of group development, group goals will address specific self-regulation competencies, skills, and needs that may be required for the individual and the group to move successfully through that particular stage. As the individual within the group attains the constructed goals, individual and group goals are then modified.

Self-monitoring

Self-monitoring is an important subarea of self-regulation. It refers to the level of recognition, awareness, and capacity to respond related to an internally or externally experienced situation. Self-monitoring is a process whereby the individual becomes aware of internal and external cues that trigger reactions and of the potential outcomes and consequences of the reactions. The individual then selects a response to the cue, consistent with his own temperament, emotional range, personal needs, understanding of the situation, and problem-solving capacities. At its simplest level, it is the choice of what the individual thinks or feels will be "best" for him. At its most complex level, it involves the awareness of one's individual functioning and capacities as related to the seven core areas of development and as related to the situation and circumstances that exist. It also relates to the selection of a deliberate, well-conceived response that takes into consideration all the internal and external information available to the individual at that moment.

Within the emotion area, self-monitoring refers to the awareness of one's own emotions at a particular point in time, of the emotional experiences that are being triggered by the situation, of the decision-making and problem-solving process, and of the response that is generated in that situation. Effective self-monitoring within the emotion area generally requires the consideration and effective use of other areas (e.g. cognitive, social) together with an appropriate level of emotion competence. Emotion competence allows the individual to recognize and be aware of an emotion, to label and categorize it accurately, and to understand the effects of that particular emotion on the individual. Emotion regulation allows the individual, following his accurate recognition, labeling, and understanding of the emotion, to consider and respond with a deliberate, controlled, and appropriate response and reaction to the particular emotional situation.

In a group situation, members address and confront emotions and emotional content, learn to label and categorize them accurately, and understand their use and meaning within group situations. Group members are also required to learn and use appropriate emotion regulation strategies so that relationships can be maintained, group process can continue, and goal and task focus can be maintained.

In addition to the focus on emotion competence and its components, effective strategies for stress and anxiety control and management are also targeted. Group members are taught to recognize and attend to increases in their own personal arousal level as it occurs within the group situation and to understand the situation and/or individuals which provide their triggers. They are provided with a range of strategies and techniques for stress and anxiety control and management that are learned and practiced during each group session and subsequently embedded within tasks and activities that are likely to generate stress and anxiety.

Because of the central role that core variables play in the development of individuals with ASD, each individual considered for placement in a group is assessed regarding self-regulation during the intake and assessment phase (described in Chapter 14). Information on the ability of the individual with ASD to self-regulate is collected from parent, teacher, and professional data sources together with all interview and observation data. Following this process, the SCEP Individual Profile: Self-Regulation Assessment (see Form 14.3) is completed as part of the SCEP Initial Evaluation and Interview Form. Individual goals are then created based on the presence or absence of the individual's self-regulation capacities. If then placed in a group, group goals and related group activities are formulated based on the individual's capacities and the needs of the group as a whole.

Chapter 5

Emotion Competence: A Core Variable

Emotion competence is the ability to understand emotions. It consists of the ability to recognize emotions, to provide and use the appropriate labels and descriptions for these emotions, to express them in appropriate personal or interpersonal ways, to understand how and why emotions occur, and to control and regulate their impact on the individual's life. Emotion competence is considered a core variable and fundamental to attaining and maintaining social competence. As a core variable, emotion competence is embedded within the core area of emotions and involves the complex process of awareness, communication, comprehension, and regulation and control of emotional and affective experiences.

Emotion competence consists of four interrelated components, all considered critical in the processing and experiencing of emotions, especially as they relate to social-interpersonal and group-based interactions. These are:

1. emotion recognition
2. emotion labeling and expression
3. emotion understanding
4. emotion regulation.

Emotion recognition refers to the individual's own acknowledgement of his emotional and affective experiences, both personally ("I feel sad") and interpersonally ("You are making me upset," "You sound angry"). Emotion recognition specifically relates to awareness of emotions and feelings, the first component in this core variable.

Emotion labeling and expression is a twofold process, generally occurring simultaneously. It involves emotion labeling: the ability to provide and use appropriate labels and descriptions for emotions once they are recognized and acknowledged. Often, but not always, once the individual is able to recognize and label an emotion, he may seek to express it in some manner. Emotion expression is the specific ability to give some means of expression to the emotions that the individual recognizes, experiences, and labels. In fact, labeling emotions is known to enhance and facilitate emotion expression. Labeling emotions accurately allows the individual to collect sets of emotions or feelings that can then be given expression in any number of ways. Thus once the individual recognizes and acknowledges the experience of emotions (both in himself and in others), he is capable of applying labels to those emotions and finding ways to express them more clearly and accurately ("I am not angry, I am upset!"). Emotions, when labeled and expressed, are most often communicated verbally ("I am happy") or behaviorally (e.g. a tantrum) or in combination across several core areas simultaneously (e.g. hitting a person when upset (emotion and behavior areas), smiling at someone and responding, "I like you" (emotion, communication, and social areas)).

Emotion understanding is the ability to recognize, label, and express emotions in a range of ways, and to understand how these emotions affect the individual and their interactions with others in social-interpersonal and group situations. This understanding then influences subsequent emotional experiences, further enhancing the individual's ability to quickly recognize, accurately label, and appropriately express emotions, and at the same time understand the impact and effect this process has on the individual as well as others involved in a social-interpersonal or group interaction.

Emotion regulation is the ability to regulate and control one's emotions in keeping with the situation and environment within which one is experiencing them. Emotion regulation relies on the effectiveness of emotion recognition, labeling, expression, and understanding. The more effectively one masters these emotional abilities, the more one is likely to attain and maintain emotion regulation. Emotion regulation is considered a sequential process, including strategies to modulate emotions and to maintain control and regulation. Emotion competence is considered a core variable primarily related to emotional development. However, it also is directly connected to other areas such as cognitive/executive functioning (attention, joint attention, memory, perspective taking, abstraction), communication (receptive and expressive language), and social development (relatedness).

Because of the central role that core variables play in the development of individuals with ASD, each individual considered for placement in a group is assessed regarding emotion competence during the intake and assessment phase (described in Chapter 14). Information on the ability of the individual with ASD to manage emotions is collected from parent, teacher, and professional data sources together with all interview and observation data. Following this process, the SCEP Individual Profile: Emotion Competence Assessment (see Form 14.4) is completed as part of the SCEP Initial Evaluation and Interview Form. Individual goals are then created based on the presence or absence of the individual's emotion competence capacities. If then placed in a group, group goals and related group activities are formulated based on the individual's capacities and the needs of the group as a whole.

Chapter 6

Stress and Anxiety Control and Management: A Core Variable

Overview

In the individual with ASD, stress and tension appear to occur more frequently, more intensely, with more adverse outcomes, particularly in social situations, and with anxiety levels that are reported to be significantly higher than the general population (Bellini 2004). Significant levels of anxiety have been noted in children with ASD across a range of daily experiences, including school (Coupland 2001) and home, social, and behavioral situations (Gillott, Furniss and Walter 2001; Groden *et al.* 1994; Kim *et al.* 2000; Muris *et al.* 1998; Tonge *et al.* 1999), and individuals with ASD have been reported to experience anxiety levels that are as much as three times that of a comparison group (Gillott 2007).

This chapter reviews a model (Cotugno 2009) for understanding, managing, and controlling stress, tension, and anxiety as experienced by the individual with ASD. This includes how the individual with ASD attempts to maintain equilibrium and to manage and fend off stress and tension and how, when overwhelmed, a downward spiral through a stress–tension–anxiety continuum can occur, and how effective strategies for stress and anxiety control and management can be learned and implemented. A second pathway resulting from increased stress and tension, a shift into a mode of rigidity/inflexibility in managing stress, tension, and change, is addressed in Chapter 8.

Stress is considered to be a state of disequilibrium (i.e. the stress response), triggered in an individual by a broad range of internally or externally generated stimuli (i.e. the stressor), which create a state of heightened arousal in the individual (Selye 1993). Coping is the capacity of the individual to manage the heightened state of arousal without compromising performance or functioning and without exceeding the available resources of the individual (Lazarus and Folkman 1984) while responding effectively and within the range of expected demands of the situation (Suldo, Shaunessy and Hardesty 2008). Stress may be triggered by new, novel, or unfamiliar situations, by situations which have previously been associated with stress and tension, by social and emotional situations, or by combinations of these factors and may contain cognitive, sensory, social, emotional, behavioral, and physical elements. If the heightened arousal level is managed and controlled effectively, then equilibrium returns. Otherwise, stress will increase as the individual senses his vulnerability to the situation and his inability to control or manage effectively his heightened arousal level.

Anxiety is defined as a specific state of overarousal triggered by an internal or external situation (i.e. the stressor), creating stress (i.e. the stress response) which cannot be managed, controlled, or coped with in any effective way. Anxiety emerges during this state of increased stress and when effective management or coping strategies are unavailable to stabilize the individual or to reduce stress, thus resulting in stress overload, the state of anxiety. In most individuals, certain levels of stress and tension are a normal and frequent occurrence, requiring tolerance at lower levels and control, management, and adaptation (i.e. coping) at higher levels. Although maintaining a general state of internal/external equilibrium is the preferred state for most individuals, managing and adapting to the frequent shifts in stress levels that regularly occur in the course of day-to-day experiences are necessary abilities. While these typically require a broad range of strategies and techniques, key components include: self-awareness, self-regulation, and self-monitoring; stress and anxiety management techniques; cognitive, behavioral, and emotional flexibility; and the use of external supports when needed and available.

For the individual with ASD, many of these strategies and techniques may not be consistently available to the individual or, when available, may be difficult to implement. For example, self-regulation/self-monitoring in a stress-free environment may occur relatively smoothly, but when an individual is contending with external change or disruption that results in increased internal stress states, self-regulation/self-monitoring mechanisms may operate less efficiently, whereupon the individual must rely upon additional combinations of stress/tension-reducing mechanisms or contend with stress overload.

While there is no clear understanding regarding why individuals with ASD experience such high levels of stress, tension, and anxiety, there is some research support for the view that the majority of individuals with ASD may experience a social competence deficit in modulating arousal levels, particularly to social and sensory stimuli (Dawson 1991; Dawson and Lewy 1989; Kinsbourne 1987; Ornitz 1989), thus explaining the chronic states of stress, tension, and anxiety that are observed and reported in new and unfamiliar situations by individuals with ASD, particularly those involving social interactions or high levels of sensory input. These situations are likely to contribute to a circular pattern involving a sequence which includes social interaction, increased stress and tension, poor social response, increased stress, anxiety, etc. In other words, in the individual with ASD, these concerns may each operate as triggers for one another (i.e. social interaction triggers stress, stress triggers anxiety, anxiety rises in relation to the demands of the social interaction); in an attempt to cope with the increased stress, tension, and anxiety, the social situation may be avoided. As a result, the individual with ASD may need significantly more time to adapt or adjust to normal arousal levels prior to learning to cope with heightened arousal levels (i.e. learn to cope with "normal" stress) (Stevens and Gruzelier 1984).

Understanding, anticipating, and managing stress are all critical aspects necessary for negotiating one's personal and social environments effectively. For example, social interactions, generally viewed as part of normal day-to-day existence, will likely produce some level of stress. Therefore, when an individual with ASD is in a group setting, issues and problems related to the stress experienced in interpersonal interactions are more likely to occur and can be addressed and targeted immediately. Strategies and techniques for stress management can be taught, practiced, and reinforced for use as necessary when problems arise within the group situation and then can be generalized to experiences out of group.

Cautious contentment

For most individuals, the absence of stress is associated with a state of calmness and relative equilibrium. The neurotypical individual expects and anticipates some level of stress (heightened arousal) in moment-to-moment and day-to-day experiences and deals with these as they occur without significant disruption in his overall state of relative equilibrium. For the individual with ASD, this is described as a state of "cautious contentment," because this state appears to rely primarily upon the maintenance of "sameness and the avoidance of change," rather than to be a dynamic, ongoing state of frequent adjustment and adaptation to change. In other words, the individual with ASD strives to keep things from changing in order to avoid stress, whereas the neurotypical individual "goes with the flow," adjusting to the minor changes that occur readily and fluidly without significant stress. At times, an individual may even encourage or seek out change to excite or arouse internal systems.

This state of "cautious contentment" often includes the seeking out or repeating of known, repetitive situations and activities that are internally calming or relaxing. These may be solitary, isolated situations where the individual is in control, where sensory input is managed and controlled, where others do not intrude or try to change the situation, and when the individual can alter, change, or adjust his activities at his own discretion to maintain this state of "cautious contentment." To others, this may appear as existing with states of low arousal or the absence of arousal (i.e. no change); for the individual with ASD, it is managing, controlling, and maintaining his own state of arousal at tolerable levels.

These calming, relaxing tasks or situations become self-reinforcing and may be repeated over and over, becoming habituated, stereotypic, ritualized, and repetitive, in an effort to reconstruct and maintain the state of calm they are intended to induce. These may be specific situations (i.e. playing with legos, making up own games, reading, etc.) or they may be specific repetitive and stereotypic play scenarios (i.e. repeating exactly the words to a book, reenacting a *Star Wars* battle exactly as created, repeating exactly a stepwise progression of activities to complete a game).

When individuals with ASD are presented with external demands and expectations (from parents, siblings, peers, school, play), this appears to intrude upon and threaten their "cautious contentment," triggering a state of heightened alert and arousal and of potential disequilibrium. Typically, the individual attempts to adjust by returning to or reconstructing the state of equilibrium (calm/low stress) previously experienced. If the environmental stimulus continues to push the issue, two things are likely to occur, both of which send the situation into a downward spiral: first, a movement toward increased stress/tension, and next, a shift toward increased rigidity/inflexibility. When the individual's preferred arousal level is disturbed, increased stress and tension is triggered, generally referred to as increased "anxiety." The individual's heightened stress and tension trigger reactions by the individual to try to cope with and manage the situation (an emotional reaction) and by the environment to cope with and manage a now stressed, "anxious," upset individual (a behavioral reaction).

The stress–anxiety continuum

The stress–anxiety continuum (see Figure 6.1) provides a representation of specific states or levels of arousal along a continuum ranging from equilibrium to breakdown. At each point along the continuum, an individual makes "decisions" or "choices" as to how best to manage and deal with the stressful situation, event, or interaction that is occurring. These decisions or choices will differentiate between effective or adaptive coping and management strategies and ineffective and maladaptive management strategies. Various points along the stress–anxiety continuum represent different levels of arousal, each with multiple triggers and response patterns and with varying individual-to-individual thresholds which determine the degree and intensity of the response/reaction.

In this approach, stress is viewed as a function of increasing arousal levels associated with potential disequilibrium or distress, ultimately either being "managed" effectively or breaking through a stress threshold and moving to a higher level on the continuum. Stress, tension, and anxiety themselves are each complex concepts involving combinations of physiological, cognitive, social, and emotional components. Although these components may occur in isolation, they are most likely to occur in multiple or overlapping combinations.

This progression along a stress–anxiety continuum presents itself in the following ways:

- Level 1: Cautious contentment.
- Level 2: Stress/tension.
- Level 3: Anxiety.
- Level 4: Overload.
- Level 5: Breakdown.

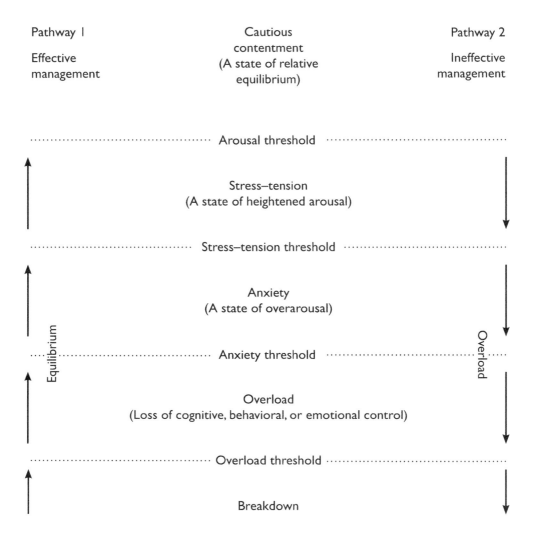

Figure 6.1 Stress–anxiety continuum

At each level, the individual is confronted with experiences, situations, and interactions which create a state of heightened arousal and which trigger a reaction (of coping/managing or of stress/tension, anxiety, or overload). These reactions may occur related to separate or to interacting experiences (e.g. physiological, cognitive, social, behavioral, emotional). At each level, there appear at least two clear pathways, with one resulting in the evoking of management and coping strategies to sufficiently and effectively deal with, defuse, and control the experience within manageable levels, resulting in decreased arousal. As this occurs, the individual gradually returns to a state of equilibrium and proceeds to move forward in normal ways.

The second pathway results from the inability to adequately or effectively manage the experience, situation, or interaction (increasing arousal levels), moving through threshold levels and resulting in a state of overload and ultimately breakdown. As thresholds are broken through and overload occurs, the individual loses significant cognitive and emotional control over internal states and external variables. At this point, if the individual is unable to evoke any useful or effective strategies or to rely on external controls in order for a state of equilibrium to be regained, then he will be unable to prevent an inevitable "meltdown" or breakdown.

Stress–anxiety assessment

Establishing the strengths and weaknesses of the individual with ASD relative to the management and control of stress, tension, and anxiety as it occurs along the stress–anxiety continuum occurs next. In this context, prominent signs/signals, triggers, and responses to stress, tension, and anxiety are assessed in order to evaluate the individual's response for adaptability in social and group interactions, and to construct plans and interventions to serve a more adaptive response to the stress, tension, and anxiety that the individual with ASD experiences. Information on the individual's experience of stress, tension, and anxiety is collected from available data sources and observations and is reported on the SCEP Individual Profile: Stress–Anxiety Assessment (see Form 14.5) that is part of the SCEP Initial Evaluation and Interview Form (described in Chapter 14).

From this information, individual goals can then be constructed which relate specifically to the needs of the individual with ASD in the management and control of stress, tension, and anxiety (described in Chapters 13 and 14).

Next in this chapter, techniques for stress and anxiety control and management are discussed: how they relate to stress and anxiety in individuals with ASD, how they can be taught and learned within the group structure and process, and how they can be implemented effectively in group and peer interactions.

Stress and anxiety control and management

Stress and anxiety are pervasive and often debilitating factors in the day-to-day functioning of individuals with ASD. It is particularly prominent in the social interactions of individuals with ASD where the recognition, attention to, and understanding of another person's needs is vital to effective and satisfying social communication. In addition, the individual with ASD may also be struggling to manage, cope with, and overcome deficits in all or some aspects of attention (especially joint attention), to understand the perspectives and views of others (theory of mind), to use pragmatic communications effectively (correctly interpreting verbal and nonverbal cues), to use aspects of cognitive and executive functioning (initiating, planning, organizing, self-monitoring) effectively, and, at the same time, to manage high degrees of stress, tension, and anxiety.

In the process of social interaction, the individual with ASD must learn to experience, recognize, monitor, and control the stress, tension, and anxiety that are typically evoked in social interactions. A group-focused, peer-based, and adult-monitored setting, such as the SCEP approach, provides opportunities for social interactions and exchanges to take place in a safe and supportive environment where the primary goals for each group participant are to acknowledge that stress and anxiety are an inevitable aspect of social interaction, to recognize when these states are triggered for the individual, and to learn both individual and group-based strategies to manage and cope with stress, tension, and anxiety effectively. Participants must also learn to recognize and manage their own approach to threshold level, overload, and breakdown.

Within the SCEP approach, at each stage of group functioning, group participants are educated about how these issues may play out, are taught strategies and techniques to manage stress and anxiety effectively, and are given multiple opportunities to use and practice these skills in real-life, peer interactions. Following each stress/anxiety event, group discussion, processing, and debriefing can occur, together with priming of the group for the inevitable "next event."

The effective management of stress and tension, of approaches to threshold levels, of anxiety, and of overload involves specific techniques which employ both cognitive and emotional control over a range of internally and externally generated stress- and anxiety-producing reactions. These techniques address the range of responses/reactions that may occur along the stress–anxiety continuum, beginning with initial experiences or interactions which create stress or tension, then the management of building and escalating stress and tension which produce anxiety, anxiety reactions, and, finally, effective management and coping so as to avoid poorly controlled anxiety responses which result in overload and breakdown.

Techniques for stress and anxiety control and management should include aspects of both cognitive control and emotional control which can be brought to bear on reactions occurring anywhere along the stress–anxiety continuum (see Figure 6.1). All individuals, including individuals with ASD, can learn to recognize heightened arousal and stress signals and approaches to threshold levels and to manage, control, or prevent anxiety reactions. They can also learn to manage and cope with anxiety adequately and effectively when it occurs, and to recover from emotional overload and breakdown when necessary.

Stress and anxiety control and management is considered a core variable primarily embedded within the core area of emotional development, but also with a critical role in the development of all other core areas of development. Within SCEP, a focus on the core variable of stress and anxiety control and management allows the individual to experience emotions and emotional information without debilitating stress. Stress and anxiety control and management provides the capacity to address emotions in adaptive, growth-fostering ways, and as outlined within this model, to directly address and connect the experience and management of emotions to social-interpersonal and group situations.

In considering movement through each stage of group development (discussed in Chapter 16), SCEP focuses specifically on facilitating the management and regulation of stress and anxiety so that other group processes can proceed with less interference. Stress and anxiety prevention, control, and management are connected to all group goals and embedded within both early and later sessions of all groups through stress management and relaxation techniques. Stress-management and self-calming techniques are geared toward the goals which help individuals manage stress when it arises, manage anxiety that is stress-generated, and regain equilibrium and stabilization once overload and meltdown is approached.

Training within the SCEP model for each specific technique for stress and anxiety control and management follows a consistent pattern and series of steps:

1. Group members are "educated" about the meaning of stress, tension, and anxiety and how, when, and why it occurs.

2. Group members are taught specific techniques at the appropriate points within each group stage and are given multiple practice opportunities.

3. Specific (first mild, then moderate) stress- and anxiety-producing situations are leader-constructed and implemented, then managed, with the group then discussing, practicing, and debriefing what specific strategies and techniques would be most effective in the specific situation confronted.

4. The group as a whole participates in practicing the learned strategies and techniques in group-constructed, play-acted, and modeled situations.

5. As naturally occurring stress- and anxiety-producing situations play out in the group, members are prompted to employ learned strategies and techniques appropriate for the specific situation and to share these experiences with their peers in group.

6. Appropriate use of techniques for stress and anxiety control and management is reinforced consistently.

Stress and anxiety control and management training

Within the SCEP model, several different types of stress and anxiety control and management can be used. Several that have been found most successful in use with individuals with ASD are briefly described here because of the importance of this core variable for individuals with ASD. When used within the SCEP method, these techniques can be adjusted, modified, and embedded within the tasks and activities developed at each stage of group development. The goal of this training is to effectively manage, cope with, and reduce levels of stress, tension, and anxiety when they arise by evoking states of increased calmness and decreased muscle tension, to increase self-awareness, and to increase self-control.

Group participants are provided with brief, simple, easy-to-learn, modified stress-reduction techniques sufficient to help them manage and cope with stress and tension as they arise in interactive group situations. Techniques provided and taught focus on helping each individual and the group as a whole to learn useful stress-management techniques that can be generalized for use with stress-producing situations both within and outside of group. The focus is on specific stress- and anxiety-producing situations which will arise in group interactions. Group participants are provided in advance with training and practice through "priming" for the different types of interactions which are likely to occur within the group. Specific stress-management techniques are then taught, reinforced, and practiced within group sessions and then embedded within ongoing and subsequent activities.

As the stress- or anxiety-producing situations emerge, techniques for stress and anxiety management appropriate to the situation are directed into play by the group leader. Primarily, techniques are employed which include elements of relaxation, self-calming, positive self-talk, and affective expression. Techniques such as these fit within and complement a cognitive-developmental framework within a group psychotherapeutic approach.

In initiating these techniques with children with ASD during initial group situations, group members are encouraged to settle into a comfortable spot either standing, relaxing in a chair (e.g. a beanbag or cushioned chair), or reclining on the floor within the group room, to close their eyes or to pick a point of focus, and to clear their head of any distracting or confusing thoughts. Then they begin with learning the following.

Deep breathing

The deep breathing technique involves learning to take long, slow breaths, lasting upwards of 4–10 seconds each, and drawing air into the diaphragm and abdominal area. The focus of each breath is shifted from the lungs in normal breathing to the diaphragm, and emphasis is placed on the measured, slow, paced inhaling, pauses at the peak of intake, and slow, measured, and calm exhaling. Between five and ten smooth and relaxed inhale–exhale cycles are generally sufficient once learned and practiced to lower stress and tension levels significantly to more manageable capacities.

Deep breathing is a basic, quick, efficient, and easy-to-learn relaxation technique that can be performed in any environment. The calming effects are immediate, and with practice and repetition these effects can be consistently enhanced and improved (Bourne 2005).

The Relaxation Response (Benson 1975)

The Relaxation Response is considered a form and adaptation of transcendental meditation developed by Benson (1975), originally as a non-invasive, non-medical treatment to lower blood pressure. Its positive effects have been consistently demonstrated, and more recently it has been expanded to include a broad range of mind–body connections (Benson and Proctor 2010) to be used as a broad program of physical and psychological stress reduction.

The original Relaxation Response was considered as a means to control and manage more effectively the physiological reactions triggered by the sympathetic nervous system in response to stress situations. These reactions include increases in oxygen consumption, heart rate, respiratory rate, and blood pressure. The technique involves using a quiet, controlled environment, together with a "mental device" (e.g. a word or mantra) used to control distracting thoughts and mind wandering and employed in a comfortable, relaxing state and with a passive ("not to worry") attitude. Benson (1975) reports that the subjective feelings of calm and relaxation elicited by the Relaxation Response result in decreased activity by the sympathetic nervous system and reports of an improved state of being within the deeply personal unique "relaxation experience." Individuals are trained in four basic elements which include:

1. a quiet environment

2. an object to dwell upon

3. a passive attitude

4. a comfortable position. (Benson 1975, pp.78–79)

In SCEP groups, individuals are asked to seek a quiet and comfortable spot (e.g. the floor, a beanbag chair, yoga mat, stand relaxed) away from others and with as few external distractions as possible. They are instructed to pick a private and individual focus word (e.g. "calm," "quiet," "moon," "cloud") of their choice. They are guided through a brief relaxation phase, including how to get comfortable, regulate their breathing, stay focused, and use their focus word. Over time and with repetition, they are trained to increase gradually the amount of time that they can remain in this Relaxation Response, in how to return to a relaxation state if concentration is broken, and how to maintain a passive attitude toward relaxation. Frequent and regular opportunities are provided to practice and refine the Relaxation Response technique. Discussion among group members about the individual and group experience of relaxation is encouraged and appears necessary as the group comes to understand which strategies for stress and anxiety control and management work for the individual and for the group.

Autogenic Relaxation Training

Autogenic Relaxation Training (ART) is a passive relaxation technique which employs self-initiated and self-directed hypnotic suggestion. ART was first described by Schulz in 1966 (Goldbeck and Schmid 2003) and concentrates attention on one part of the body at a time, moving in sequence to address all parts of the body. The purpose of ART is to learn to induce a physical state of relaxation on demand (i.e. by suggestion), which is experienced as passive, relaxing, and nonstressful, but with a focused awareness of existing in this state.

ART exercises involve creating a state of passive awareness focusing on physical relaxation sensations in the body. As a passive relaxation method using autosuggestion, the individual begins by settling into a comfortable, relaxed body position in a calm and quiet environment and adopting a passive, accepting attitude about his present state. The initial ART exercises involve focusing attention on the heaviness in the body parts, focusing first on the extremities and then moving through all other body parts. Next, the individual focuses on an acceptance of a sense of warmth pervading body parts as he concentrates attention sequentially on each body part. This is followed by focused concentration on breathing and finally on a sense of coolness and relaxation.

As the individual settles into a state of relaxation, he will close his eyes and draw his attention first to an extremity (arm or leg), providing the subvocal suggestion of warmth and relaxation ("I will feel warm, comfortable, relaxed"). This is repeated as all body parts are cycled through using the same autosuggestion. Each body part is addressed slowly and rhythmically, paying attention to the physical sensations (of heaviness, warmth, lightness, coolness). Often a sense of physical detachment is experienced, and is considered helpful and beneficial to the relaxation process. The individual's awareness is brought back to the body parts being focused upon before then slowly moving on. ART involves relaxed concentration and relaxed awareness of the sensations in different body parts, as the individual accepts easily and passively the experience while repeating the autogenic suggestion.

Progressive muscle relaxation

Progressive muscle relaxation, based on techniques developed by Jacobson (1974), involves the engaging of individual muscles or muscle groups in a cycle of tension–relaxation, taking 5–10 seconds each. The individual is taught to move systematically through a series of 10–20 muscle groups, each time tensing then relaxing the muscle or muscle group focused on and "learning" to recognize and mentally note the relaxation state of the muscles. Increased facility with progressive muscle relaxation allows the individual to select muscles and areas of tension for concentrated focus and relaxation efforts. Davis, Eshelman, and McKay (2000) provide a detailed description of this technique in its entirety and the adaptations described by Cautela and Groden (1978) for use with children with special needs are useful for training children with ASD in group situations.

While this particular technique requires more practice than deep breathing, many aspects of the learning process can be embedded within fun activities created specifically for young children with ASD. As with deep breathing, progressive muscle relaxation can be employed as a quick and efficient stress and tension reducer, particularly when stress-producing situations arise spontaneously within the group setting.

With both the deep breathing and progressive muscle relaxation techniques, it is helpful for individuals with ASD to designate a "cue" or signal that a relaxation, self-calming technique is required in the situation that is occurring at the moment. For example, the group leader may signal "time to relax" or "time to calm" or "slow down time" by a previously discussed hand gesture, a verbal cue (e.g. "deep breath," "inhale," "five seconds"), or a handy prescribed placard or index card.

Visualization

Visualization is a technique that involves the use of positive and pleasant experiences (created internally as mental pictures or visual images) that are evoked during times of stress, tension, or anxiety specifically to induce a state of calm and relaxation. The creation of specific visual images that are associated with calming, positive, and relaxing physical and emotional states are practiced and learned so that, when under stress, these images can be spontaneously evoked, bringing with them the associated state of calm and relaxation.

In group situations, the group members are instructed to close their eyes and select an image associated with a calm, pleasant, and relaxing experience and set of physical and emotional feelings. The members are encouraged to use as many of their senses as they can evoke as they create this set of internal images. The group members are guided through the experience of selecting an image, of experiencing and registering its calming, relaxing effects, of building the image with elaborate detail and sensation into a powerful, easily recovered association, of practicing its easy recovery from memory when needed, and of periodically reinforcing and bolstering its intensity. Generally, group members are encouraged and guided to create and elaborate at least three or four visual images, any of which could be used in a given situation depending on the individual's needs at that moment.

Positive self-talk

Self-talk is the label given to the internal monologue that accompanies various events, situations, and interactions that individuals encounter as they go through their lives. Some individuals constantly use this internal monologue as an attempt to sort out, understand, or talk through what they are experiencing. Others employ self-talk only episodically, such as when confused, anxious, excited, angry, or needing to generate alternatives to choose from. In work with individuals with ASD, self-talk is employed in its most general and global way as an internal monologue, generating thoughts and feelings, falling on a fairly broad continuum from negative to positive.

Positive self-talk represents positive self-statements, self-affirmations, motivating factors, ego boosts, and esteem builders. With individuals with ASD, it is best to address and reinforce only that subset of positive self-talk that represents reality-based interpretations by the individual. The subset of positive self-talk that represents any distorted, fantasy-based, unrealistic, or self-serving interpretations by the individual (e.g. "I'm smarter than you," "I am always happy") is typically ignored or subtly confronted (e.g. "Everyone is smart in this group," "Everyone has some down moments").

Training is provided to group participants in the appropriate use of positive self-talk through priming (e.g. "Think of the best thing that can happen in the game we are about to play"), modeling by group leaders (e.g. "You are working really hard"), rapid verbal reinforcement (e.g. "That was a great thing to say to J."), written scripts (e.g. "Let's generate a story about how our group helps J. fix his computer"), and generating scripted and repeated positive self-affirmations (both for each individual within the group and for the group as a whole). Throughout each session, group leaders closely attend to the verbal and body language of the participants, commenting, clarifying, or reinforcing the use of positive self-talk as the group proceeds through its tasks and activities.

Positive self-talk is considered a stress and anxiety management technique because of its effects in countering negative thoughts, distortions, and self-disparagement that generate stress and tension and ultimately create or increase anxiety both for the individual and for the group. As these efforts are countered and neutralized, it allows group participants to learn how to extract and experience positive aspects of interactions to use as a foundation for an improved sense of self. Positive self-talk is known to enhance and reinforce this process (Helmstetter 1987).

Affective expression

Experiencing and expressing feelings and emotions as they occur has long been known to have calming and curative effects. While this process is not completely understood, it is believed that allowing individuals to give expression to feelings, emotions, and internal states increases a sense of cognitive control over their current situation. Also, the expression of feelings and emotions to another individual opens the door for additional input into understanding and managing these feelings and emotions and in itself fosters an interactive communication process. Within the SCEP approach, group participants are given structured opportunities to address both the situations and interactions that trigger stress (and to use the group members and group process for problem-solving strategies) and the emotions aroused in stressful situations (through techniques for stress/tension control and management).

In the SCEP model, expressions of feelings, emotions, and internal states are viewed as potential stress- and anxiety-reducing techniques that can be explored and responded to in sensitive and helpful ways within the group experience. Attempts are consistently made to combine other techniques for stress and anxiety management (deep breathing, muscle relaxation, positive self-talk) with affective expression so as to address the exact level of stress that may exist within the experience, connected to the feelings being described.

From the outset of all groups, appropriate affect expression is modeled by the group leader, is encouraged and reinforced when it occurs appropriately, and is reframed, redirected, or limited when expressed inappropriately. Specific verbal or written scripts are also provided and practiced when necessary. This process emphasizes the importance of recognizing, experiencing, and expressing feelings, emotions, and internal states and that individuals can employ affective expression as a tool to manage and cope with stress, tension, and anxiety. Given the view here of these groups as therapeutically based, affective expression, affective management, and cognitive control are also considered necessary components of the therapeutic process.

Because of the prominent role that stress and anxiety play in the interpersonal functioning of individuals with ASD, strategies and techniques to manage these issues most effectively are considered critical and all groups are provided with training, practice, and reinforcement of techniques best suited for their age and level of development. Discussion and practice are initiated during the first sessions and followed up in all subsequent Stage 1 sessions. During later stages, those techniques learned are called upon as needed for the specific situations that arise.

Because of the central role that core variables play in the development of individuals with ASD, each individual considered for placement in a group is assessed regarding stress and anxiety control and management during the intake and assessment phase (described in Chapter 14). Information on the ability of the individual with ASD to control and manage stress and anxiety is collected from parent, teacher, and professional data sources together with all interview and observation data. Following this process, the SCEP Individual Profile: Stress–Anxiety Assessment (see Form 14.5) is completed as part of the SCEP Initial Evaluation and Interview Form. Individual goals are then created based on the presence or absence of the individual's stress and anxiety management capacities. If then placed in a group, group goals and related group activities are formulated based on the individual's capacities and the needs of the group as a whole.

Chapter 7

Attention and Joint Attention: Core Variables

Attention

Problems with attention and focus are frequently reported among individuals with ASD (e.g. Frith 1989; Rosenn 2002) with estimates as high as 60–70 percent (Rosenn 2002). Asperger (1991) himself reported that the "disturbance of active attention" was common in those high-functioning autistic children he observed. The few empirical studies that specifically address attention in individuals with ASD consistently report evidence of attention deficits in significant numbers among this group (Schatz, Weimer and Trauner 2002).

Available studies make clear that the underlying nature and source of these attentional concerns may vary within the ASD population. Frith (1989) has described attention in individuals with ASD as varying between "overload" states in which the individual is unable to attend to simultaneously presented information and "underload" states in which the individual is unable to focus on any important piece of information. Either state results in faulty or inadequate attention. Similar results have been reported by others with the common finding of attention deficits in focused (Pierce, Glad and Schreibman 1997), sustained, selective (Frith and Baron-Cohen 1987; Lovaas, Koegel and Schreibman 1979), flexible (Ciesielski, Courchesne and Elmasian 1990; Courchesne 1991), and joint (Wilczynski *et al.* 2007) attention. In fact, anecdotal and observational data suggest that, in general, attention may be defined much too broadly and generically to be of value when attempting to address these problems in individuals with ASD. Empirical studies to date have indicated that, to address this problem precisely, the specific attentional variable must be explicitly and operationally defined for evaluation and measurement, then considered within the individual's overall cognitive and learning style (Schatz *et. al* 2002).

Research into specific aspects of attention (Mirsky *et al.* 1991) indicates that attention is a cognitive/neurological function influenced and affected by many variables, but is also governed by underlying developmental components. The ability to employ attention appears dependent on a range of cognitive, neurological, constitutional, social-emotional, and even genetic variables. It is believed that attention is a complex set of concepts rather than having a single unitary meaning. Taking a developmental perspective, attention is viewed as a broad category encompassing specific and overlapping aspects of focused attention, sustained attention, selective attention, flexible attention, and joint attention (see Figure 7.1). Within the SCEP approach, the core variable of attention is considered to be a broad-based developmental concept, primarily embedded within the core area of cognitive/executive functioning. Joint attention is also considered as a fundamental component of attention and to be embedded within cognitive/executive functioning. However, joint attention is a concept that also has its roots in the capacity to engage other individuals in addition to the capacity to engage information. Therefore, joint attention is acknowledged here as a critical component in the developmental view of attention, but also similarly as a critical component in the process of social interaction. Because of its importance, it is given separate status from other attention variables as a core variable, with acknowledgement of its importance within both core areas of social and cognitive/executive functioning.

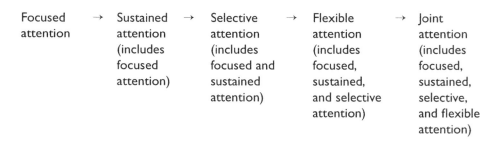

Figure 7.1 Developmental progression of attention

Within the SCEP model and based on observations and experiences with individuals with ASD, emphasis is placed on these five aspects of attention as they appear within the social interactive processes of peer-based, group situations.

The five variables of attention addressed here are as follows.

Focused attention

This is the ability to direct one's attention to a desired task or activity on demand by the individual and to hold it there for some minimal amount of time, as characterized in Figure 7.2.

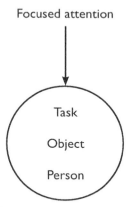

Figure 7.2 Flow of focused attention

Sustained attention

This is the ability to hold and sustain one's attention to a desired task or activity over an extended period of time (as designated from Time 1 to Time 2) which is defined either by the individual or by the task. This is characterized in Figure 7.3.

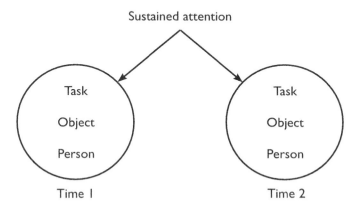

Figure 7.3 Flow of sustained attention

Selective attention

This is the ability to differentiate types of stimuli to be focused on and to direct attention selectively and purposefully to a task defined as relevant and important and simultaneously to withhold attention from other stimuli defined as irrelevant, unimportant, or distracting to the task currently focused on. This is characterized in Figure 7.4.

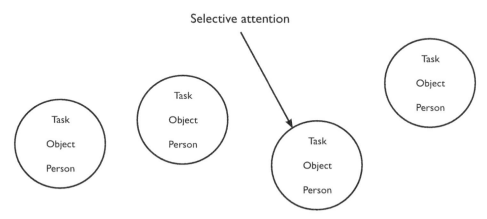

Figure 7.4 Flow of selective attention

Flexible attention

This is the ability to shift attention flexibly and spontaneously from one task or activity to another task or activity without the prior task or activity disrupting focus or attention to the task or activity being shifted to. Flexible attention may at times involve multiple and frequent shifts of attention between two or more tasks or activities and is characterized in Figure 7.5.

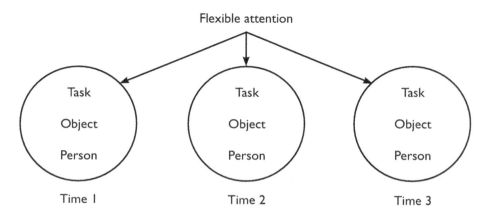

Figure 7.5 Flow of flexible attention

Joint attention

This is the ability to recognize and respond to the requests, demands, or needs for attention elicited by others. This joining with another person results in a mutual and reciprocal focus of attention on a particular experience, task, or activity. This is characterized in Figure 7.6.

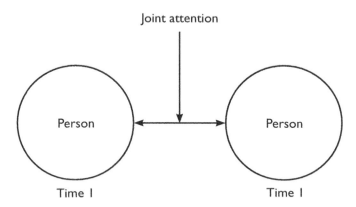

Figure 7.6 Flow of joint attention

Although based on the limited research in this area, a developmental view of attention begins with the inherent and innate ability at birth of the child to locate and attend to stimuli of need, interest, and importance (i.e. the breast, mother's voice, light, etc.) with focused attention. Once able to focus attention on stimuli and objects of choice, the capacity to sustain that attention for increasing amounts of time develops, followed by the ability to attend selectively—that is, to specific aspects of available stimuli designated as important, while ignoring other aspects considered irrelevant, contradictory, or distracting. Following the development of focused, sustained, and selective attention comes the ability to shift attention spontaneously and flexibly to other stimuli, objects, or activities deemed relevant or important, as internal or external factors dictate.

This developing capacity to shift attention flexibly between tasks or stimuli assumes the capacity to focus and direct attention at will, to sustain that attention on a task for some period of time sufficient to complete the task, and to focus and sustain attention on a specific selective task, withdrawing or withholding attention from other stimuli that might command attention. The capacities to focus, sustain, attend selectively, and shift attention flexibly all appear as necessary components of the most developmentally complex aspect of attention—that is, joint attention.

Joint attention

Joint attention is the capacity to direct and employ attentional capacities as they relate to shared interpersonal requirements and expectations. It requires a mutual recognition of shared and reciprocal interactions that make significant demands on the individuals involved. Joint attention involves a variety of social, cognitive/executive function, communication, behavioral, and sensory components and includes eye gaze, facial expressions, gestures, and verbal and nonverbal cues in the presence of related and relevant input from others (Wilczynski *et al.* 2007). To recognize, understand, and respond to these demands in an interpersonal interaction requires each of the developmental components of attention, moving from focused attention through to joint attention. Several studies have addressed the issue of joint attention in individuals with ASD and consistently found deficits that inhibit or impede social interactions and shared experiences (Loveland and Landry 1986; Sigman *et al.* 1986; Wilczynski *et al.* 2007).

Joint attention is considered primarily a social and cognitive construct that engages another individual or group of individuals through receptive and expressive information processing chains. This involves the awareness, recognition, understanding, regulation, and management of both verbal and nonverbal sets of information available to the individual. Earliest forms of joint attention are apparent in the nonverbal interactions and communications of neurotypically developing infants that are further developed with the addition of language. Deficits in joint attention have been correlated with overall severity of ASD symptoms, particularly in cognitive and language development (Mundy, Sigman and Kasari 1994). Still relatively unclear is the impact of undeveloped or underdeveloped joint attention abilities on overall development and outcomes as they occur in the individual with ASD. It also appears clear that the variability in joint attention abilities that occurs among individuals with ASD hampers the ability to understand fully the underlying processes and how they develop in these individuals.

In the SCEP model, joint attention is considered as an endpoint on the developmental trajectory for the core variable attention. Thus, it is assumed to include the ability to focus and direct attention to another individual (focused attention), to sustain attention to that individual or group (sustained attention), to focus attention selectively on most relevant information available (selective attention), and to shift attention flexibly back and forth as needed within the interactions (flexible attention). While some of these aspects of attention may not be fully developed (each operates on its own developmental continuum), all are required in some form for some degree of joint attention to occur.

Joint attention, as a core variable, is embedded simultaneously within the social area (it requires awareness of and connection to another individual or group) and the executive function area (the capacities for the full range of focused, sustained, selective, and flexible attention) and is a cornerstone of effective social interaction and social competence. Within SCEP, group goals are constructed at each stage of the group process around the development and enhancement of joint attention. In particular, the focus is on joint attention as a necessary competency for effective reciprocal interchange and communication within interpersonal group settings. Goals are constructed and activities selected which foster shared interactions and experiences, mutual and reciprocal cooperative learning tasks, and active listening and responding skills between group participants.

Because of the central role that core variables play in the development of individuals with ASD, each individual considered for placement in a group is assessed regarding attention during the intake and assessment phase (described in Chapter 14). Information on the ability of the individual with ASD to focus, sustain, select, and direct attention flexibly as well as engage in joint attention is collected from parent, teacher, and professional data sources together with all interview and observation data. Following this process, the SCEP Individual Profile: Attention Assessment (see Form 14.6) is completed as part of the SCEP Initial Evaluation and Interview Form. Individual goals are then created based on the presence or absence of the individual's attentional capacities. If then placed in a group, group goals and related group activities are formulated based on the individual's capacities and the needs of the group as a whole.

Chapter 8

Flexibility, Change, and Transition: A Core Variable

Cognitive and behavioral flexibility is defined here as the capacity to cope with, manage, and adapt to changes, shifts, and transitions, as they occur within an individual's personal and interpersonal environments (i.e. internal or external) and as they alter the demands and expectations placed upon the individual.

From its earliest description, the insistence on sameness, resistance to change, and behavioral inflexibility have been defining characteristics of ASD (Kanner 1973) and have been consistently linked to social impairment (Berger *et al.* 1993; McEvoy, Roger and Pennington 1993; Szatmari *et al.* 1989; Wing and Gould 1979). Thus, in order to facilitate engagement in appropriate social interactions, a critical issue arises around the inability of the individual with ASD to engage the world, especially the social-interpersonal world, in flexible ways. The issue of flexibility appears to have its origins in neurological (Delis, Kaplan and Kramer 1999; Lezak 1995) and cognitive (Klein 1970) processes, with the outcome manifested in either or both of cognitive and behavioral inflexibility or rigidity. This issue also appears to have a strong relationship and connection to flexible attention processes, although there is limited research to date in this area.

With individuals with ASD, Flannery and Horner (1994) assert that increased rigidity may reflect a need for predictability (i.e. sameness) and, when joined with the individual's lack of awareness of surrounding informational cues signaling the need for change, characteristic restrictive and stereotypic patterns of behavior may arise. When change was made more predictable (i.e. signaled), problem behaviors were reduced. Similarly, increased availability of adult interaction (Kern and Vorndran 2000), increased contingent attention (Repp and Karsh 1994), and manipulation of environmental variables (Sterling-Turner and Jordan 2007) also appear to reduce the intensity of inflexibility/rigidity when change is introduced.

Antecedent intervention techniques also have demonstrated positive effects in reducing inflexibility/rigidity in both individual and group situations and have been employed successfully in a variety of group therapeutic situations. These include signaling change (Flannery and Horner 1994), verbal prompts (Tustin 1995), auditory inputs (Ferguson *et al.* 2004), behavioral momentum (Singer, Singer and Horner 1987), visual inputs (Schmit *et al.* 2000), physical guidance, activity schedules (Dettmer *et al.* 2000), and videotape modeling (Schreibman, Whalen and Stahmer 2000).

Within the SCEP model, a primary goal is to foster and encourage an increased flexibility in thinking, behaving, and interacting with other individuals and with the environment, since inflexibility and rigidity are known to reduce the quality and quantity of an individual's interactions with the world around him. Behaviors involving inflexibility/rigidity as manifested by individuals with ASD may include isolation, noncompliance, aggression, stereotypic movements or activities, transition problems, and tantrums. These difficulties may ultimately limit the individual's independence.

With individuals with ASD, requirements for cognitive and behavioral flexibility, change, and transitions are often reported to result in a state of increased internal tension, often labeled in the literature as an increase in "anxiety," but best described here as a state of heightened arousal. This is based on an understanding of cognitive and behavioral rigidity as a response to a request or demand for change, causing a heightened state of arousal, triggering increased tension, and creating a state of disequilibrium or distress. If the individual is unable to manage or cope effectively (i.e. make the adjustment) and regain equilibrium, then stress and tension will continue to increase. In many situations, cognitive and behavioral inflexibility appears to be an attempt to maintain a preferred state of equilibrium actively initiated by the individual as a reaction to the increased stress and tension created by demands for change, shifts, or transitions.

Demands or requirements placed on the individual with ASD for flexibility, change, or transition are likely to heighten arousal and trigger movement along the stress–anxiety continuum (as discussed in Chapter 6), resulting in either the invoking of coping and adaptation strategies or in progression toward overload.

When unable to manage or cope with a situation requiring change or flexibility, the individual moves from a state of internal equilibrium, prior to a request or requirement for change, to a heightened state of arousal or disequilibrium after a change request is made. This change in state triggers stress and tension with the anticipated or approaching situation (change). The individual attempts to regain equilibrium and to reduce the tension being created by remaining at (or returning to) the previous (preferred) state of (lower) arousal (a state of cautious contentment), solely by remaining involved in the same task or activity with no consideration for other alternatives. This attempt to return to a state of cautious contentment (lower arousal/equilibrium) by the individual with ASD does not serve as an adaptive strategy to manage stress or tension, but rather as part of a more fixed and rigid system to maintain equilibrium through "sameness." Thus, in a change situation involving the individual with ASD, he moves from a state of perceived calm to a state of increased tension, triggering a state of inflexibility/rigidity in the hope of returning to the preferred state of calm (sameness). When the external environment cannot or will not comply with the individual's attempts to maintain the status quo and pushes for further change, then "stress" behaviors for the individual are likely to emerge (e.g. isolation, refusal, noncompliance, anger/aggression, tantrums) as manifestations of the individual's altered internal state—that is, a state of increased stress/tension and state of heightened arousal. Given the fixed and rigid qualities to this sequence, overload and meltdown are often inevitable cognitive and behavioral outcomes.

In the SCEP approach, the attempts to help individuals with ASD manage these states, which are likely to differ from individual to individual, are multifaceted. First, attempts are made to help the individual manage his stress and tension, not by a solution of inflexibility/rigidity, but by first reducing tension in order to allow the individual to reconsider his options, usually with previously learned stress and anxiety control and management techniques. Second, attempts are made to intersperse into the situation demands that have a positive reinforcing capacity and a high likelihood of compliance, further reducing the individual's tension state. This intervention, characterized as behavioral momentum (Nevin 1996), has been shown to increase compliance during change situations (Ray, Skinner and Watson 1999; Romano and Roll 2000; Singer *et al.* 1987). Third, interventions with individuals with ASD that approach the problem from a number of different directions are considered, depending on the individuals involved, the group makeup, and the specific individual and group goals that might apply. This is considered a key aspect of the specific individual and group goal-oriented approach used here (described in Chapter 13).

The following are examples of tasks requiring flexibility that have been observed to trigger reactions of inflexibility/rigidity in individuals with ASD. Generally, these are actions or behaviors initiated by others or in the external environment and when the individual with ASD appears to be in a state of cautious contentment.

- Object movement (e.g. "I'm going to move this over here"). This involves another individual disrupting a certain order or sequence constructed by the individual with ASD.

- Attention shift (e.g. "I need you to stop that and answer my question"). This involves a request for a shift in focus requiring flexible attention capacities.

- Task change (e.g. "I need you to come to the table now"). This involves flexible attention, mental shifting, and acceptance of change.

- New information (e.g. "Today we are going to do things a little different"). This involves the introduction of new, unknown, or unfamiliar tasks requiring change or transition.

- Sensory inputs (e.g. more confined space/louder noise levels than usual). This requires focused and selective attention capacities involving primarily sensory inputs and stimuli.

- Consistency/sameness (e.g. "You cannot do that today/anymore"). This involves a task transition from a preferred activity to another (often non-preferred) activity.

- Activity interruption (e.g. "Just listen to me for a minute"). This requires cognitive or behavioral delay (i.e. "Stop!"), flexible and joint attention, additional information processing (i.e. the task request), and decision making.

Regarding movement along a flexibility–rigidity continuum, individuals with ASD appear to follow a path of: comfort zone/cautious contentment; a stimulus event, typically requiring change, transition, or adjustment which triggers stress/tension; marked increases in stress/anxiety; attempts to return to the original stimulus or original state of equilibrium (e.g. comfort zone/ cautious contentment); repeated, often perseverative, attempts (even when unsuccessful) to return to the original state of equilibrium; further increases in stress/tension, resulting in anxiety states, which may occur until thresholds are broken through and overload occurs; and inflexibility/rigidity to alternative tasks presented which may occur along with resistance and sustained anxiety. Thus, the requirement for change will occur as shown in Figure 8.1.

External change/external triggers increased stress/anxiety:

Individual assesses expectation for flexibility/change and personal willingness for flexibility/change and moves to one of the following:

Most adaptive
- immediate and cooperative adjustment to change
- excitement and stimulation with change
- exaggerated rule following.

Somewhat adaptive
- quick adaptation with little thought to change, its meaning, or its consequences
- slow adaptation with hesitation and reluctance, but eventual compliance
- alternative approaches.

Least adaptive
- repetitive, perseverative attempts to reduce stress/anxiety with refusal to change
- repetitive, perseverative attempts to return to status quo with refusal to change
- avoidance of new stimulus
- becomes overwhelmed.

Figure 8.1 Patterns of inflexibility/rigidity

In approaching the issue of flexibility, change, and transition, attempts are made to apply the following in individual and group goal setting and in task construction within the group:

1. predictability in upcoming tasks, unique situations, and transitions

2. signaling, preparation, and priming used as upcoming changes and transitions approach

3. consistent use of verbal cues, auditory cues, behavioral momentum techniques, visual supports, and activity schedules.

Finally, it is most helpful and most highly reinforcing to pay close attention to how each individual responds to particular kinds of information regarding change and adjustment within the group and the stress it may induce, and then to provide that individual with specific strategies and techniques that can be used to effectively manage the situation. Also, regarding interactions and responses within the group situation, attention to other related variables—such as how many individuals are involved, the number and sequence of steps in a task, the length of a task, the nature of the activity, the degree of choice-making, and the extent of involvement required by other group members—is an important factor in moving individuals with ASD toward more flexible and resilient response patterns.

Within the SCEP approach, the specific techniques and interventions used within the group to address coping and management strategies for the core variable of flexibility, change, and transition are initially dictated by information received through a review of the detailed developmental histories, reports of test functioning, behavioral observations, and completion of parent/caretaker and teacher social competence checklists, including information regarding the flexibility, change, and transition variables recorded on the SCEP Individual Profile: Flexibility, Change, and Transition Assessment (see Form 14.7) which is one part of the SCEP Initial Evaluation and Interview Form (described in Chapter 14).

Each individual considered for group placement will be evaluated based on this information obtained during the intake and assessment phase for their specific flexibility, change, and transition needs and capacities, with subsequent individual goals created and based on these capacities. If then placed within a group, goals specific to the individual are then constructed in this area based on this information and ultimately combined with individual goal information of other individuals to form sets of group goals, focusing on behaviors emphasizing flexibility and using modeling, rehearsal and feedback, practice and repetition, and integration with other process and skill variables (e.g. anxiety/stress management and reduction).

Chapter 9

Perspective Taking: A Core Variable

Perspective taking is the ability to understand that other people have different thoughts, emotions, and experiences from our own. Perspective taking is considered a core variable embedded primarily within the cognitive/executive function area and the social area because it consistently requires thought processes relative to self and other, generally relating to an engagement or interaction with another individual or group. Clearly, if emotions and emotional experiences, communications, sensory experiences, motor issues, or behavior are involved, then perspective taking would also relate directly to these areas as well. It is common that perspective taking may involve all core areas of development, operating at different levels of involvement and complexity.

While joint attention recognizes the social and cognitive requirements necessary to engage another individual or group, the core variable perspective taking requires the recognition and understanding that another individual or group distinct from ourselves possesses particular and unique ways of thinking or points of view that are different from our own. Both joint attention and perspective taking are directly related to social and cognitive/information processing abilities of the individual; however, age and developmentally appropriate joint attention appears to be a necessary component for effective perspective-taking capacities (Moore and Corkum 1994; Mundy *et al.* 1993; Sheinkopf 2005).

As with other core variables, perspective taking is not a unitary concept, but one that has several layers of complexity. Consideration must be given to the individual's ability to recognize, identify, and understand his own thoughts and emotions (i.e. self-perspective) as the preliminary step to gaining a broader perspective of the world. Next is the process of recognizing and understanding that others have thoughts, emotions, and experiences and that these are based on sets of information that the other individual possesses or has access to, but not always the observing individual. Next, as the observing individual develops and matures and becomes capable of processing, understanding, and taking more information into account, that individual is better able to recognize and consider that others separate from himself act, think, and feel differently and that others consider, analyze, and use information differently and in their own unique way. The final step in this process of achieving mature perspective taking is the observing individual's ability to consider and use multiple and complex sets of thoughts, feelings, and experiences in order to understand what other individuals or groups may be thinking, feeling, and experiencing and then to use this information to constantly monitor and adjust his own interactions with those other individuals or groups. At the same time, this process exists within a broad social and cultural process.

Because perspective taking is a complex and abstract concept, individuals with ASD often experience difficulty with it on several levels. For example, they may have difficulties recognizing and identifying their own thoughts, feelings, or behaviors or may hold on to an overly rigid view of the meaning of these, and therefore also have difficulty understanding or tolerating others' thoughts, feelings, or behaviors. Some individuals with ASD may be able to identify and understand their own thoughts, feelings, or behaviors, but may have difficulty when these are set against (e.g. compared to, contrasted with) another individual's or group's. Some may have difficulty with the fact that thoughts and beliefs of other individuals change over time and without the observing individual's awareness.

The source of these and other difficulties in perspective taking is likely varied and multidimensional. These difficulties may have their roots in difficulties in emotion competence (an inability to recognize, identify, or understand one's own feelings or the feelings of others), in attention/joint attention (an inability to "pay attention" to the communications of another individual and to link up or "sync" with them), in flexibility, change, and transition (an inability to consider or tolerate the thoughts, feelings, or behaviors of others if they disagree with one's own), or in relatedness (the inability to connect or relate to another individual prevents consideration of the validity of the other's thoughts, feelings, or behaviors). In practice, problems in perspective taking relate to combinations of these (or other) issues and often must be addressed in a deliberate, systematic, and sequential manner. Understanding the status and role of related core variables in the development of perspective taking is critical.

Because of the central role that core variables play in the development of individuals with ASD, each individual considered for placement in a group is assessed regarding perspective taking during the intake and assessment phase (described in Chapter 14). Information on the ability of the individual with ASD to engage in perspective taking is collected from parent, teacher, and professional data sources together with all interview and observation data. Following this process, the SCEP Individual Profile: Perspective-Taking Assessment (see Form 14.8) is completed as part of the SCEP Initial Evaluation and Interview Form. Individual goals are then created based on the presence or absence of the individual's perspective-taking capacities. If then placed in a group, group goals and related group activities are formulated based on the individual's capacities and the needs of the group as a whole.

Chapter 10

Relatedness: A Core Variable

Relatedness is considered a core variable embedded primarily within the social area. It is defined as the ability to connect or relate to an individual or group and, in that process, provides each individual involved with some mutual, interpersonal benefit and a general sense or feeling of social-emotional "well-being." Relatedness between two or more individuals is based on some degree of emotional and social reciprocity and on elements of basic trust which together result in a deeper connectedness. The ability to create or establish a sense of relatedness or connectedness is regarded as an innate capacity for human beings and provides the fundamental basis for relationships to form and develop in order to experience interpersonal satisfaction and gratification.

For the individual with ASD, the capacity for relatedness appears to emerge and develop in very different ways than for neurotypical individuals. The individual with ASD often has difficulty recognizing and identifying the shared thoughts, feelings, and values of others (a form of perspective taking) that would connect him to those other individuals and that would serve as the basis for mutually satisfying ongoing relationships. When viewed as a problem of perspective taking or theory of mind, relatedness is embedded primarily within the social area. When viewed as a problem of understanding emotions and emotional connections, relatedness is embedded primarily within the emotional area.

The capacity for relatedness is part of the ongoing process of social development with roots that develop very early. Newborns use caretaker interactions, need satisfaction and gratification, and attachment and bonding experiences, together with their own innate personality and temperament characteristics, to shape a path of social development. When any (or all) of these social developmental experiences are developmentally deficient or derailed, as may happen with individuals with ASD, then the subsequent capacities for appropriate social experiences will be influenced and affected. For example, the derailment of appropriate eye contact, of attention to facial cues, of social communication, of social comprehension, or of joint attention capacities will ultimately affect the capacity for high-quality experiences of relatedness and connectedness. While relatedness is considered a core variable, it is also viewed as one endpoint of social development, resulting from a "good enough" progression through stages of social development and social competence (Cotugno 2009).

Overall, relatedness has to do with the connections between self and others (Maslow 1954) where those connections reciprocally influence all the individuals involved. Group experiences provide structured opportunities to experience and learn about others, to develop and use lower level social competencies (self-regulation, emotion competence, stress management, attention, flexibility) in interpersonal interactions, and to experience the connections between self and others that may be lacking. Experiences within a group provide opportunities to focus on those specific areas of social development and social competence considered deficient within a supportive, structured, peer-focused, therapeutic environment.

Because of the central role that core variables play in the development of individuals with ASD, each individual considered for placement in a group is assessed regarding relatedness during the intake and assessment phase (described in Chapter 14). Information on the ability of the individual with ASD to relate to others is collected from parent, teacher, and professional data sources together with all interview and observation data as part of the SCEP Initial Evaluation and Interview Form. Individual goals are then created based on the presence or absence of the individual's relatedness capacities. If then placed in a group, group goals and related group activities are formulated based on the individual's capacities and the needs of the group as a whole.

Part III

The Use of Group Interventions in the Treatment of Individuals with Autism Spectrum Disorders (ASD): The Social Competence Enhancement Program (SCEP)

Part III describes the Social Competence Enhancement Program (SCEP), a group model that was developed to make use of and combine group therapy principles, a process-oriented approach, structured cognitive-behavioral techniques, and skill-based instruction. Within the SCEP model, an environment is created in which the focus is on both the individual within the group and the group as a whole. Within a group structure, SCEP follows a cognitive-developmental model that tracks and builds upon the individual's development through stages within the group. This approach systematically builds an understanding of the individual's own capacities and abilities to engage others as well as his areas of difficulties and weakness, then uses this information to develop a plan to address these issues and concerns in a developmentally sequenced manner.

First, the integration of social competence and social skills is discussed, including how these concepts connect to the SCEP model. This is followed by an understanding of how the connections between emotion competence and social competence influence the structuring of a group.

Then, the SCEP model is described in detail, with emphasis on its group therapy underpinnings, on the rationale for group-focused and peer-based interventions for individuals with ASD, and on the specific types of group interventions chosen for use within this model. Next is a description of how data and information are collected on potential group members to define areas of interest and to construct individual goals. Once a set of individual goals is constructed and the individual is placed within a group, then this information is integrated with information of other group members in the formulation of group goals.

Stages of group development are then described and defined within this context. As the group proceeds through the stages of group development and as the group members focus on individual and group goal attainment, group participants are taught the necessary and relevant skills to interact effectively and in age-appropriate ways with peers in the natural group setting. In this context, the group's strengths and relationship capacities are engaged to enable and facilitate the necessary skill building that follows.

Chapter 11

Basic Principles in the Development of Social Competence and in Social Skill Building

Primary focus of this model

The primary emphasis of the SCEP model is the development of social competence and social skills necessary for age-appropriate social functioning in a dynamic and ever-changing peer environment. However, for the individual with ASD, this must occur with an understanding of functioning within each core area and how this may relate to deficits in core variables. As the group maintains an overall focus on the development of social competence, individual strengths and weaknesses within core areas and related core variable deficits are integrated into a structured goal-directed plan of intervention. This plan initially takes a broad view in developing social competence in the group, narrows to consider each individual's functioning in core areas and any related core variable deficits, then broadens again as this information is used to construct social skill-building tasks and activities.

Social competence

Social competence is the ability to combine cognitive, social, and emotional components in ways that enable an individual to engage in spontaneous, socially acceptable, and mutually satisfying social interactions and to adapt to the constantly changing, dynamic nature of these interactions. Social competence is considered to consist of three critical elements, each necessary for successful social interaction, and includes:

1. the situation—the ability to recognize and understand the social situation as it exists, as it unfolds, and as it moves forward

2. the interchange—the ability to recognize, understand, and engage in the elements of social interchange with others (individuals or group)

3. the response—the ability to recognize, understand, and implement an appropriate response in that specific situation with all the participants involved.

This model views social competence as the ability to read and understand the types of interchange occurring and to understand situations and respond with appropriate thoughts, behaviors, and communications for specific social situations as they exist at that moment (they are changing constantly and may require different responses at each subsequent moment).

Social skills

Social skills are complex sets of behaviors which allow an individual to engage in positive mutually reciprocal and beneficial social interactions (Gumpel 1994). Social skills follow from social competence in that they are the specific tools that make an effective social interchange happen. While social competence has to do with the recognition and understanding that a social situation exists and that it requires an interaction that has parameters of social appropriateness, social skills are the actual repertoire of behaviors that the individual possesses which fit appropriately the specific situations being encountered. These social skills enable an individual to initiate, maintain, manipulate, or solidify a social interaction, thereby creating "a social relationship" (Gumpel 1994).

Research completed to date makes clear connections between social skill development and school achievement (Brown, Odom and McConnell 2008). However, there are few specific social competence or social skill curricula or related assessment tools that can identify which particular social skills are most necessary for effective development and contribute most to healthy and satisfying interactions, achievement, and life satisfaction. It is assumed, then, that a necessary initial step in this process is the adequate assessment of the strengths and deficits of the child with ASD, followed by the development and implementation of an intervention plan that uses the individual's strengths to target specific deficits.

Planning for social competence and social skill development

In addressing the remediation or management of deficiencies in social competence, it is necessary first to assess the social competence of the individual in order to gain an understanding of which social abilities exist and which are absent or deficient. This information is considered together with information on how the individual manages core variables necessary for social interaction, paying specific attention to those that are often deficient (core deficits) in individuals with ASD. With information on an individual's social competence (social abilities) and functioning on core variables (core deficits of ASD), a plan for social skill development can be constructed and implemented within a group-based, peer-focused, stage-based, cognitive-developmental framework. This plan begins with the collection of "areas of interest" from information provided by parents, teachers, and observers of the individual in social situations. Areas or topics of interest typically fall into two broad, but separate, categories: those relating to underlying process, structure, or competence variables and those relating to specific skill or function variables (a more common designation, often including both process and skill variables). Areas or topics of interest are designated based on the needs of the individual as they relate to social-interpersonal functioning and as they are expected to occur within group and interpersonal situations. They are gleaned from information provided during the initial intake and evaluation process and collected from parents, teachers, and previous evaluators and providers. They relate specifically to areas of deficit or deficiency that undermine effective social interaction and that will be necessary for successful completion of social interchanges.

Areas of interest for an individual with ASD may include any combination of social competencies and social skills deemed of importance by parents, teachers, professional evaluators, and interviewers. Typically, areas of interest will be those recognized as important by multiple members of the individual's team. These areas of interest will form the basis for the construction of individual goals. As individuals are considered for group participation, group participants are selected based on their similar areas of interests, both in terms of social competencies and social skills. Next, individual goals are constructed based on the individual's areas of interest. If subsequently placed in a group, the individual goals of all the participants are reviewed together and specific group goals are formulated, typically in a process that involves all group members during initial group sessions.

During these initial sessions, group members are provided with an understanding of how their individual and group goals relate to specific social competencies and how they impact one's understanding of social situations. Group participants are also provided with an understanding of the importance of specific skills, what situations they are important and necessary for, and how to implement these specific skills. This will occur within the group through discussion, group leader or peer modeling, role play, direct instruction, group leader and group member feedback, and reinforcement of specific target behaviors.

General social competence and social skill-building techniques in the development of core variable tasks and activities

When addressing specific core variables in the development of social competence and the building of social skills, a broad general structure is used which guides thinking about the presentation of information relative to specific core variables. In keeping with the view that all aspects of group interventions, group processes, group interactions, and group tasks maintain inherent structure, the development of tasks and activities follows a consistent pattern and set of steps which include the following:

- An area or topic of interest focusing on a core variable, such as emotion competence (recognition, labeling, understanding, and regulation), is introduced with a "topic plan" for how it will be addressed in the group. This includes providing group members with a preview of what will be expected of them as the group addresses the topic and discussing the specific tasks involved, the specific leader and group member roles, the expected benefits, some likely problems, and the desired outcomes.

- Next, group members are provided with information ("are educated") about the topic or area of interest, how it affects the group, what its meaning and purpose may be, and how it may occur in negative and in positive ways.

- Specific techniques that address the area or topic are discussed and their suitability, individual fit, and group appropriateness are considered. Group decisions are made about what techniques and strategies will be most beneficial and useful in addressing the particular area or topic of interest.

- Group members are taught specific techniques and provided with multiple practice opportunities that address the specific area or topic of interest.

- The group as a whole participates in practicing the learned strategies and techniques in group-constructed, play-acted, and modeled situations.

- Specific situations which address the particular topic or area are constructed by the group leader and implemented within the flow of the group.

- The group discusses and debriefs what strategies and techniques were most effective in the specific situation confronted.

- As naturally occurring situations play out in the group, these are brought to the group's attention and the group is prompted to consider and employ any of the learned strategies and techniques appropriate for the specific situation.

- Appropriate use of these techniques is consistently reinforced.

Chapter 12

Joining Emotion Competence and Social Competence

Individuals with ASD struggle to understand how their own and others' affective and emotional responses relate to and affect social interactions and social situations. This may include how to process and understand incoming information relating to the situation at hand (inputs), how to formulate and select an appropriate response, and how to implement a response appropriately, based on the environmental and social cues available (outputs). The effective management and regulation of affective and emotional responses as they arise in social situations requires an accurate understanding of the situation one is involved in, a varied repertoire of responses available for that situation, the selection of an appropriate response for that situation, the effective implementation and follow-through with that response as the situation dictates, and the processing or debriefing of how effective the situation was managed (i.e. what was learned).

In helping individuals with ASD to address and manage affective and emotional responses appropriately in social situations, the SCEP approach attempts to provide a structured, safe, and supportive peer-based environment where issues and concerns related to understanding, managing and regulating, and expressing affects and emotions can be addressed. Within a safe and supportive peer-based group, emotional risk taking, constructive feedback, implementation of peer suggestions, and self-managed emotional monitoring are encouraged and reinforced. Issues of stress, anxiety, frustration, and anger are anticipated and are addressed, and specific strategies to manage these emotions effectively are taught. Learning how to rely on peers for help and support in the group situation is also addressed.

Developing an understanding of the social situation

Within the group situation, group participants are provided with a structure where they will experience different types of interactions (e.g. meeting unfamiliar individuals, sharing information about themselves, gathering information about others, confronting and resolving conflict with peers, feeling stressed and anxious, saying goodbye and experiencing loss), each of which stir up a range of feelings and emotions that are pointed out to group members, are addressed directly and labeled, and are discussed, processed, and understood. The group leader maintains a focus on the feelings and emotions surrounding specific situations by constructing tasks and activities which are stage-based and which focus on specific interactive situations.

In this way, group members will proceed through stage-based social situations, being confronted with and learning about the feelings and emotions connected to these situations. Group members are taught to recognize and experience the feelings and emotions associated with specific social situations (e.g. choosing a peer to team up with, confronting an obstinate peer, savoring the successful completion of a difficult group activity). Of particular focus in this approach is the recognition and awareness of situations involving core variables for the individual with ASD of self-regulation, emotion competence, stress, tension, and anxiety, attentional demands, flexibility, adjustments, and transitions, perspective taking, and relatedness.

Group participants are taught that, as part of a group working on developing, maintaining, and improving the quality of their social interactions and social relationships, they will inevitably be faced with situations where self-regulation is necessary, stress and tension will occur, anxiety and overload will be triggered, the need for a range of attentional capacities will be required, the need for flexibility and accommodation to change requirements and expectations will be confronted, and other perspectives must be considered. It is in this context of addressing the core variables and deficits of ASD that individuals will not only learn and rely on strategies and techniques that directly address these issues, but will also acknowledge and address the importance of their affective and emotional experiences and reactions in these situations.

Having a repertoire of responses available

As group members become more aware of and capable of recognizing and addressing feelings and emotions as part of the social interactive process, they are taught strategies and techniques to manage these feelings and emotions in effective, sensitive, and respectful ways. Group members are encouraged to apply the adaptive strategies and techniques learned in group to situations where feelings and emotions occur. Group discussions are ongoing about what strategies may be employed and which are best for the different situations confronted. Group members are encouraged to problem-solve as a group in the search for new or additional ways to manage and regulate feelings and emotions effectively.

Within the group structure, individuals are encouraged to focus upon and enhance individual capacities to focus and sustain attention within the peer interactions taking place and to participate actively in sharing and explaining thoughts, ideas, feelings, and emotions within the solution-focused environment. As cohesiveness is attained, the group participants are encouraged to actively engage one another, to learn when and how to confront one another respectfully, and to view each group session as a shared experience. Group members are expected to learn about one another, to guide each other in the consideration of problems and their solutions, and to support each other during times of stress. As problems are approached, group members participate fully in exploring the range of available alternatives and possibilities and are encouraged to develop flexible approaches to problem solving.

Choosing the appropriate response for the situation

With increased awareness of the emergence of feelings and emotions in group situations and with training and practice in basic management strategies and techniques, the group members are encouraged to consider and attempt the application of different strategies when emotions arise and must be managed. These attempts are discussed and processed, and members are encouraged to develop their own "toolbox" of strategies for the management and regulation of their own feelings and emotions as they might arise in group interactive and social situations.

Following through using the right tool for the situation

As the group proceeds through progressive stages, a range of different social situations are confronted and must be managed together with the coinciding feelings and emotions. Group members are taught to recognize the situation and its components (cognitive, social, emotional, behavioral), to choose a way to manage the situation, to implement the strategy, and to evaluate the success and benefits for the individual and the group. As these situations emerge, they are discussed and processed, and additional strategies may be considered. The group is encouraged to work together to formulate a "group approach" as well as to support each individual group member in their struggles to find effective strategies to manage and regulate their feelings and emotions. At each step, the group leader prepares and primes the group to anticipate the next level of stress, attentional issue, or flexibility concern that is likely to emerge as the group proceeds through stages of development.

In this group-based approach, where emphasis is placed on addressing underlying core variables and deficits and improving specific social skill development within a cognitive-developmental framework, aspects of emotional development, related to management, control, and regulation, can be addressed.

This approach follows a stepwise progression in focusing on these needs through:

1. raising awareness about affects and emotions: what they are, how they are experienced, and what forms of expression they may take

2. learning strategies and techniques to personally manage, control, and regulate one's own affects and emotions

3. learning how to recognize, experience, and use affects and emotions in interactions with peers, such as group-based situations

4. learning how to use one's increased awareness and understanding of affects and emotions to help others who may be struggling with their own management and control of affects and emotions.

Chapter 13

A Group-Based Therapeutic Model of Intervention for Children with ASD

Overview

As discussed in previous chapters, individuals with ASD present with many unique developmental issues. This includes uneven or derailed development in many of the seven critical core areas, resulting in deficits in related core variables. The most prominent concern is the pervasive core deficit of social impairment. To address these issues, the SCEP approach was developed, employing a group-focused approach to address the interpersonal, interactive aspects of the social impairment, a cognitive-developmental framework to address, discuss, problem-solve, and confront issues as they change and evolve over time, a social-competence/social-skill-based model to address the underlying structure-based and skill-based deficits, and a psychotherapeutic approach to address affective and emotional elements that come into play in an intervention program.

In this chapter, aspects of group-based psychotherapeutic approaches are considered and applied within the SCEP model. This is followed by descriptions of several key components that support a group-based psychotherapeutic approach for individuals with ASD, including fundamental therapeutic principles, the rationale for a group psychotherapeutic approach, and specific types of intervention techniques employed within this approach.

Group therapeutic approaches, while requiring some adaptation and modification, in many ways appear as the most appropriate and well-suited interventions to address the personal and interpersonal social impairments of individuals with ASD. By recognizing the impact and effects of weaknesses and deficits in core areas and related core variables, structures can be put in place within a group setting to address and overcome these issues. Issues that can be addressed include the core variables of self-regulation, emotion competence, anxiety and stress management, attention and joint attention, flexibility, change, and transitions, perspective taking, and relatedness. Because the SCEP model is considered a therapeutic approach, appropriate training for the group leader is necessary. While group psychotherapy should only be conducted by appropriately trained and credentialed professionals, psychotherapeutic process and psychotherapeutic approaches have much to offer in understanding how to consider and to address the issues that individuals with ASD present.

Psychotherapeutic approaches with ASD

Psychotherapy is a communication process in which an individual learns how to share and explore problems with another individual—the therapist—and together they work toward solutions. The individual with ASD must often learn first *how* to communicate, how to express himself accurately and appropriately, and how to read and understand the communications of others, again accurately and appropriately. Psychotherapy for the individual with ASD is about learning how and what to communicate, how and why to express and articulate problems, and how best to solve these problems with the strengths and limitations that the individual himself possesses. This is the therapeutic process for the individual with ASD.

Psychotherapy is a process of self-awareness and of interaction, where the individual learns about specific aspects of himself, including his own individual needs, and then must decide when and how to modify certain aspects of himself to address these needs. For the individual with ASD, it is also a process of self-awareness, of learning about his own unique issues and concerns, how they are related to ASD, and how they may affect his interactions with the world around him. It is this process of self-awareness that leads the individual with ASD to understand his disorder and its effects, to learn how to express these issues accurately and appropriately to others, and to take ownership and responsibility for his own thoughts, behaviors, and actions, whether related to ASD or not.

Psychotherapy is an interaction process that occurs between an individual and a therapist in a process of communication, exploration, and self-awareness. Psychotherapy with the individual with ASD must also address and explore the unique problems that will arise in interactions and communications resulting from the ASD itself. Given the problems inherent in ASD, the therapist must join with the individual with ASD in understanding the individual's problems and concerns, in how they relate to the issues of ASD, and in seeking solutions that best fit the individual and his needs.

The focus within the SCEP model is on how these principles relate specifically to group psychotherapeutic processes with individuals with ASD. As such, modifications of these processes for use with individuals with ASD must be considered and tailored to the needs of these individuals.

Therapeutic principles guiding group interventions

Axline (1964) outlined the basic principles necessary for effective psychotherapy with children which are adapted here to apply to group interventions for children with ASD. These form the psychotherapeutic basis for the SCEP approach described in this book. They include:

1. The group leader as therapist develops a warm empathic relationship with each group member.

2. The group leader recognizes and encourages each group member's right to express himself through thoughts, emotions, and appropriate behaviors.

3. The group leader and group participants understand and explicitly agree to engage and interact with one another on the basis of honesty and respect.

4. The group setting and environment will be a safe, supportive, open environment where thoughts and emotions can be shared and expressed in an open, honest, and respectful way between group participants without concern for one's physical or emotional safety.

5. Each group participant is expected to take ownership and responsibility for his own statements and behaviors and to attempt to understand how these are understood and interpreted by other group participants.

6. The primary rule in group therapy relates to *respect*—respect for the group leader, respect for oneself, respect for others in the group, respect for things that are brought into or used in the group, and respect for one's own and others' thoughts and emotions.

7. The group leader maintains responsibility for creating and maintaining the group structure, including setting, clarifying, and enforcing rules, boundaries, and limits when necessary.

8. A group structure is established, agreed upon, and adhered to by all group participants. (Axline 1964)

Within the group approach discussed here, consistent emphasis throughout is placed on the structure and progression within the group as it relates specifically to:

- the recognition of and adherence to the need for respect in all facets of interaction within the group

- the need to build and maintain rapport and cohesion within the group

- the need for rules and limits and an understanding of what is allowed and what is not allowed

- the importance of and focus on relationships and connections established, fostered, and maintained within the group

- a willingness to recognize, process, and understand what happens within the group, such as: attending to issues of self-regulation, emotions, anxiety, attention, flexibility, change, and transition, perspective, and relatedness; learning skills necessary to make relationships work.

The rationale for group interventions with individuals with ASD

ASD involves an impairment of social interaction and social communication. Individuals with ASD typically demonstrate significant problems in multiple areas of social functioning, and while there may be variation from individual to individual in how this manifests itself, impairment in social-interpersonal functioning is a core deficit. Therefore, it is important to understand the strengths and limitations of the individual with ASD and how these affect and influence social-interpersonal interactions. In this context, it is also believed that the learning and development of appropriate social-interactive skills is best achieved within a group environment that is sensitive to the issues, concerns, and needs of both individuals within the group and of the group itself.

Group interventions provide its participants with opportunities to address issues related to behavior, emotions, and thinking that can be enhanced through the use of:

- homogeneous grouping
- individual and group goal setting
- ongoing and consistent peer connections
- therapeutic interactions.

Homogeneous grouping

Homogeneous grouping—that is, grouping that is based on common factors and variables shared by all members of a group—forms the basis for the group structure employed within the SCEP model. A combination of age and developmental level serves as the first criterion for homogeneous grouping. Groups are constructed having a two-year age span (e.g. 6–7 years, 7–8 years, 8–9 years) allowing for a developmentally "more mature" seven-year-old to be placed in a 7–8 year old group where issues will more accurately reflect his developmental level, or for a developmentally "less mature" seven-year-old to be placed in a 6–7 year old group for the same reasons.

Also, during the application process, all group members are evaluated on the SCEP Initial Evaluation and Interview Form (see Form 14.2), described in Chapter 14, for the presence or absence of several individual, personal, and interpersonal variables considered important for social interaction. As described in previous chapters, these core variables include regulation (the ability to manage and control physical and emotional impulses as they arise in increasingly stimulating environments), emotions (recognition, labeling, expressing, understanding, and regulation), anxiety (its experience, expression, control, and management), attention (individual capacities for focused, sustained, selective, flexible, and joint forms), flexibility, change, and transition (its speed and efficiency), perspective (of self and others), and relatedness (the capacity to find a way to connect interpersonally and emotionally with another individual who is physically present at that moment). Other variables assessed include sensory issues (the toleration of stimulation involving the internal and external environmental needs of the individual, including sound/noise levels, physical space issues, visual inputs), general social-interpersonal capacities (the range of skills used to interact with another individual on verbal, physical, emotional, and behavioral levels), theory of mind (the capacity to take or understand another individual's point of view, way of thinking, or position on an issue or topic), and peer relationships (the demonstration in the real world—i.e. school, neighborhood, afterschool activities—of the ability to establish, maintain, and nurture extended and meaningful relationships and friendships).

With a general understanding of the functioning of the individual with ASD on these variables, a general profile of group proficiency (abilities and skills) is established. This profile is then used as the primary tool for understanding how the individual may function in a group situation, with consideration given to how this particular individual with ASD will "match" with other individuals with ASD. On this basis, group members are selected based on their ability to "match" with others on similar variables.

Within the SCEP model, great significance is placed on establishing and maintaining group balance—that is, that group members complement one another's strengths and deficits. Thus, group members may share similarities on some variables, but may contrast on other variables, as these are considered in a "good fit" approach. The ability of each individual considered for group placement to match with at least one peer in a core area is considered critical for the establishment of an appropriate group therapeutic environment. A particular group member may match with one member on a cognitive level, with another member on a communication level, with another on an emotional level, and so forth. One goal of this approach is to provide an environment where group members can recognize and acknowledge similarities and differences, can learn to relate to one another and to establish connections at their own pace, to learn how to make social-interpersonal contacts, to take social-interpersonal risks, to feel accepted within a group, and to express and learn from positive and negative emotions.

The homogeneous grouping of individuals with ASD assumes that when individuals are matched on similarities in core areas, particularly cognitive/ executive function, social, communication, and emotional functioning, identification, connection, and cohesion with other group members will be facilitated and enhanced. An understanding and awareness that others within the group may share similar experiences and perspectives enhances a sense of safety and support as issues and concerns emerge which generate stress and tension. As individuals within the group come to understand that they share similarities in thoughts, emotions, and experiences, a sense of mutual sharing and trust develops, allowing for a reduced sense of isolation, increased interpersonal risk taking, and enhanced self-exploration (Brown, Hedlinger and Mieling 1995).

Homogeneous grouping, by age, developmental level, and personal/ interpersonal characteristics, also allows for the construction of SCEP tasks and activities that are geared for particular stages of group development (described in Chapter 16).

Individual and group goal setting

Individual and group goal setting is a twofold process and includes, first, the establishment of individual goals for each member, and then, as the group forms and develops, the creation of group goals by all participants as they join in a common focus and recognize a common set of needs. The initial step in this goal-setting process is for each member to understand why he is in the group and what he is there to work on. This begins in the initial interview with each individual and family, where there is a discussion of parent issues and concerns, teacher data on school-based issues and concerns, information from checklists, and the individual's own expressed interests and concerns. This is followed by the creation of a list of "areas of interests" for the individual which provides a preliminary understanding of each individual's capacities to function with others in a group situation and of the ways in which individuals would "match" in a group situation with other similar individuals. Each individual's areas of interest form the basis for the creation of their own individual goals that will be focused on within the group (see Chapter 14, Forms 14.17 and 14.18). These goals are developed based on assessments from core areas and of core variables (areas of concern or need noted by child, parent, professional, or interviewer) and designate specific issues relating to peer interactions and group performance that interfere with effective social-interpersonal functioning. Examples of individual goals are contained in Appendix 2.

These areas of interest and individual goals are discussed and clarified with the individual with ASD and his parents/caretakers, with the understanding that these are issues that may be addressed in the group. Each participant then enters the group with a basic understanding of his own areas of interest, of his own individual goals, and of the importance of the goal-setting process. Member selection is determined by combinations of matches for age, developmental level, personal/interpersonal characteristics, and areas of interest. Following the construction and initiation of a group with participants who "match" and who share similar and consistent individual goals, group members must recognize and understand that they will be part of a group and must join with other participants in the establishment and setting of group goals—that is, goals that apply to the ongoing development of the group as a whole. As this process unfolds, group goals can be addressed and focused on.

Typically, groups are constructed of individuals with ASD who have similar individual goals to be worked on at the outset of the group experience. The individual goals for each group member are then used to construct group goals for that particular group. Initially, group leaders construct group goals as the group gets started, and eventually, through group discussion, the group itself accepts the task of creating and implementing appropriate group goals. Early on, groups typically create group goals that are similar to their individual goals, but relatively quickly they recognize the differences between individual and group goals and join together, led by the group leader, in the establishing of group goals based on shared intersections of interests, needs, issues, and concerns. The group goals are constructed based on the specific stage of group development that the group is at (as described in Chapter 16). For example, each group beginning at a Stage 1 level of *Group formation and orientation* will have constructed specific group goals relating to this stage. For example, a Stage 1 group goal may be "The group will learn what each member's favorite hobby (food, TV show, etc.) is." As the group moves through a particular stage and the next stage is approached, group leaders review individual goals with each participant, then, in discussion with the group, modify group goals or construct new goals as needed. It is this process of shared discussion and interaction on how to create group goals and what they will address that signals forward progress.

While groups proceed at different rates and function at different levels, it is necessary for the group leader to be active in encouraging and fostering the establishment and modification of ongoing group goals. At the same time, the group leader must be patient as the group members initially rely on their own individual goals to get themselves going before getting to the point of being ready and able to join together in the creation of group goals. Throughout, however, the group leader is aware of each participant's areas of interest and individual goals, so that the group leader may steer and direct the formation of the group goals in keeping with the developmental, cognitive, behavioral, emotional, and social needs of the group. Examples of individual and group goals are provided in Appendix 2 and Appendix 3.

Ongoing and consistent peer connections

The group format is intended to provide a safe haven for group members to establish connections at their own pace with each individual group member and to the group as a whole. Opportunities are provided for indepth peer connections and for each member to learn about social interactions, how to take social-interpersonal risks, how to express and experience both positive and negative affects and emotions in group situations, and what it is like to be accepted and understood by peers. Within the group, individual members are able to address stress- and anxiety-related issues as they arise within each stage of group development and as the result of various group interactions. New and previously experienced stress- and anxiety-producing situations that are related to individual interpersonal interactions and to specific situational or environmental triggers can also be addressed.

In the group situation, members may also address how variable attentional capacities (focused, sustained, selective, flexible, joint) affect and influence peer connections and interactions and how best to manage these situations. Group members are also provided with real-life opportunities to address issues of flexibility, change, and transition, as they arise in the moment-to-moment life of the group. Over time, internal comfort and security are established within the group, allowing members to experience and to express emotions, to receive honest and constructive feedback, and to learn and to employ new strategies and techniques to manage and cope more effectively in the social domain.

Therapeutic interactions

Therapeutic interactions make use of the group setting to provide opportunities for individuals to learn about what it means to be part of a group, to learn how to be a more effective group member, and to learn how to support and reinforce self and peers positively and respectfully within a group setting. The setting provides ongoing and frequent opportunities for the group leader to use existing situations and to create new situations which allow therapeutic interchanges to be experienced both directly and indirectly by all group members. The therapeutic value of the group experience for individuals with ASD exists within the interactions themselves, in learning how to communicate with others more effectively, in gaining increased self-awareness, and through repeated interpersonal interactions and experiences. From there, new responses can be constructed (Mishna and Muskat 1998).

Therapeutic interactions in this context occur between the group leader and individuals, between the group leader and the group as a whole, between an individual group member and another individual group member, and between individual group members and the group as a whole. Therapeutic interactions are always embedded within a relationship, emphasizing the relatedness and connectedness that occurs between individuals separately or as a group. They are respectful and accepting of the individual as a person or as part of a group and as existing with a range of thoughts, emotions, behaviors, and impulses, many of which seek expression. Therapeutic interactions are genuine and convey honest communication in a safe and supportive manner.

Implementation of the SCEP model

The SCEP model uses several different types of interventions to support the development of social competence and social skill building. Each of the interventions or techniques was chosen because of its ability to function effectively within a group setting and to enhance the benefits of grouping, goal setting, peer interactions, and therapeutic interactions, to allow for cognitive-developmental progression in core areas, both for individuals and for the group as a whole, and to be sensitive to the varying social, emotional, and behavioral aspects of individuals with ASD. Some are broad-based approaches, while others are specific techniques with demonstrated effectiveness with certain aspects of intervention or training with individuals with ASD. Each adheres to the underlying rationale of the SCEP model that uses group approaches to address the social impairment of individuals with ASD and emphasizes the importance of homogeneous grouping, individual and group goal setting, peer connections, and therapeutic interactions.

While the types of interventions employed here may differ in significant ways from each other, they also overlap in many other ways and appear best suited to emphasize the key concepts and support the underlying rationale of SCEP. Those that have been found particularly helpful and are used extensively within the SCEP model include:

1. small-group format
2. developmental leveling
3. self-management
4. peer-mediated approach
5. priming
6. pivotal response training
7. direct instruction
8. written scripts.

Small-group format

Within SCEP, the small-group format employed typically consists of four or five individuals with ASD with one group leader or, alternatively, five or six individuals with ASD with two group leaders. Since group members are also selected on the basis of "best fit" in core areas and core variables and similar areas of interest and individual group goals, the likelihood of strong and positive connections is increased. Keeping group membership at low and manageable levels is intended to encourage and create more relationship opportunities between group participants early in the group experience, to encourage ongoing group cohesion and peer connections, and to foster more intense interactions and connections later in the group experience.

The small-group format allows for the construction and maintenance of a group structure that meets the needs and individual goals of each group member while also emphasizing the needs and goals of the group as a whole. Initially, this includes setting up a structure to encourage and foster interaction, later a structure that requires addressing and managing conflict and confrontation, and still later a structure that includes understanding, processing, and integrating interactional information. With a small, limited number of group participants, it is possible to focus specifically on each individual's areas of interest and individual goals and gradually to join these with the group goals constructed for the particular stage of group development. The small-group format also makes possible the construction of more specific and directed group goals as well as allowing the broader group goals to shift more quickly and readily, based on the group's development as it moves through different stages of group evolution.

The small-group format also ensures a close connection between group members and the group leader, utilizing a constant feedback loop of what works and what doesn't as the group leader initiates and facilitates appropriate task and activity selection consistent with the current stage of group development. It also allows each individual member to be more involved directly in task and activity construction and selection, forces members to discuss issues and work together, and requires the addressing and resolution of differences and conflicts. In this format, the group leader is better able to focus on developing group cohesion, peer connections, and interactive intensity in therapeutically useful and beneficial ways, to stay attuned to the variety of interactive experiences, and to respond to situations in timely and informed ways.

Developmental leveling

Developmental leveling occurs when, following assessment in one or more areas, individuals are grouped together based on similarities or (complementary) differences in those areas, in the belief that those similarities or (complementary) differences will facilitate both individual and group progress. The SCEP model emphasizes an ongoing understanding of the overall developmental level in core areas for each group member as well as the overall developmental level of the group as a whole. Within the SCEP model, information from a variety of sources is collected as part of the intake, interview, and assessment process in order to assess general performance in each core area, to understand the strengths and weaknesses of each individual, to specify areas of interest, and ultimately to make informed decisions about group placement. Information from past and current evaluations, parent and teacher observations, and interview data provides the basis for understanding an individual's cognitive, behavioral, learning, and emotional styles and for understanding an individual's general developmental level in the areas covered. When information for several potential group participants has been collected and reviewed, considerations about the likelihood of an effective "developmental fit" can begin. For example, individuals with similar levels of cognitive-development may share similar interests in this area, individuals at similar levels of behavioral development may require similar levels of external structure, individuals with similar levels of emotional development may benefit from certain types of support and feedback, and individuals with similar levels of learning and skill development may share educational interests.

While homogeneous grouping, based on group members' overall similarities, provides one basis for forming a group, the SCEP model also requires an understanding of both the individual's and the group's complementary differences, areas of interests, individual and group goals, and individuals' specific needs for tasks and activities (i.e. skill instructional levels). As groups proceed, increasing emphasis is placed on group leader observations, the quality and types of group member interactions and feedback to one another, and a constant monitoring of the group's session-to-session performance on the specific tasks and activities selected based on group goals. Group goals and activities are adjusted and modified frequently to stay in line with the overall developmental level of both individuals and the group.

Self-management

Within the SCEP model, heavy emphasis is placed on self-management and self-control by individual group members, with the goal of developing strategies to understand, manage, and control their own behavior, thoughts, and emotions. Discussions, tasks, and activities are constructed specifically to address and consider within the group how self-management requires an understanding of oneself and one's typical responses to different situations, how it requires an understanding of the nature of social situations, and how it requires an understanding of what responses are required in which situation. The expectation and requirement for self-management and self-control in social situations is directly connected to the core variables of self-regulation, the effective management of varying degrees and states of stress and anxiety related to both individual and group social situations, to needs for close and directed attention, and to needs for flexibility and change depending on the situation. As such, self-management and self-control in social situations are understood as the most important and often the most difficult facets of social competence for individuals with ASD.

The SCEP model requires group members to become aware of and assume increasing responsibility for understanding, managing and controlling, and directing their own personal and interpersonal communications and interactions with others. From the outset of group, both individual and group goals focus on increasing personal and interpersonal self-management and self-control through training, practice, and reinforcement. Group members are expected to take increasing ownership and responsibility of this individual and group process and to learn and implement strategies that can be applied consistently and effectively in natural group settings. This includes learning and practicing how to self-monitor and self-reinforce with both tangible and intangible reinforcers.

Peer-mediated approach

Peer-mediated approaches emphasize the power and importance of peer-to-peer interactions when peers are placed in active, instructional roles, learning and teaching one another skills for effective advancement. The SCEP model employs a structured peer-mediated approach utilizing the extensive research and positive results of this approach with instructional groups. Within the SCEP model, peer-mediated interactions emphasize structure, direction, self-awareness and self-management, systematic skill building, consistent monitoring, and frequent feedback within a sequential and progressive model that places increasing responsibility on the group members themselves to move their group forward.

Within the small-group setting, with group members placed based on similar developmental levels, and with an emphasis on self-management and self-control, the group leader gradually places increasing expectations on group members to be aware of their own individual and group goals, to take an active role in meeting then reconstructing their individual and group goals, and to learn how to participate in taking control and running their group so as to achieve these mutual, reciprocal goals. The small-group format with significant leader involvement allows group members to gradually assume roles of increasing self and group responsibility and to actively and cooperatively work with other group members in moving the group forward. The peer-mediated approach within SCEP emphasizes setting and holding to a clear structure and set of expectations, significant practice and orientation to all tasks and activities provided, including a discussion and understanding of the rationale and purpose of their use, clear instructions and skill building in ways to succeed, close monitoring of performance and progress with adjustments and modifications as necessary, and constant and consistent feedback to group members.

Priming

The concept of priming is used to introduce new information and new skills, to reduce and manage related anxiety and stress, and to provide a consistent and predictable approach. Priming involves preparing the group members for the introduction of new information, a new task or activity, or a new way of approaching and managing a problematic situation. Within SCEP, this is done by breaking complex tasks into simple steps, then preparing and training the group to manage the initial parts of the new information with previously learned skills and strategies. Following this, subsequent steps are introduced and merged with previously learned steps, until the task is completely learned.

Group members are prepared in advance to anticipate and respond to the new information to be presented and are desensitized to any stress or anxiety related to the upcoming information by the use and practice of techniques for stress and anxiety control and management. They are encouraged to rely on learned strategies and techniques and skills that have been successful and reinforcing as they develop and consider new strategies and skills. When presenting new information, initial steps in the task are introduced in low-stress situations, with reduced cognitive, behavioral, and social demands. Initial successes are heavily reinforced, then gradually followed with subsequent steps, reinforced and supported as needed and with stress and anxiety management techniques as indicated. As new tasks are moved into, additional strategies are taught and employed to address the new information or situations, and attempts are made to integrate any new information and skills with previously learned skills. This process is repeated with each new task and each new step in the learning process, constantly making use of previously employed strategies and techniques to learn and master the new information and tasks.

Pivotal response training (PRT)

Within SCEP, principles of pivotal response training (PRT) are used and adapted for individuals with ASD to fit with other aspects of this peer-based, group-focused, skill-directed intervention program. PRT, an intervention that primarily employs applied behavioral techniques, focuses on training in pivotal areas, such as behavior, language, and social interaction, through the use of motivation, multiple cues, and self-management (Koegel and Frea 1993). The PRT focus within SCEP is on learning and increasing the frequency of social interaction while managing behaviors that could interfere with this process.

The small-group, peer-based SCEP approach described here focuses on and encourages group member initiation and agreement on tasks and activities, group member direction of tasks and activities when appropriate, and mutual reinforcement of success and of appropriate behaviors, as motivating influences. The group leader facilitates a task and activity selection process that begins with less demanding, more manageable tasks with a higher likelihood for success and gradually moves toward more demanding, challenging, and anxiety-arousing tasks and activities. Group members are provided with strategies and techniques to manage stress and anxiety as it arises related to both the tasks and activities and the group and individual interaction process, with self-motivating and peer-motivating affirmation statements and techniques, and with learned positive optimism approaches.

Other PRT components emphasized throughout SCEP are active choice, clear instructions, goal focus, consistent reinforcement, and multiple presentations in slightly different form of the same skill. Throughout this process, principles of PRT are merged with priming concepts. PRT provides the group leader with techniques to understand, target, and respond to important areas of social interaction and related behaviors, while priming concepts encourage the group leader to move sequentially and systematically through the steps of teaching specific social skills. PRT and priming both allow the "spiraling effect" to take hold and influence the recognition and learning of process variables (self-regulation, emotion competence, stress/anxiety management, joint attention, flexibility/transitions, etc.) and the learning of specific social skills (initiating conversation, asking questions, providing feedback, etc.). There is some research evidence that with consistent effort these components support generalization across settings and activities (Pierce and Schreibman 1995, 1997).

Direct instruction

Initially, the group leader selects specific skills to be taught based on information collected, observations, and the construction of individual and group goals. The SCEP model assumes that group members possess a wide range of interactive skills, but also with significant and varied areas of deficit requiring direct skill instruction. Attempts are made to use and build on areas of strength to target these deficit areas and to specify the necessary skills to be taught, practiced, reinforced, and generalized, employing principles of priming and PRT. Specific skills to be taught are selected by the group leader based on areas of interest and individual and group goals. The group leader then breaks down complex social skills into simple steps that can be learned, practiced, and reinforced within each weekly group as well as over time. The specific skills presented are intended to fit the cognitive, language/communication, and social-emotional capacities of each group member.

Group members are also encouraged to interact with one another about their experiences, to discuss strategies that they find useful and successful, to help their peers understand and manage points or areas of difficulty, and to work together in developing additional strategies to succeed and move forward. Direct skill instruction within SCEP requires group members to learn how to understand and work with both their strengths and limitations in group interaction and to take increasing responsibility for their group behavior and social-interpersonal interactions.

Written scripts

The use of written scripts as a specific type of intervention (Charlop-Christy and Kelso 2003; Volden and Johnston 1999) has been used successfully with individuals with ASD to focus on and teach specific skills and appropriate behavior as they relate to specific events and situations. These events and situations can be initiated by adults working with individuals with ASD or can be taken from the individual's own daily interactions. Written scripts are then constructed either by an adult or together with the individual with ASD which include characters, themes, certain environments and situations, a range of possible social behaviors, outcomes, and feedback. Written scripts provide opportunities for individuals with ASD to address specific issues and concerns that may be encountered or, in many instances, situations that may be of ongoing concern (i.e. teasing, bullying, approaching unfamiliar situations, etc.).

The use of Social Stories™ is a specific intervention developed by Carol Gray (1998, 2000) that has been found useful for some individuals with ASD. Social Stories are intended to address what is happening, who is involved, where it is occurring, why it is happening, when the situation is taking place, and what the most age-appropriate responses or outcomes for the specific situation may be. Social Stories employ the use of written scripts, direct instruction, self-management, developmental leveling, priming, and managing and regulating affective reaction and responses, and have been demonstrated to be most effective when used in combination with other types of interventions (Scattone, Tingstrom and Wilczynski 2006).

Chapter 14

Assessment in the SCEP Model: Understanding Individuals with ASD

Overview

The SCEP model emphasizes a thorough and comprehensive understanding of the ongoing needs and areas of concern of the individual with ASD, specifically as these needs relate to the presence or absence of social competencies and social skills. This includes an understanding of functioning in each core area and of any difficulties in related core variables. Related to these issues, relevant information is collected from history and previous evaluations, past and present intervention reports, and current parent and teacher observational data. This includes information related to diagnostic considerations and questions and the individual's cognitive, emotional, behavioral, and learning styles and patterns of existing strengths and limitations. When these sets of information and observations have been acquired, specific questions are then generated for face-to-face interviews. Ultimately, this information will be used to determine areas of interest and to construct goals for each individual, and, finally, group goals when the individual is placed within a group.

Collecting information relevant to group interventions

Referrals to the SCEP program begin with an initial direct contact from the family or referring professional to discuss the appropriateness of the program for the individual with ASD. All available relevant background medical, developmental, educational, and mental health histories are requested, with a particular focus on social interactions and social skill development.

This process requires that parents/caretakers of the individual with ASD provide documents, medical records, previous assessments and evaluations, pertinent school records, and information regarding previous interventions. A face-to-face interview is also required of both parent/caretaker and individual with ASD, with at least part of the time being a joint interview of the parent/caretaker and individual with ASD together in interaction. These interviews include a complete developmental and family history. At this point, arrangements are also made for the collection of teacher observations as well as those of any other professionals or paraprofessionals working with the individual with ASD.

Next, but prior to beginning group, parents and teachers are required to complete several formal and informal checklists that address core areas and related core variables and aspects of social competence and social interactions in both group and individual home and school settings. These checklists were created or selected specifically to assess the particular needs of individuals with ASD, to understand areas of interest, and to guide the construction of appropriate individual and group goals within the SCEP model. They are used to assess and measure functioning in various individual and group situations and at different points in time, and to compare the functioning of these individuals to both neurotypical and nontypical standardized populations. They may also be used to assess an individual's progress over time regarding the group interventions provided when administered at different points in the group process (e.g. beginning, middle, and end of an individual's group participation).

Checklists were constructed to assess each core area and related core variables. In assessing core variables, the focus is on those variables considered most important and critical for social-interpersonal development. Necessarily, there is significant attention paid to those variables whose development has been derailed and that prevent or inhibit age-appropriate development and progress in social development and interactions. As stated throughout this book, core variables do not usually function independent of one another, nor are they discrete. They are complex, overlapping constructs that function in consequence and simultaneously with one or more other core variables. Generally, several core variables will be considered simultaneously in the construction of a SCEP program, whether related to a single individual or to a cluster of several group participants. The SCEP Test Information and Data Sheet (Form 14.1) is used to compile this information in a useable manner. The SCEP Initial Evaluation and Interview Form (Form 14.2) requires that core variables and related issues be specifically considered and addressed in the interview process with parent/caretaker and the individual with ASD.

Following the interview process, the interviewer/evaluator is encouraged to complete the 11 brief assessments (Forms 14.3–14.13) which cover all core areas and core variables. At times, for specific reasons or with certain individuals, the interviewer/evaluator may select only specifically relevant assessments to complete, but this should always include core variable assessments for those core variables being considered as a focus of the group.

Following completion and consideration of the core area and core variable assessments, the interviewer/evaluator is now able to evaluate the child's appropriateness for SCEP group intervention. Several forms are used to collect summary data from the interview forms and core area and core variable assessments and include the SCEP Assessment for Group Placement (see Form 14.14), SCEP Core Strengths and Weaknesses Form (see Form 14.15), and SCEP: Would This Child Benefit from a Social Competence/Social Skills Group? (see Form 14.16). If appropriate for a group, then the SCEP Groups: Areas of Interest Form (Form 14.17) and the SCEP Groups: Individual Goals Form (Form 14.18) are completed and group placement issues are addressed. When a group is formed, the SCEP Groups: Group Goals Form (Form 14.19) for the group of the individuals to be included is completed.

The intent of gathering such extensive information is multifaceted. The primary goal is to assess and understand the social competence and social skill development of the individual with ASD in order to construct an appropriate plan of action for a successful group experience. Given the nature of ASD as a significant impairment in social interaction with related problems in understanding and engaging in age-appropriate peer relationships, the requested information is a necessary component in addressing the individual's issues in social relationships in a systematic way, fully informed by all available diagnostic and treatment information. Following interview, data collection, and review of this necessary information, decisions about appropriate structure and implementation of behavioral and treatment interventions are then considered. The SCEP model was created specifically to address the broad range of social, cognitive, emotional, and behavioral needs demonstrated by individuals with ASD within the social-interactive, therapeutic peer group setting.

All the information collected is reviewed by the group leader prior to the start of the group, forming the basis for the construction of areas of interest and individual and group goals for each child. Areas of interest are defined as issues of concern designated by both parents and teachers—that is, concerning or problematic behaviors or interactions noted both at home and at school by adult observers in situations prior to beginning in the group. Examples of areas of interest selected may be broad, such as "tries to control discussions," to the more specific, such as "refuses to share personal information." Additionally, the data collected provide information regarding appropriate group placement as well as informing the process of individual and group goal development.

In working with individuals with ASD within the SCEP model, the following forms have been developed and have proven useful in understanding the social competence and social skill needs of the individual and to guide decisions about acceptance for a group experience, placement in a specific social competence group, and construction of appropriate individual and group goals.

SCEP Test Information and Data Sheet
(Form 14.1, page 144)

This form collects in one place information considered relevant to the SCEP model and is completed as soon as all past and current evaluations, reports, and communications have been received and reviewed. This form includes test data and information about learning, cognitive, and social-emotional styles as demonstrated on previous evaluations completed. An attempt is made to understand the individual's cognitive abilities and style, language and communication patterns, neurocognitive capacities (i.e. visual-spatial, attentional, memory, organizational capacities), academic skill development, and social-emotional functioning. Emphasis is placed on understanding the level of development of underlying structures and the attainment and precision of specific skills. This information is generally obtained from parents and other professionals working with the individual with ASD prior to the initial interview and provides a general sense of the individual's overall profile of strengths and limitations as well as allowing for the construction of specific questions for the face-to-face interviews.

SCEP Initial Evaluation and Interview Form
(Form 14.2, page 145)

This form is completed during or shortly after the face-to-face interview with the parent/caretaker and individual with ASD. It includes observational data that is considered important for group placement decisions and for understanding the individual's areas of interest—that is, those issues or concerns to be addressed within the group.

The Initial Evaluation and Interview Form focuses primarily on specific personal and interpersonal issues which appear to be of critical importance for the individual with ASD and necessary for social interchange. Nine specific issues are addressed on the form, and relevant examples of each are recorded when observed in the interview, particularly those areas (referred to as "core variables") known to be deficient in individuals with ASD. (Each is rated on a scale from 1–5, low–high.) Also, observations, collected information, and examples of several other key concepts important for an understanding of the individual with ASD are obtained and noted on this form with a final global statement about the individual's appropriateness for placement in a group.

In addition to the history taking, interviewing, and the review of previous data and evaluations, a number of specific core area and core variable assessments are completed. The checklists are constructed so that they can be completed by multiple individuals involved with the individual being assessed and considered for placement in a group (parents, teachers, clinician/interviewers, and group leaders). They are constructed to be brief checklists of 5–20 items, intended to provide information on the individual's functioning in core areas and on core variables for use in group placement and goal construction, group task and activity development and selection, and pregroup and postgroup evaluations. A total of 11 assessments are included and a description of each follows.

SCEP Individual Profile: Self-Regulation Assessment (Form 14.3, page 146)

The Self-Regulation Assessment (also discussed in Chapter 4) is a checklist containing 15 items that parents/caretakers are requested to complete at or shortly following the initial intake interview. Teachers, clinician/interviewers, and/or group leaders are also requested to complete the assessment after having had an opportunity to work with the individual for a period of time sufficient to understand general levels of functioning. The 15 items provide the group leader with specific information about how the individual with ASD manages and copes with different self-regulation-related issues. Each item is rated on a scale from 1 to 5, ranging from *never* (a score of 1) to *always* (a score of 5). The total of these 15 ratings is summed and a *total self-regulation score* is obtained. A general *self-regulation assessment scoring continuum* is included at the end of the assessment to provide a general guide to the group leader as to where the individual will fall on the continuum which ranges from *poorly regulated internal and external capacities* (a score of 15) to *well-regulated internal and external capacities* (a score of 75). The information from the Self-Regulation Assessment provides the group leader with additional data with which to understand areas of interests and to develop individual and group goals.

SCEP Individual Profile: Emotion Competence Assessment (Form 14.4, page 147)

The Emotion Competence Assessment (also discussed in Chapters 3 and 5) is a checklist containing 20 items that parents/caretakers are requested to complete at or shortly following the initial intake interview. Teachers, clinician/interviewers, and/or group leaders are also requested to complete the assessment after having had an opportunity to work with the individual for a period of time sufficient to understand general levels of functioning. The 20 items are divided into four sections, each relating to specific areas of emotion competence (emotion recognition, labeling and expression, understanding, and regulation) and consisting of five items each. The five items within each area provide the group leader with specific information about how the individual with ASD functions in that specific area of emotion competence. Each item is rated on a scale from 1 to 5, ranging from *never* (a score of 1) to *always* (a score of 5). The total of the five ratings within each area is summed and an *emotion competence score* for each area is obtained. The total sum of the 20 items provides a *total emotion competence score*. A general *emotion competence assessment scoring continuum* is included at the end of the assessment to provide a general guide to the group leader as to where the individual will fall on the continuum for both the specific emotion competence areas and for the total score. This ranges from *poor emotion competence* (a score of 5 for the specific areas, a score of 20 for the total score) to *excellent emotion competence* (a score of 25 for the specific areas, a score of 100 for the total score). The information from the Emotion Competence Assessment provides the group leader with additional data with which to understand areas of interests and to develop individual and group goals.

SCEP Individual Profile: Stress–Anxiety Assessment (Form 14.5, page 148)

The Stress–Anxiety Assessment (also discussed in Chapter 6) is a checklist containing 12 items that parents/caretakers are requested to complete at or shortly following the initial intake interview. Teachers, clinician/interviewers, and/or group leaders are also requested to complete the assessment after having had an opportunity to work with the individual for a period of time sufficient to understand general levels of functioning. The 12 items provide the group leader with specific information about how the individual with ASD manages and copes with different stress–anxiety issues. Each item is rated on a scale from 1 to 5, ranging from *never* (a score of 1) to *always* (a score of 5). The total of these 12 ratings is summed and a *total anxiety score* is obtained. A general *stress–anxiety assessment scoring continuum* is included at the end of the assessment to provide a general guide to the group leader as to where the individual will fall on the continuum which ranges from *high stress/anxiety and low coping/ management* (a score of 12) to *manages stress/anxiety and good coping/management* (a score of 60). The information from the Stress–Anxiety Assessment provides the group leader with additional data with which to understand areas of interests and to develop individual and group goals.

SCEP Individual Profile: Attention Assessment (Form 14.6, page 149)

The Attention Assessment (also discussed in Chapter 7) is a checklist containing 20 items that parents/caretakers are requested to complete at or shortly following the initial intake interview. Teachers, clinician/interviewers, and/ or group leaders are also requested to complete the assessment after having had an opportunity to work with the individual for a period of time sufficient to understand general levels of functioning. The 20 items are divided into five sections, each relating to a specific area of attention (focused, sustained, selective, flexible, and joint attention) and each consisting of four items. These five areas of attention follow the developmental progression of attention described in Chapter 7. The four items within each area provide the group leader with specific information about how the individual with ASD functions within specific areas of attention. Each item is rated on a scale from 1 to 5, ranging from *never* (a score of 1) to *always* (a score of 5). The total of the four ratings within each area is summed and an *attention score* for each area is obtained. The total sum of the 20 items provides a *total attention score*. A general *attention assessment scoring continuum* is included at the end of the assessment to provide a general guide to the group leader as to where the individual will fall on the continuum for both the specific attention areas and for the total score. This ranges from *low attention* (a score of 4 for the specific areas, a score of 20 for the total score) to *high attention* (a score of 20 for the specific areas, a score of 100 for the total score). The information from the Attention Assessment provides the group leader with additional data with which to understand areas of interests and to develop individual and group goals.

SCEP Individual Profile: Flexibility, Change, and Transition Assessment (Form 14.7, page 150)

The Flexibility, Change, and Transition Assessment (also discussed in Chapter 8) is a checklist containing five items that parents/caretakers are requested to complete at or shortly following the initial intake interview. Teachers, clinician/interviewers, and/or group leaders are also requested to complete the assessment after having had an opportunity to work with the individual for a period of time sufficient to understand general levels of functioning. The five items provide the group leader with specific information about how the individual with ASD deals with issues and situations requiring flexibility, change, and transition. Each item is rated on a scale from 1 to 5, ranging from *never* (a score of 1) to *always* (a score of 5). The total of these five ratings is summed and a *total flexibility, change, and transition score* is obtained. A general *flexibility, change, and transition assessment scoring continuum* is included at the end of the assessment to provide a general guide to the group leader as to where the individual will fall on the continuum which ranges from *high inflexibility, low capacity for change or transition* (a score of 5) to *high flexibility, good capacity for change or transition* (a score of 25). The information from the Flexibility, Change, and Transition Assessment provides the group leader with additional data with which to understand areas of interest and to develop individual and group goals.

SCEP Individual Profile: Perspective-Taking Assessment (Form 14.8, page 150)

The Perspective-Taking Assessment (also discussed in Chapter 9) is a checklist containing 15 items that parents/caretakers are requested to complete at or shortly following the initial intake interview. Teachers, clinician/interviewers, and/or group leaders are also requested to complete the assessment after having had an opportunity to work with the individual for a period of time sufficient to understand general levels of functioning. The 15 items provide the group leader with specific information about how the individual with ASD manages and copes with different perspective-taking issues. Each item is rated on a scale from 1 to 5, ranging from *never* (a score of 1) to *always* (a score of 5). The total of these 15 ratings is summed and a *total perspective-taking score* is obtained. A general *perspective-taking assessment scoring continuum* is included at the end of the assessment to provide a general guide to the group leader as to where the individual will fall on the continuum which ranges from *poor perspective taker, does not understand others' thoughts, feelings, or behaviors* (a score of 15) to *good perspective taker, good understanding of others' thoughts, feelings, or behaviors* (a score of 75). The information from the Perspective-Taking Assessment provides the group leader with additional data with which to understand areas of interests and to develop individual and group goals.

SCEP Individual Profile: Social Interaction Assessment (Form 14.9, page 151)

The Social Interaction Assessment (also discussed in Chapter 3) is a checklist containing ten items that parents/caretakers are requested to complete at or shortly following the initial intake interview. Teachers, clinician/interviewers, and/or group leaders are also requested to complete the assessment after having had an opportunity to work with the individual for a period of time sufficient to understand general levels of functioning. The ten items provide the group leader with specific information about how the individual with ASD manages and copes with different social interaction issues. Each item is rated on a scale from 1 to 5, ranging from *never* (a score of 1) to *always* (a score of 5). The total of these ten ratings is summed and a *total social interaction score* is obtained. A general *social interaction assessment scoring continuum* is included at the end of the assessment to provide a general guide to the group leader as to where the individual will fall on the continuum which ranges from *limited social interactive capacities* (a score of 10) to *excellent social interactive capacities* (a score of 50). The information from the Social Interaction Assessment provides the group leader with additional data with which to understand areas of interests and to develop individual and group goals.

SCEP Individual Profile: Cognitive/Executive Function Assessment (Form 14.10, page 151)

The Cognitive/Executive Function Assessment (also discussed in Chapter 3) is a checklist containing 12 items that parents/caretakers are requested to complete at or shortly following the initial intake interview. Teachers, clinician/interviewers, and/or group leaders are also requested to complete the assessment after having had an opportunity to work with the individual for a period of time sufficient to understand general levels of functioning. The 12 items provide the group leader with specific information about how the individual with ASD manages and copes with different cognitive issues. Each item is rated on a scale from 1 to 5, ranging from *never* (a score of 1) to *always* (a score of 5). The total of these 12 ratings is summed and a *total cognitive/executive function score* is obtained. A general *cognitive/executive function assessment scoring continuum* is included at the end of the assessment to provide a general guide to the group leader as to where the individual will fall on the continuum which ranges from *limited cognitive capacities and understanding* (a score of 12) to *high cognitive capacities and understanding* (a score of 60). The information from the Cognitive/Executive Function Assessment provides the group leader with additional data with which to understand areas of interests and to develop individual and group goals.

SCEP Individual Profile: Pragmatic Language Assessment (Form 14.11, page 152)

The Pragmatic Language Assessment (also discussed in Chapter 3) is a checklist containing 15 items that parents/caretakers are requested to complete at or shortly following the initial intake interview. Teachers, clinician/interviewers, and/or group leaders are also requested to complete the assessment after having had an opportunity to work with the individual for a period of time sufficient to understand general levels of functioning. The 15 items provide the group leader with specific information about how the individual with ASD manages and copes with different pragmatic language issues. Each item is rated on a scale from 1 to 5, ranging from *never* (a score of 1) to *always* (a score of 5). The total of these 15 ratings is summed and a *total pragmatic language score* is obtained. A general *pragmatic language assessment scoring continuum* is included at the end of the assessment to provide a general guide to the group leader as to where the individual will fall on the continuum which ranges from *poor understanding and use of verbal/nonverbal language* (a score of 15) to *excellent understanding and use of verbal/nonverbal language* (a score of 75). The information from the Pragmatic Language Assessment provides the group leader with additional data with which to understand areas of interests and to develop individual and group goals.

SCEP Individual Profile: Sensory Assessment (Form 14.12, page 153)

The Sensory Assessment (also discussed in Chapter 3) is a checklist containing eight items that parents/caretakers are requested to complete at or shortly following the initial intake interview. Teachers, clinician/interviewers, and/or group leaders are also requested to complete the assessment after having had an opportunity to work with the individual for a period of time sufficient to understand general levels of functioning. The eight items provide the group leader with specific information about how the individual with ASD manages and copes with different sensory issues. Each item is rated on a scale from 1 to 5, ranging from *never* (a score of 1) to *always* (a score of 5). The total of these eight ratings is summed and a *total sensory score* is obtained. A general *sensory assessment scoring continuum* is included at the end of the assessment to provide a general guide to the group leader as to where the individual will fall on the continuum which ranges from *limited sensory capacities and understanding* (a score of 8) to *good sensory capacities and understanding* (a score of 40). The information from the Sensory Assessment provides the group leader with additional data with which to understand areas of interests and to develop individual and group goals.

SCEP Individual Profile: Motor Assessment (Form 14.13, page 153)

The Motor Assessment (also discussed in Chapter 3) is a checklist containing five items that parents/caretakers are requested to complete at or shortly following the initial intake interview. Teachers, clinician/interviewers, and/ or group leaders are also requested to complete the assessment after having had an opportunity to work with the individual for a period of time sufficient to understand general levels of functioning. The five items provide the group leader with specific information about how the individual with ASD manages and copes with different motor issues. Each item is rated on a scale from 1 to 5, ranging from *never* (a score of 1) to *always* (a score of 5). The total of these five ratings is summed and a *total motor score* is obtained. A general *motor assessment scoring continuum* is included at the end of the assessment to provide a general guide to the group leader as to where the individual will fall on the continuum which ranges from *undeveloped or poor motor capacities* (a score of 5) to *coordinated motor capacities* (a score of 25). The information from the Motor Assessment provides the group leader with additional data with which to understand areas of interests and to develop individual and group goals.

SCEP Assessment for Group Placement (Form 14.14, page 154)

This form requires the interviewer/evaluator to rate the child in ten areas (eight specific core areas and core variables and two general), each on a continuum ranging from low-functioning to high-functioning, using collected evaluation, interview, and assessment data. This form is intended to narrow the interviewer/evaluator's thinking regarding how the particular child may function in specific areas when placed in peer-based, group situations.

SCEP Core Strengths and Weaknesses Form (Form 14.15, page 155)

The Core Strengths and Weaknesses Form is a checklist designed to highlight a prospective group member's strengths and weaknesses in specific core areas and specific core variables based on reviews of information provided and assessments completed. All major areas focused on within the SCEP model are addressed and considered. This information is used for decision making on the appropriateness of group participation, in the construction of "best fit" groups, in the placement of specific children with others of similar strengths/ weaknesses, and in the construction of individual and group goals.

SCEP: Would This Child Benefit from a Social Competence/ Social Skills Group? (Form 14.16, page 156)

This form provides a final checklist in the decision of the appropriateness of a SCEP group intervention for this child. It includes a review of all areas considered and assessed.

SCEP Groups: Areas of Interest Form (Form 14.17, page 157)

This form is used to compile areas of interest collected from parents/caretakers, teachers, other professionals, interviewers of the individual with ASD, and, when appropriate, the individual with ASD himself. This information is also gathered from previous reports and evaluations provided, telephone consultations, interview information, and observational material.

Areas of interest are issues of concern defined by the individual with ASD, parents/caretakers, teachers, or other observers of the individual as requiring focus and attention in order to function more effectively in social interactions. Areas of interest may be concerning or problematic behaviors or interactions which would benefit from intervention. The Areas of Interest Form notes specific points that may be addressed in considering these issues. Attempts are made to categorize these points by their apparent importance, designating areas of interest as most significant, somewhat significant, or "other" significant. These categories are intended to facilitate translation into individual and group goals for the individual with ASD. An area of interest is considered more significant (i.e. more important, more problematic) if it is noted by several observers and rated as less significant (i.e. less important, less problematic) if it is noted by fewer observers or observable only in certain defined, controlled situations. Some examples of general and specific areas of interest are provided in Appendix 1.

SCEP Groups: Individual Goals Form (Form 14.18, page 158)

This form is used to indicate specific goals based on areas of interest indicated by parents/caretakers, others working with the individual with ASD, observers of the individual, and, when appropriate, the individual with ASD himself. It is the focus of the SCEP model to create feasible goals for the individual with ASD that can be worked on within the group. As such, not all areas of interest, even when designated as most significant, may be chosen for translation into goals. This may occur when the designated area of interest cannot feasibly and appropriately be addressed within the group setting constructed. Some examples of individual goals constructed by specific stage are provided in Appendix 2.

SCEP Groups: Group Goals Form (Form 14.19, page 159)

Group goals are created by the group leaders based on the sets of individual goals for each individual with ASD entering the group. Once the Individual Goals Form is completed, the goals for each individual with ASD being considered for possible group placement are then aligned with those of other individuals being considered and emphasis is given to the "best fit" clustering within the group setting. Individual goals may be specific to the individual with ASD, but must also be related to overall group goals with consistency and synergy between individual goals and group goals maintained. All individual goals must have some connection to a group goal and to a specific stage of group development.

Group goals must be specific and related to the whole group's needs and to the specific stage of group development within which they will be focused. Forward progression on group goals should coincide with individual goal attainment and relate to the specific stage of group development that the group has achieved. Some examples of group goals constructed by specific stage are provided in Appendix 3.

The forms are available for download at www.jkp.com/catalogue/book/9781849058483.

Form 14.1 SCEP Test Information and Data Sheet

Name: _____   Grade: _____

Date of birth: _____   School: _____

Age: _____   City/town: _____

Dates of testing: _____

Diagnoses (include all given and dates): _____
_____

Cognitive functioning

Wechsler (or Stanford-Binet, Kaufman, Woodcock-Johnson, etc.) scores

Verbal score: _____   Index scores: _____   Subset scores: _____

Performance score: _____

Full scale: _____

Verb-perf diff: _____

Overall level of cognitive functioning: _____

Language processing

Receptive: _____

Expressive: _____

Other communication issues: _____

Overall level of language processing and functioning: _____

Visual–perceptual–spatial–motor functioning

Motor: _____

Visual perceptual: _____

Visual motor: _____

Visual motor perceptual integrative: _____

Overall level of visual–perceptual–spatial–motor processing

| **Attention** | Visual: _____ |
| | Auditory: _____ |

| **Memory** | Visual: _____ |
| | Auditory: _____ |

Executive functioning	Inhibition/delay _____	Mental shifting _____	Initiation _____
	Idea generation _____	Planning _____	Organization _____
	Working memory ____	Decision making _____	
	Problem solving _____	Self-monitoring/self-checking _____	

Social-emotional	Depression _____	Self-concept/sense of self _____
	Anxiety _____	Understanding of emotions _____
	Quality of thinking ___	

Academic skill development	Reading _____	Recognition _____	Comprehension _____
	Mathematics _____	Computation _____	Concepts _____
	Written expression ___	Spelling _____	Writing _____

Summary	Learning style _____
	Cognitive style _____
	Social-emotional style _____

Strengths: _____

Weaknesses: _____

Specific questions for face-to-face interviews

Parents: _____

ASD individual: _____

Other relevant information:

Clinician name: _____   Date: _____

Form 14.2 SCEP Initial Evaluation and Interview Form

Name: _____ Grade: _____

Date of birth: _____ School: _____

Age: _____ City/town: _____

Interview attendees: _____ Date of interview: _____

Diagnoses (provide all given with dates): _____
_____

Relevant history (family, developmental, medical, academic): _____
_____

Appearance/presentation of ASD individual: _____
_____

Issues profile (provide relevant examples; rate 1–5, low–high):

> **Self-regulation (self-control, self-management, self-awareness, impulse management):** _____

> **Emotion competence (emotion recognition, labeling, expression, understanding, and regulation):** _____

> **Attention (focused, sustained, selective, flexible):** _____

> **Joint attention (ability to attend to and connect with others):** _____

> **Stress and anxiety control and management (strategies):** _____

> **Flexibility/ability to change and transition (stereotyped behaviors, rituals, OCD):** _____

> **Perspective taking (awareness of others, sensitivity to others, sympathy, empathy):** _____

> **Relatedness (emotional connections, quality of relationships):** _____

> **Communication (expressive, receptive language):** _____

> **Sensory issues (tactile, visual, auditory, taste, olfactory, body touch, body space):** _____

> **Motor control issues (activity level, directedness):** _____

> **Peer relationships/friendships (none, one, two, more friends); isolated play (not effective, mildly effective, moderately effective, very effective):** _____

> **Other concerns or issues:** _____
> _____
> _____

Appropriateness for group (rate 1–5, low-high): _____

Clinician/interviewer name: _____ **Date:** _____

Form 14.3 SCEP Individual Profile: Self-Regulation Assessment

Please code: Never—1; Rarely—2; Sometimes—3; Often—4; Always—5

		N	R	S	O	A
1.	Labels and understands own different emotions and feelings	1	2	3	4	5
2.	Never overwhelmed by strong emotions	1	2	3	4	5
3.	Waits turn in interactions	1	2	3	4	5
4.	Thoughtful and deliberate in planning and problem solving	1	2	3	4	5
5.	Engages cooperatively with peers and adults	1	2	3	4	5
6.	Makes and keeps friends easily	1	2	3	4	5
7.	Never interferes with others' physical space	1	2	3	4	5
8.	No repetitive, stereotypical, or self-stimulating behavior	1	2	3	4	5
9.	Not fidgety, not constantly or always on the go	1	2	3	4	5
10.	Never touches, takes, or uses others' possessions without asking	1	2	3	4	5
11.	Never hits, pushes, shoves others without apparent awareness	1	2	3	4	5
12.	Never responds with impulsive behavior or actions	1	2	3	4	5
13.	Uses voice intonation and emphasis appropriately	1	2	3	4	5
14.	Never talks too much or over others in conversation	1	2	3	4	5
15.	Quickly and easily calms self after eruption	1	2	3	4	5

Total score _____

Self-regulation assessment scoring continuum

	Poorly regulated internal and external capacities		Moderate regulated internal and external capacities		Well-regulated internal and external capacities
Scores	15	30	45	60	75

Form 14.4 SCEP Individual Profile: Emotion Competence Assessment

Emotion recognition
Please code: Never—1; Rarely—2; Sometimes—3; Often—4; Always—5

	N	R	S	O	A
1. Recognizes and comments when emotions emerge in others	1	2	3	4	5
2. Recognizes when emotions are affecting own behavior	1	2	3	4	5
3. Recognizes own emotional experiences	1	2	3	4	5
4. Notices intense emotional reactions in others	1	2	3	4	5
5. Speaks up for/defends himself appropriately when wronged	1	2	3	4	5

Score _____

Emotion labeling
Please code: Never—1; Rarely—2; Sometimes—3; Often—4; Always—5

	N	R	S	O	A
1. Labels emotions accurately when they occur in self	1	2	3	4	5
2. Labels emotions accurately when they occur in others	1	2	3	4	5
3. Possesses and uses 2–4 emotion names appropriately	1	2	3	4	5
4. Possesses and uses 10–15 emotion names appropriately	1	2	3	4	5
5. Has a broad, varied, and consistent emotions vocabulary	1	2	3	4	5

Score _____

Emotion understanding
Please code: Never—1; Rarely—2; Sometimes—3; Often—4; Always—5

	N	R	S	O	A
1. Discusses and talks about his emotions readily	1	2	3	4	5
2. Understands own and others' emotional reactions	1	2	3	4	5
3. Uses emotions vocabulary consistently and appropriately	1	2	3	4	5
4. Interprets meaning of emotions and affects for self and others	1	2	3	4	5
5. Anticipates accurately when situations are getting out of control	1	2	3	4	5

Score _____

Emotion regulation
Please code: Never—1; Rarely—2; Sometimes—3; Often—4; Always—5

	N	R	S	O	A
1. Emotions always under control and well regulated	1	2	3	4	5
2. Rarely gets upset/reactive in games/discussions	1	2	3	4	5
3. Manages stress and pressure effectively and without overload	1	2	3	4	5
4. Helps others calm and regulate emotions when needed	1	2	3	4	5
5. Regains emotional control when at the point of losing it	1	2	3	4	5

Score _____

Emotion competence assessment scoring continuum (for each individual area)

	Poor emotion competence		Moderate emotion competence		Excellent emotion competence
Scores	5	10	15	20	25

Total score _____

Emotion competence scoring continuum—Total score

	Poor emotion competence		Moderate emotion competence		Excellent emotion competence
Scores	20	40	60	80	100

Form 14.5 SCEP Individual Profile: Stress–Anxiety Assessment

Please code: Never—1; Rarely—2; Sometimes—3; Often—4; Always—5	N	R	S	O	A
1. Can recognize and acknowledge general situations that cause tension and stress	1	2	3	4	5
2. Can recognize and acknowledge social situations that cause tension and stress	1	2	3	4	5
3. Looks forward to new social situations and to meeting new people	1	2	3	4	5
4. Warms up easily to a new environment	1	2	3	4	5
5. Introduces self to unfamiliar peers	1	2	3	4	5
6. Converses freely with others once introduced	1	2	3	4	5
7. Shares information about self	1	2	3	4	5
8. Appears comfortable and relaxed with peers in group situations	1	2	3	4	5
9. Uses stress- and anxiety-management strategies	1	2	3	4	5
10. Has a variety of stress- and anxiety-management strategies available	1	2	3	4	5
11. Always manages to avoid overload	1	2	3	4	5
12. Always manages to avoid meltdown/breakdown	1	2	3	4	5

Total score _____

Anxiety assessment scoring continuum

	High stress/anxiety Low coping/ management		Moderate stress/anxiety Moderate coping/ management		Manages stress/anxiety Good coping/ management
Scores	**12**	**24**	**36**	**48**	**60**

Form 14.6 SCEP Individual Profile: Attention Assessment

Focused attention

Please code: Never—1; Rarely—2; Sometimes—3; Often—4; Always—5

		N	R	S	O	A
1.	Can locate items, objects, or people in environment at will	1	2	3	4	5
2.	Can choose a task or activity when many choices are available	1	2	3	4	5
3.	Can recognize different aspects of tasks/activities that are focused on	1	2	3	4	5
4.	Attends to name being called	1	2	3	4	5

Total score _____

Sustained attention

Please code: Never—1; Rarely—2; Sometimes—3; Often—4; Always—5

		N	R	S	O	A
1.	Can complete more than one step of a multistep task	1	2	3	4	5
2.	Stays with tasks for extended periods of time	1	2	3	4	5
3.	Can complete all steps of a multistep task of choosing	1	2	3	4	5
4.	Can complete all steps of multistep task when directed by others	1	2	3	4	5

Total score _____

Selective attention

Please code: Never—1; Rarely—2; Sometimes—3; Often—4; Always—5

		N	R	S	O	A
1.	Focuses on tasks of interest with other things going on around him	1	2	3	4	5
2.	Ignores peripheral stimuli or distractions when task-focused	1	2	3	4	5
3.	Can redirect self to important activities when pulled off task	1	2	3	4	5
4.	Spontaneously recognizes and focuses on most relevant tasks at hand	1	2	3	4	5

Total score _____

Flexible attention

Please code: Never—1; Rarely—2; Sometimes—3; Often—4; Always—5

		N	R	S	O	A
1.	Tolerates shifts, changes, and transitions with significant stress	1	2	3	4	5
2.	Follows directions of others for shifts, changes, or transitions	1	2	3	4	5
3.	Initiates shifts from one task or activity to another without rigidity	1	2	3	4	5
4.	Quickly shifts, moves from one task to another as situation requires	1	2	3	4	5

Total score _____

Joint attention

Please code: Never—1; Rarely—2; Sometimes—3; Often—4; Always—5

		N	R	S	O	A
1.	Locates people of interest to him	1	2	3	4	5
2.	Initiates exchanges with others	1	2	3	4	5
3.	Recognizes and responds to verbal/nonverbal (social) cues from others	1	2	3	4	5
4.	"Engages" or connects with others in reciprocal ways	1	2	3	4	5

Total score _____

Attention assessment scoring continuum (for each individual area)

	Low attention		Moderate attention		Excellent attention
	___	___	___	___	___
Scores	4	8	12	16	20

Attention assessment scoring continuum—Total score

	Low attention		Moderate attention		Excellent attention
	___	___	___	___	___
Scores	20	40	60	80	100

Form 14.7 SCEP Individual Profile: Flexibility, Change, and Transition Assessment

Please code: Never—1; Rarely—2; Sometimes—3; Often—4; Always—5	N	R	S	O	A
1. Does not require significant preparation and predictability for small or moderate changes or transitions	1	2	3	4	5
2. Can tolerate change and transition with external structure	1	2	3	4	5
3. Tolerates changes to preset plans and schedules without help	1	2	3	4	5
4. Suggests alternatives when personal plans/suggestions thwarted	1	2	3	4	5
5. Adjusts easily to any change or transition or alteration in plans	1	2	3	4	5

Total score _____

Flexibility, change, and transition assessment scoring continuum

	High inflexibility, low capacity for change or transition		Moderate inflexibility, moderate capacity for change or transition		High flexibility, good capacity for change or transition
Scores	**5**	**10**	**15**	**20**	**25**

Form 14.8 SCEP Individual Profile: Perspective-Taking Assessment

Please code: Never—1; Rarely—2; Sometimes—3; Often—4; Always—5	N	R	S	O	A
1. Is sensitive to other people's feelings	1	2	3	4	5
2. Recognizes other people's needs	1	2	3	4	5
3. Engages in give-and-take interactions	1	2	3	4	5
4. Anticipates others' actions	1	2	3	4	5
5. Understands own and others' emotional reactions	1	2	3	4	5
6. Friendships are mutual and reciprocal	1	2	3	4	5
7. Can recognize the change in others' facial expressions	1	2	3	4	5
8. Waits turn in interactions	1	2	3	4	5
9. Repairs breaks in relationships	1	2	3	4	5
10. Comments with understanding on others' behavior	1	2	3	4	5
11. Recognizes and understands others' intentions	1	2	3	4	5
12. Never deceived, fooled, or manipulated	1	2	3	4	5
13. Understands and accepts others' points of view	1	2	3	4	5
14. Appropriately negotiates for what he wants	1	2	3	4	5
15. Does not get upset/reactive in games/discussions	1	2	3	4	5

Total score _____

Perspective-taking assessment scoring continuum

	Poor perspective taker, does not understand others' thoughts, feelings, or behaviors		Fair perspective taker, is able to understand others' thoughts, feelings, or behaviors		Good perspective taker, good understanding of others' thoughts, feelings, or behaviors
Scores	**15**	**30**	**45**	**60**	**75**

Form 14.9 SCEP Individual Profile: Social Interaction Assessment

Please code: Never—1; Rarely—2; Sometimes—3; Often—4; Always—5	N	R	S	O	A
1. Makes good eye contact	1	2	3	4	5
2. Shows high interest in peer social interaction	1	2	3	4	5
3. Demonstrates no problems with peer social interactions	1	2	3	4	5
4. Interacts actively and collaboratively with peers	1	2	3	4	5
5. Has a best friend	1	2	3	4	5
6. Has many reciprocal friendships	1	2	3	4	5
7. Gets invited to peer birthday parties	1	2	3	4	5
8. Prefers same-age peers to younger and/or older children or adults	1	2	3	4	5
9. Engages toys/things in creative ways	1	2	3	4	5
10. Never isolates self/never plays alone when others are around	1	2	3	4	5

Total score _____

Social interaction assessment scoring continuum

	Limited social interactive capacities		Moderate social interactive capacities		Excellent social interactive capacities
Scores	10	20	30	40	50

Form 14.10 SCEP Individual Profile: Cognitive/Executive Function Assessment

Please code: Never—1; Rarely—2; Sometimes—3; Often—4; Always—5	N	R	S	O	A
1. Presents information in an ordered and sequential manner	1	2	3	4	5
2. Processes information accurately	1	2	3	4	5
3. Processes information quickly and without unnecessary delay	1	2	3	4	5
4. Readily injects acquired and related knowledge into situation	1	2	3	4	5
5. Play is appropriate and abstract with symbolic thinking and usage	1	2	3	4	5
6. No unusual, detached, or "splinter" skills	1	2	3	4	5
7. Has excellent memory for facts or details	1	2	3	4	5
8. Easily integrates information from different sources	1	2	3	4	5
9. Is sought out by others for knowledge and information	1	2	3	4	5
10. Demonstrates consistent school performance	1	2	3	4	5
11. Works to academic potential	1	2	3	4	5
12. Completes homework without difficulty	1	2	3	4	5

Total score _____

Cognitive assessment scoring continuum

	Limited cognitive capacities and understanding		Moderate cognitive capacities and understanding		High cognitive capacities and understanding
Scores	12	24	36	48	60

Form 14.11 SCEP Individual Profile: Pragmatic Language Assessment

Please code: Never—1; Rarely—2; Sometimes—3; Often—4; Always—5	N	R	S	O	A
1. Spoke by age three	1	2	3	4	5
2. Greets interviewer without parent/caretaker prompting	1	2	3	4	5
3. Initiates conversation	1	2	3	4	5
4. Makes consistent eye contact (>50% of time)	1	2	3	4	5
5. Stops speaking/looks when name is called	1	2	3	4	5
6. Makes appropriate requests to use objects (not own)	1	2	3	4	5
7. Asks related questions	1	2	3	4	5
8. Responds appropriately when spoken to	1	2	3	4	5
9. Waits turn in interactions	1	2	3	4	5
10. Never interrupts	1	2	3	4	5
11. Responds to questions concisely	1	2	3	4	5
12. Does not use peculiar, hard-to-understand language/words	1	2	3	4	5
13. Does not perseverate or repeat self over and over	1	2	3	4	5
14. Uses voice intonation and emphasis appropriately	1	2	3	4	5
15. "In sync" with interviewer	1	2	3	4	5

Total score _____

Pragmatic language assessment scoring continuum

	Poor understanding and use of verbal/ nonverbal language		Moderate understanding and use of verbal/ nonverbal language		Excellent understanding and use of verbal/ nonverbal language
Scores	15	30	45	60	75

Conversational skills ___adequate ___deficient

Suggested need areas: _____

_____

Listening skills ___adequate ___deficient

Suggested need areas: _____

_____

Form 14.12 SCEP Individual Profile: Sensory Assessment

Please code: Never—1; Rarely—2; Sometimes—3; Often—4; Always—5

	N	R	S	O	A
1. Easily comforted by others	1	2	3	4	5
2. Enjoys/seeks out appropriate physical contact from others	1	2	3	4	5
3. Enjoyed playing peek-a-boo or bouncing on caretaker's knee	1	2	3	4	5
4. Does not engage in self-stimulating behaviors	1	2	3	4	5
5. No unusual or extreme sensitivities	1	2	3	4	5
6. Does not overreact to sensory input or stimulation	1	2	3	4	5
7. Does not get easily overexcited or overstimulated	1	2	3	4	5
8. Sensory capacities are well integrated	1	2	3	4	5

Total score _____

Cognitive assessment scoring continuum

Limited sensory capacities and understanding	Moderate sensory capacities and understanding	Good sensory capacities and understanding

Scores   8   16   24   32   40

Form 14.13 SCEP Individual Profile: Motor Assessment

Please code: Never—1; Rarely—2; Sometimes—3; Often—4; Always—5

	N	R	S	O	A
1. Adequate muscle tone	1	2	3	4	5
2. Well coordinated for age, not clumsy	1	2	3	4	5
3. No unusual motor mannerisms	1	2	3	4	5
4. Is not easily moved to hyperactivity or hyperarousal	1	2	3	4	5
5. Motor activity is well regulated for task/activity	1	2	3	4	5

Total score _____

Motor assessment scoring continuum

Undeveloped or poor motor capacities	Moderate motor capacities	Coordinated motor capacities

Scores   5   10   15   20   25

Form 14.14 SCEP Assessment for Group Placement

Name: _____   Grade: _____   DOB: _____

Self-regulation		
Cannot self-regulate or self-monitor any aspects of life. Needs consistent structure and support.	Needs some structure and some supports. Regulates thinking, emotions, and behavior in age-appropriate ways.	Works well without structure and supports.
Stress and anxiety management		
Highly stressed, anxious, and reactive in most situations.	Mild–moderate anxiety, but usually appropriate to situation.	Manages and controls anxiety effectively.
Joint attention		
Unable to attend to others. No eye contact.	Attending to others as needed and when directed. Good, but variable, eye contact.	Always appropriately attends to others. Always consistent eye contact.
Communication		
Unable to communicate. Very limited use of language.	Age-appropriate language and communication.	Excellent language usage and communication.
Cannot pick up or process nonverbal communication.	Age-appropriate awareness and understanding of nonverbal communication.	Extremely effective and very attentive to and processing of nonverbal communication.
Cannot/very delayed in processing language.	Average processing of language and communication.	Effective, efficient, and spontaneous language processing.
Flexibility, change, and transitions		
Inflexible, rigid, resistant, and stressed with change and transitions.	Appropriate flexibility and ability to change and transition with preparation.	Highly flexible and easily and consistently able to change and transition with people or activities.
Perspective taking		
Highly self-centered, unable to understand or tolerate others' views.	Age-appropriate understanding of others' opinions and points of view.	Always recognizes connections between own and others' points of view, understands others' perspectives.
Relatedness		
Unable to relate or connect interpersonally to peers or adults.	Relates in age-appropriate ways to peers and adults.	Highly related and connected in all interpersonal situations.
Emotion competence		
Unable to regulate, recognize, label, or understand emotions.	Age-appropriate regulation, recognition, labeling, and understanding of emotions.	Consistent and very effective regulation, recognition, labeling, and understanding of emotions.
Play skills		
No interactive play skills.	Able to engage in age-appropriate peer play.	Easily and effectively engages familiar and unfamiliar peers.
Cognitive capacity		
Low.	Average.	High.

Form 14.15 SCEP Core Strengths and Weaknesses Form

Core area/core variable	Core strength	Core deficit
Self-regulation		
Self-regulation/self-management/self-control	☐	☐
Social		
General social competence	☐	☐
Relatedness	☐	☐
Social skills	☐	☐
Communication		
Language mechanics (phonics, syntax)	☐	☐
Language—complex (pragmatic, semantic)	☐	☐
Emotion		
Self-management/self-regulation	☐	☐
Emotion competence	☐	☐
Recognition	☐	☐
Labeling and expressing	☐	☐
Understanding	☐	☐
Regulation	☐	☐
Stress and anxiety control and management	☐	☐
Cognitive/executive functioning		
Attention (focused, sustained, selective, flexible)	☐	☐
Joint attention	☐	☐
Flexibility/transitions	☐	☐
Executive functioning (e.g. planning, organization)	☐	☐
(List) _____		
_____		
_____		
_____		
Perspective taking	☐	☐
Behavior		
Self-management/self-regulation	☐	☐
Sensory		
General sensitivity threshold	☐	☐
Specific areas	☐	☐
(List) _____		
_____		
_____		
_____		
Awareness, regulation/management	☐	☐
Motor		
Primary motor areas	☐	☐
Secondary motor areas (e.g. awkward, clumsy)	☐	☐

Form 14.16 SCEP: Would This Child Benefit from a Social Competence/Social Skills Group?

Has an adequate review and assessment of all available material on the child been completed? This will include:

- parent, teacher, professional, and interviewer input ☐
- review of all past and present formal and informal evaluations ☐
- developmental and health history ☐
- current parent and teacher behavioral data/checklists ☐
- parent and child interview ☐
- areas of concern. ☐

Do assessments indicate that the child lacks specific social competencies in any of the following areas?

- In social areas: relatedness ☐
  - joint attention ☐
  - emotional recognition, labeling, understanding, and regulation ☐
  - social regulation ☐
  - motor regulation ☐

- In emotional areas: self-management/self-control ☐
  - stress and anxiety management and control ☐
  - emotion recognition, labeling, understanding, and regulation ☐
  - social regulation ☐
  - motor regulation ☐

- In cognitive/executive function areas: attention/joint attention ☐
  - flexibility/transitions ☐
  - perspective taking/theory of mind ☐
  - Self-management/self-monitoring ☐

- In communication areas: verbal impulsivity ☐
  - expressive language ☐
  - receptive language ☐
  - emotion labeling ☐

- In behavioral areas: self-management/self-control ☐
  - repetitive, stereotypic behaviors ☐

- In sensory areas: hypersensitivities ☐
  - hyposensitivities ☐
  - sensory awareness ☐
  - sensory integration ☐

- In motor areas: motor control ☐
  - motor regulation ☐
  - motor integration ☐

Do assessments indicate that the child lacks specific social skills?

Conversational skills	☐	Listening skills	☐
Discussion skills	☐	Assertiveness skills	☐
Problem-solving skills	☐	Conflict management skills	☐
Understanding relationships skills	☐	Empathy skills	☐

Could the child work with peers at a similar level?

Age ☐   Developmental ☐   Emotional ☐   Cognitive ☐   Social ☐   Behavioral ☐

Form 14.17 SCEP Groups: Areas of Interest Form

Name: _____   Grade: _____

Date of birth: _____   School: _____

Age: _____   City/town: _____

Diagnoses: _____
_____

Areas of interest: Issues of concern defined by ASD individual, parents, teachers, and/or observers: _____
_____

Concerning or problematic behaviors or interactions noted by parents, teachers, and observers: _____
_____

Most significant overall areas of interest noted by all (ASD individual, parents, teachers, observers): _____
_____
_____

Other somewhat significant areas of interest noted by two (ASD individual, parents, teachers, observers): _____
_____
_____

Other less significant areas of interest noted by any (ASD individual, parents, teachers, observers): _____
_____
_____

Additional concerns noted: _____
_____
_____

Clinician: _____   Date: _____

Form 14.18 SCEP Groups: Individual Goals Form

Name: _____   Grade: _____

Date of birth: _____   School: _____

Age: _____   City/town: _____

Diagnoses: _____
_____

Stage 1 Group formation and orientation goals: _____
_____
_____
_____

Stage 2 Group cohesion goals: _____
_____
_____
_____

Stage 3 Group stability, relationships, and connections goals: _____
_____
_____
_____

Stage 4 Group adaptations and perspective-taking goals: _____
_____
_____
_____

Stage 5 Group termination, loss, and ending goals: _____
_____
_____
_____

Additional concerns noted: _____
_____
_____
_____

Clinician: _____   Date: _____

Form 14.19 SCEP Groups: Group Goals Form

Group members: _____
_____
_____

Age range of group: _____   Grade range of group _____

Diagnoses of group members: _____
_____

Stage 1 Group formation and orientation goals: _____
_____
_____
_____

Stage 2 Group cohesion goals: _____
_____
_____
_____

Stage 3 Group stability, relationships, and connections goals: _____
_____
_____
_____

Stage 4 Group adaptations and perspective-taking goals: _____
_____
_____
_____

Stage 5 Group termination, loss, and ending goals: _____
_____
_____
_____

Additional concerns noted: _____
_____
_____
_____

Clinician: _____   Date: _____

Chapter 15

Introduction to a Stage Model of Group Development for Individuals with ASD

The Social Competence Enhancement Program (SCEP) was constructed specifically to address the social interaction deficits exhibited by individuals with ASD within group settings. Within this model, social competence groups emphasize the range of strengths and assets that individuals with ASD bring to these situations as well as address directly the social interaction deficits exhibited. Through group-based intervention, the focus is placed on the following broad group goals:

1. Recognize and understand the complexity of social interchange and experience and understand what it means to be part of a group.

2. Manage group experiences, situations, and interactions effectively as they arise.

3. Emphasize and develop effective self-regulation functions and strategies, such as self-awareness, self-management, and insight, that are necessary for effective personal and interpersonal group interactions.

4. Develop and enhance the capacity to create and sustain meaningful interpersonal relationships with others, especially peers.

5. Understand and integrate the perspective of others into one's own thinking, feeling, and behavior.

6. Address directly key issues which inhibit or prevent successful group interactions.

7. Learn and use consistently the basic social skills necessary for successful social engagement.

To achieve these goals, processes which underlie the development of social competence and social skills are addressed and actively engaged. The SCEP approach emphasizes an understanding of the key structures (related to core areas and core variables) necessary to learn and perform skills involved in group interaction. If the structure is present, then the skill can be taught and learned. If the structure is not present, emphasis must first be placed on developing and enhancing the appropriate structures, thus providing the capacity for the individual to subsequently learn the skills deemed necessary for the particular skill set. Core variables, such as self-regulation, emotion competence, stress and anxiety management, attention/joint attention, flexibility/transitions, perspective taking, and relatedness, are viewed as important underlying structures that must be developed before related, specific skills can be learned.

The intervention process

In approaching social competence through the SCEP model, a peer-based, group-focused, cognitive-developmental model is considered most effective in providing for the range of social-interactive needs demonstrated by individuals with ASD. Primary emphasis in this model is placed on the construction of settings that foster and encourage structure, interaction, mutual support, sharing, respect, competence development, skill instruction, cooperation, and collaboration. In addressing social competence and social skills training, the concept of structure within settings is essential in this model. The employment of homogeneous grouping, development of targeted individual and group goals, encouragement of positive peer connections, and emphasis on therapeutic and supportive interactions allows for the construction of the most efficient and effective structures necessary for the group to progress and to learn and practice new interactive strategies. Providing a peer-based, group-focused setting for this structure further enhances each group member's capacity to learn about himself and about being part of a group. Within this model, the SCEP approach employs the following overlapping principles:

- general structure: providing a general structure within which the group can operate

- specific structure: allowing the group to develop its own unique and specific structure

- peer-based settings: encouraging the group to use peer-based settings to develop its own identity

- group-focused settings: providing emphasis on group-focused interactions and settings where group process takes precedence and overshadows individual status.

General structure

Emphasis is given to principles of structure and consistency within SCEP as it relates to each aspect of group formation and development. This includes structure and consistency in the assessment and consideration of individuals for group, in the placement of individuals into groups, in the planning and constructing of individual and group goals, and in the setting and maintaining of an appropriate atmosphere and tone for group.

While emphasizing structure and consistency, the group process must at the same time allow for flexibility and resiliency in order for the group flow to activate and engage members when appropriate and useful to the group. This includes the use of specific tasks and activities which emphasize the development of core competencies and the learning of specific skills. This model creates an environment for the repetition and reinforcement of core variables and learned skills and develops and maintains an environment that allows the group increasingly to take ownership and responsibility for each step in the group development process. Emphasis is placed on structure and consistency within each weekly group and on structure and consistency over the entire course of year-long groups.

Initially in early sessions, the group leader more actively directs these structures, but as the group forms and orients and as it moves to subsequent stages, the group itself is expected to assume the task of decision making and follow-through. Therefore, initial groups are more highly structured, more leader-directed, more focused on learning about one another and how to relate as a group, and more focused on defining an effective format for the group to proceed.

In later group sessions, the leader serves to guide the group through the structure set in place during early sessions. As the group practices and internalizes this structure, the leader becomes less active and directive, increasing expectations that group members self-initiate and move through the steps previously practiced. As the group matures, it will demonstrate its own areas of strengths and weaknesses as it struggles with leadership issues, decision making, task selection, conflict resolution, and follow-through. Although the group leader becomes less active and directive as the group proceeds, depending on the group's capacities to self-manage, the leader maintains a primary role of facilitating key process and skill development through encouragement, constructive criticism, reinforcement, modeling, and identification.

As the group moves toward the final stages, the group leader ensures that needed issues are addressed, clarified, and processed as necessary. In these settings, the group structure provides the consistent foundation for the group to move from session to session, the group leader ensures that the group develops the tools necessary for the group to move continuously forward, the group members provide the power and energy (through bringing issues to the forefront) to address and confront interactional issues, and the group as a whole develops and exerts a stabilizing influence in keeping the group on course and working on its group goals toward a meaningful outcome.

Specific structure

The specific structure of SCEP sessions focuses on the moment-to-moment connections and interactions, cognitively, socially, and behaviorally. Initially, this is dictated by the group leader's assessment and understanding of the group members' needs and concerns and how these are translated into individual and group goals. Tasks and activities are also constructed and/or selected based on these group needs. As the group proceeds and develops increased cohesion and connectedness, the group leader gradually provides increased opportunities for the group to become more active in the decision-making process. The specific structure of groups initially uses an imposed schedule to create an atmosphere of unity, cooperation, respect, openness, and predictability.

The group structure generally follows this sequence:

- introductions/greetings
- sharing, announcements, discussion items, and brief review of previous session
- selection and decision making of competence/skill-based group task/activity, performing and completing task/activity focusing

on group goals, related core variables, and the stage of group
development attained to that point

- snack time, debriefing of group task/activity, and group comments

- goodbyes.

Introduction/greetings
The initial segment of the group involves the greetings and introductions of
group members with one another. Each group session begins with the group
members orienting to the group room and coming to a table or common
meeting area, typically in a circle, to convene the group. The purpose of this
segment is to create, foster, and practice the coming together as a group, the
transitions, the separations, and the re-entries that occur for an individual when
they are part of a group that has a common purpose of connecting with others
around social-interpersonal goals.

Each group begins with each member of the group greeting by name
each of the other members of the group, thereby respectfully recognizing
and acknowledging each member's presence and place in group. This simple
exercise is intended to serve several specific purposes which include: to promote
peer-to-peer, group interactions between members; to develop focused and
joint attention competencies; to focus on overall relationship-building issues
as they occur within group interactions; to acknowledge and recognize each
group member's reconnection with the group and with the group process that
constitutes it as a unique entity; and to recognize the commitment of time and
energy necessary to transition back into a group process begun in previous
sessions. These issues also contribute to the ongoing development of group
cohesion and group connectedness.

Sharing, announcements, and discussion items
Introductions are followed by the sharing by each group member of significant
experiences, events, or interactions that may have occurred since the last
group. The purpose of sharing time in the group is to facilitate, encourage, and
practice the process of giving others personal information about ourselves so as
to recognize similarities and differences among group members and to explore
and establish relationship-building opportunities.

Within the SCEP model, the sharing of new personal information by each
group member allows increased awareness, understanding, and knowledge of
what is important to each group member, allowing a heightened degree of
intimacy to develop between group members for the purpose of creating a

distinct and unique group experience. Sharing time also allows the group to engage in shared experiences, to request and provide elaboration of shared experiences in order to learn more about one another, to sort out and adjust to shared similarities and differences, and to learn about what is meaningful and important in relationships.

When sharing is completed, there is a brief period of general discussion, announcements, etc., to reinforce and model the appropriate interaction process and allow group goals to be addressed and articulated, then sorted out by the group for that specific session. Sharing is followed by a decision-making process of how the activities for that session will be selected, based on group goals and the stage of group development attained to that point.

Task/activity

Prior to each group session, the group leader selects several tasks/activities that will address the individual and group goals, the stage of group development attained to that point, and the specific core variables being focused upon. The group is given choices from several topic areas (games, movement, visuals, writing, competitive or team-oriented activities, etc.) and can select from several of the tasks/activities previously prepared and selected by the group leader. The specific tasks and activities are constructed with knowledge of the individual and group goals, of the stage of development the group has attained to that point, and of the specific core variables that the group is working on. The group leader can create and construct specific tasks and activities or draw from those in Chapter 19. With several targeted choices available to the group, the group leader guides the group in a decision about which task/activity best meets their needs for that session.

The purpose of the task/activity provided by the group leader or initiated/developed by the group is to address in sequence particular aspects of focused social competence or social skill development necessary for both individual and group development. The task/activity is specifically selected or constructed to encourage and enhance developmentally sequenced, social-interpersonal experiences with other group members, to recognize and acknowledge the importance of these experiences, to practice and repeat the task/activity until mastery occurs, and to acknowledge and understand the importance of the task/activity and its connection to the specific aspect of social competence or necessary social skill on which it focuses. This part of the group structure is intended to foster the active involvement of the group in the task-selection process, to encourage understanding and acting within group goal structure, and to create, define, and follow through flexibly on the roles that develop within the group. Over time, the group itself is expected to assume the task of decision making and follow-through as the group leader becomes less active and directive and as the group demonstrates increased capacities to self-manage and self-direct.

Following the activity, attention is given to how the task/activity was completed, to the level of ease or difficulty with which it was carried out, and to the ways in which it encouraged or interfered with interactive group process. The group members also address how the task/activity helped them to work on their own individual goals and how it helped the group as a whole progress on group goals. In the discussion of group goals, these may be adjusted and modified depending on the task/activity performance and with a view toward future development. The task/activity is also processed in the context of the stage of group development attained by the group to that point.

Snack, debriefing/discussion, and goodbyes

Following completion of the task/activity, the group members direct their attention to a period of winding down prior to exiting group. This includes some brief self-calming, arousal-reducing stress and anxiety management techniques, followed by a brief snack time. During snack time, the group assembles together at a table to eat and drink and to discuss the task/activity and how they experienced it. The purpose of snack/discussion is to provide an opportunity for the group to come together for an open but unstructured discussion of the group process that has just taken place in that session, of the level of social interactions, and of the task/activity just completed.

Within the SCEP model, snack/discussion is an important part of the group session and group process as it provides an understanding of what the group and its members may have learned from the session, of the benefits and shortcomings of the particular task/activity focused upon, and of the quality of the overall group experience on this day as it connects with previous group experiences. The snack/discussion provides a close and direct view of what and how much the group understood about the purposes of that day's group experiences and provides information about how to plan and structure subsequent group sessions. The time is used to debrief the task/activity relative to its connection to individual and group goals, to the specific stage of group development the group is at, and to the core variables focused upon. The group is given some indication of what will occur at the next group and that task/activity may be previewed if necessary. This last phase of group structure is intended to model and reinforce appropriate socialized endings, to maintain joint attention to the end of group, and to engage in endings that foster ongoing connections from one group session to the next.

The SCEP model of group intervention places importance on the consistent aligning and structuring of segments which include introductions and previewing, decision making and implementation, and reviewing and closing during each group session, while the ongoing group experience considers and addresses aspects of group homogeneity, individual and group goal setting, specific structuring of the group experience, peer connections, and therapeutic interactions.

Peer-based settings

In a social world, the skills needed to survive and flourish are varied and extensive. An understanding and awareness of the need and desire to connect and relate to and to experience another individual in mutually reciprocal ways are necessary steps. This model emphasizes the importance of peer-to-peer interactions as a driving force and impetus for change in individuals within a group. The desire to connect to, to relate to, and to experience another individual or group of peers in mutually reciprocal ways is considered the underlying force in social interaction and communication. Peer-based settings provide structured situations for these interactions to take place. They are purposefully constructed with consideration given to each individual's social competence, developmental level, and emotional needs. They emphasize peer interactions over individual or group-to-adult interactions. They provide ongoing opportunities to engage peers, while at the same time provide an understanding of an individual's own needs to acquire and develop underlying structures or key processes and to learn the specific skills for successful peer interaction. With increased individual self-skills (self-awareness, self-regulation, self-monitoring, and insight), group participants are encouraged and taught how to ally with and join their peers in the process of mutual and reciprocal interaction, negotiation, decision making, and group reflection. While groups are initially adult-monitored so as to be structured to increase and positively reinforce mutual contacts, increasing responsibility is transferred gradually over the course of the group to peer members for the structuring of their own interactions in more effective ways as new and more complex social-interactive skills are learned and as new and more complex social-interactive situations are confronted.

Peer-based settings provide opportunities to experience others, to develop self-awareness of one's needs in these situations, and to consider how these needs can be responded to and met within peer-based interactions. Within peer-based settings, individuals are able to experience and understand the social rules and expectations which govern social interactions. They are able to learn and experiment with new ways to adapt to these interactions and to learn how to get their own needs met in these peer-based situations. Individuals must understand not only the rules and expectations of interaction (appropriate and inappropriate) and how they apply, but that these rules can be highly fluid and rapidly changing, based on a range of social, interactional, and contextual factors. Peer-based settings allow individuals to exist within a group and to share their experiences with peers in a naturalistic setting that closely mirrors real life.

Group sessions are purposefully constructed with consideration given to the social competence, developmental level, and emotional needs of each individual and how these will influence their interactions with other group members. This model emphasizes and encourages peer interactions over individual or group-to-adult interactions, provides ongoing opportunities for each member to engage peers directly, provides an understanding of an individual's own needs to acquire and develop underlying structures and core variables, and teaches the specific skills necessary for successful peer interaction. The goal of peer-to-peer interactions is to experience others, to develop self-awareness of one's needs in these situations, and to consider how these needs can be responded to and met within peer-based interactions. The group structure is intended to enhance peer-to-peer interactions and to allow for the experience and understanding of the social rules and expectations which govern social interactions, for the learning of and experimenting with new ways to adapt to a range of social interactions, and for the learning processes through which one's individual needs can be met within peer-based situations.

Group-focused settings

Membership in groups allows similar-aged peers to come together for the common purposes of sharing experiences, learning from them, recognizing and addressing areas of social difficulty, and learning and practicing new skills to manage the social interactions which arise within a group more effectively. The experience of positive group membership has been consistently demonstrated to be a powerful force and contributing factor in influencing behavioral change, contributing to increased self-esteem, and building social-interactive skills (Yalom 2005).

Group interactions provide structured situations in which individuals can interact with others with a focus on common issues and concerns while monitored by an adult facilitator and while working toward change and growth in specific, designated areas. These interactions provide opportunities for sharing of information, experiences, thoughts, and emotions. They allow for the establishment of cooperative, mutual, esteem-building, and often enduring relationships. They provide a setting for collaborative efforts directed toward individual and shared goals, and they can provide opportunities for direct instruction and practice in needed skills to accomplish these group-based objectives. Group members become aware of and learn that the group process follows certain predictable patterns that can be anticipated, managed, and worked through, but that this group flow can also trigger concerns and issues related to core variables and deficits, such as stress/anxiety, attention issues, inflexibility, narrowness of thinking, and even distortions. Since these are considered group issues, they are addressed through the group (e.g. group goals) and by group members as a group, not as individuals.

In summary, the group structure provides the consistent and ongoing foundation for the group to come together, to set, meet, and modify goals, to confront, manage, and solve problems in interactions as they arise, and to move systematically and sequentially from session to session. Within this structure, the group leader ensures that the group members develop the competence and skills necessary for the group to move continuously forward. The group members provide power and energy (through bringing issues to the forefront) to address and confront interactional issues and to make clear how this should happen. As the group progresses, the group as a whole develops and exerts a stabilizing influence in keeping the group on course and in working on its group goals toward a meaningful outcome. At the same time, the group members learn how to support one another in this process.

Chapter 16

Stages of Group Development

Over the years in SCEP groups structured around social competence and social skill development, children have been observed moving through a series of stages during the course of both the short-term (6–8 weeks) and long-term (30 weeks) group programs. These stages follow a consistent sequence and appear related to specific processes, sets of skills, and modes of behaviors that occur at each stage. These elements are necessary to pass through the particular stage effectively in order to move forward and make use of subsequent stages.

The following stages are observed within SCEP group interventions with ASD children:

Stage 1 Group formation and orientation

Stage 2 Group cohesion

Stage 3 Group stability, relationships, and connections

Stage 4 Group adaptations and perspective taking

Stage 5 Terminations, loss, and endings

Stage 1: Group formation and orientation

The stage of *Group formation and orientation* relates primarily to the task of several individuals coming together in the process of forming a group. This group will eventually develop a unique identity, a set of common goals, its own style of interaction, and its own set of group norms. During this first stage, the group leader takes a very active role in encouraging and facilitating opportunities, including the constructing of specific tasks and activities that foster sharing and learning about one another, especially around common interests. The group leader actively directs and guides discussion and activities that accentuate the interactive process during this stage.

This process of group formation includes establishing group rules and expectations, dealing with stress and anxiety management, and making the group a structured, predictable, safe place where feelings and emotions can be expressed without attack, where resistance is addressed openly and directly, and where a sense of togetherness, connectedness, and community will develop and strengthen over the course of many group meetings. This stage relies heavily on the group leader's understanding of each individual's background and history, their areas of strength and weakness, and multiple interrelated cognitive, behavioral, social, and emotional variables.

During the initial sessions, the group leader observes and attends to key behaviors, with particular attention paid to information previously obtained during the application and interview phase and provided by parents and teachers relating to the group formation and orientation process. Group leader observations are then combined with the previously obtained information and with the set of individual areas of interest collected for each child prior to starting group to form individual goals for each group participant.

Individual goals are constructed at the outset of Stage 1, particularly in relation to core areas and related core variables, such as emotion competence, stress/anxiety control and management, attention, and flexibility/transitions, based on the specific defined areas of interest indicated for each group member. As each child progresses through his individual goals and as the group moves through Stage 1 goals, then the group leader reviews current areas of interest for each child and constructs adjusted or modified individual goals for each child as needed as the group moves into Stage 2.

Group goals are also constructed at the outset of Stage 1 and are formed with an understanding of each group participant's individual goals. These individual goals are "pooled" to form more general group goals that will relate to the broader issues that the group as a whole will focus on. Group goals will also address as needed key process areas from this broader group goal perspective and will be reviewed frequently for adjustment and modification. These steps are repeated as the individual and group goals are met and as the group readies to move into each subsequent stage.

The initial stage of *Group formation and orientation* can last anywhere from 1–2 sessions to 10–12 sessions. It is characterized by several key components which are translated into group goals. These goals are constructed with input from the group members and become the basis for structuring subsequent group activities.

Setting group goals for Stage 1

The group goals for Stage 1 *Group formation and orientation* will often include:

General

- building the group culture
- learning and practicing basic anxiety- and stress-reduction techniques
- encouraging members to actively attend to each other
- tolerating multiple kinds of input

Specific

- setting the rules
- defining the boundaries
- developing and describing this group's social code
- identifying with the group leader
- managing anxiety that arises around joining a group, meeting new people, and sharing information about oneself
- paying attention to other members in the group
- giving everyone the opportunity to speak and to respond.

Group goals at Stage 1 focus on bringing the group members together, recognizing common areas of interest, and experiencing the normal tension and anxiety of being with others in goal-oriented, group situations. The goals are intended to provide structure about what is expected and what is and is not tolerated (e.g. setting and defining rules and boundaries), about what information, behaviors, and thoughts fit within the group setting, and about shared feelings, thoughts, and experiences common to all group members when beginning in a new situation.

Group goals provide an overall focus on the common and shared experiences and needs of all group members, while individual areas of interest focus on specific concerns or behaviors that a particular group member may be working on. These may vary from one group member to another and will form the basis for constructing individual goals for each individual within the group. The group leader uses an individual's areas of interest and individual goals as guides for setting group goals (general and specific), for constructing the appropriate group structure, and for directing the selection of group tasks and activities at the specific stage.

Setting the Stage 1 group structure

The group structure at Stage 1 relates to the specific environment created and facilitated by the group leader together with the group members to enhance the building of a group culture and the establishment of a group identity. Discussions of group and individual goals result in the creation of the structure within which group members can function and within which these goals can be met. This relates to the building of a group culture wherein the group can effectively learn about one another, establish, understand, and follow the rules it requires, and begin to test out the types of interaction it requires to function most effectively.

Gradually as the group moves through the stage of *Group formation and orientation*, members are able to demonstrate increased competence and mastery of these initial processes, and as Stage 1 goals are achieved, the group is primed and prepared to move to Stage 2. Examples of this developing mastery include the group entering the group room appropriately, being aware of and following group rules, and initiating and following through with group structures, such as directing themselves through group-orienting activities, greetings, sharing, activity selection, and decision-making processes, all with reasonable success and minimal unresolved conflict.

One major issue with the great majority of individuals with ASD that influences interactions at all stages, but particularly at Stage 1, relates to the experience and management of stress and anxiety. As described previously, the experience of stress, tension, and anxiety is prominent in nearly all interpersonal interactions with individuals with ASD and therefore must be addressed and considered within each stage. At Stage 1, the management of stress and anxiety is specifically designated as one of the group goals so that it can be addressed and discussed directly from the outset of group. These initial discussions recognize that everyone will be "stressed and anxious" in beginning a new group and meeting new people. Therefore, the group will address this and learn to control it (a long-term goal) by learning basic techniques for stress and anxiety reduction (the short-term goal).

Each initial group session and subsequent sessions in Stage 1 provide progressive and systematic training in simple techniques for stress and anxiety control and management, such as deep breathing, rhythmic counting, and visual imaging (as described briefly in Chapter 6), which are then repeated and practiced consistently within each Stage 1 session. This process also serves to trigger group discussions about what causes stress and anxiety, what it feels like, and what techniques or methods can assist in managing it, both adaptively and maladaptively. Most typically, however, specific and more elaborate discussions of stress and anxiety occur at later stages. It is necessary to emphasize here very strenuously the importance of recognizing and accommodating to the role that stress, tension, and anxiety play in social interactions with individuals with ASD. Its emergence is inevitable, must be managed through awareness, consistent training, and application of effective strategies for stress and anxiety reduction, and acknowledged and managed throughout each stage of group development with individuals with ASD.

A second major issue for individuals with ASD which emerges early in Stage 1 and which is an issue to be addressed throughout each stage relates to attention. At each stage, depending on the group and individual needs, group goals are constructed around the development and enhancement of focused, sustained, selective, flexible, and joint attention. In particular in interpersonal group settings, joint attention is an important and necessary competence for reciprocal interchange and communication. At Stage 1, each activity is constructed by the group leader to develop and reinforce joint attention among group participants. The group is primed in advance for the subsequent activities, with modeling, reinforcement, and stress management.

A third major issue that affects the majority of individuals with ASD, particularly in interpersonal and group situations, relates to the issue of flexibility and transitions. The requirements to be flexible, to adjust and accommodate to change, and to transition (i.e. shift attention) between tasks and activities are known to create significant degrees of stress and tension in the majority of individuals with ASD, triggering increased stress, tension, and anxiety, and often overload (i.e. meltdown). Attempts are made to anticipate and prepare for the stress related to the needs for flexibility and transitions by discussing the issue with the group participants at Stage 1, by constructing group goals related to the issue, and by addressing the issue specifically (through modification of group goals and developing specific directed tasks and activities) at each of the five stages.

Specific skills to be addressed at Stage 1

Since Stage 1 relates to group formation and orientation, the specific skills addressed are those necessary for the initiation of a reciprocal relationship, including basic social interaction skills. These include basic interactive skills such as eye contact, initiating a conversation, active listening, active responding, asking related and pertinent questions, and following directions.

When individuals within the group share common areas of interest or individual goals relating to any of these Stage 1 skills, then group goals are constructed and tasks and activities focusing on these skills are generated. See Appendix 4.1 for additional specific skills addressed at Stage 1.

Stage 2: Group cohesion

The stage of *Group cohesion* relates to the group's capacity to form a bond as a group and to use that bond as a force to hold the group together as it begins to deal with increasingly more stressful issues. The group leader has had the opportunity during Stage 1 to observe and influence how group members begin to connect as a group and to one another as individuals. Information learned about the group's strengths and weaknesses within core areas and related core variables will inform the construction of Stage 2 goals as the group moves forward.

Again, as at Stage 1, information obtained during the application and interview process is reviewed by the group leader and combined with group observations in order to understand better how to foster improved communication and group identification and how to anticipate, based on previous information and current observations, where problems in social interaction will occur. In reviewing this information, additional areas of interest may be considered and included as the group proceeds to setting goals for Stage 2.

During this stage of group development, all activities, tasks, and communications are viewed through the lens of developing and solidifying the group as a cohesive, self-supporting unit. The group is encouraged to take more control (or as much as it can), particularly in the setting of goals for the group, in decision-making procedures, and in fostering appropriate avenues for communication.

Setting group goals for Stage 2

The group goals for Stage 2 *Group cohesion* will often include:

General

- developing and solidifying cohesion within the group and between group members

Specific

- group members jointly trying to set their own goals
- individual members identifying with the group
- establishing group communication methods
- requiring honesty/directness
- fostering reliance on one another
- managing stress and anxiety related to increased connectedness
- attention to active listening and active responding
- understanding and utilizing cooperative and flexible interactive strategies.

At Stage 2, group goals foster interaction, while individual goals work on specific aspects of a group member's thinking or behavior that will enhance group participation or that might interfere with effective group involvement. Group goals provide the opportunity for interaction, while individual goals focus on the specific needs of the individual to make interactions successful. For example, a Stage 2 group goal may focus on group decision making, while individual goals may focus on a member being more positive, using two different cooperation strategies, or going along with the majority.

As individual stage goals are met, the group goals take on greater significance as they begin to reflect more accurately the overall group process and progress. As specific group goals are met at Stage 2, group members are encouraged to begin to think about constructing group goals for Stage 3 *Group stability, relationships, and connections*, a stage of increased group connectedness and independence.

There also is a continued emphasis on efforts to acknowledge, address, manage, and cope with the stress and anxiety that arises as individuals take risks to share personal information, join others in attempts to gain support and feedback, express needs that may feel personal and may be embarrassing, and recognize and express intimacy and affiliation needs. Following the learning and practicing of simple techniques for stress and anxiety reduction learned in Stage 1, a broader forum for stress and anxiety control and management is now provided in Stage 2. This includes additional relaxation techniques, including the refinement of deep breathing, progressive muscle relaxation, positive self-talk, and visual imaging strategies, and extensive interactive discussion of "what works for you." Ongoing discussion and reinforcement of techniques for stress and anxiety reduction play a key role in allowing Stage 2 *Group cohesion* to take hold, flourish, and move toward Stage 3.

In addition, group members are pushed to develop or to enhance their capacities for joint attention—the process of "locking on" to another while speaking, listening, or connecting—as a means to facilitate relationship development and identify with other group members. Members are provided with guidance in how to stay "tuned in," in how to follow conversational rules, and in how to become more self-aware of their own attentional style as it occurs within the group.

Group members are also provided with strategies to assess their own capacities for flexibility, change, and transitions and to understand how these impact group connections and relationships. At Stage 2, group members are cued when flexibility issues arise, are encouraged to consider suggestions and alternative approaches, and are reinforced for appropriate responses to these situations.

Setting the Stage 2 group structure

The specific environment of Stage 2 relates to the group as a whole working together on common tasks directed toward common goals. In entering this stage, the group members have acquired significant information about one another and about their strengths and weaknesses and now have the capacity to use this information in both positive and growth-fostering, and negative and destructive, ways.

Information from prior parent and teacher data and current observations is used to develop goals for each individual and for the group, both generally and specifically focused on fostering cohesion through increased intermember and group communication, through identification with the group as a whole as well as between individual members, and through the management of the tension/anxiety related to relationship building and the interactive process. Each individual is encouraged to generate specific individual goals for themselves that are linked to targeted group goals constructed with significant group involvement.

Specific skills to be addressed at Stage 2

Since Stage 2 *Group cohesion* relates to developmentally more advanced usage of social competence and social skills, those specific skills addressed represent more advanced use of skills learned at Stage 1, though still basic and necessary for common interactions. Stage 2 skills are those required to form relationships with others in basic and consistent ways. These include initiating discussions of personal information and preferences, collecting and soliciting information about other group members including their interests and preferences, acknowledging points others make, sharing related information, regulating the intensity and quality of one's interactions (e.g. voice tone, voice volume, facial expressions, joint attention, body language and cues), and taking turns.

If individuals within the group share common areas of interest or individual goals relating to any of these Stage 2 skills, then group goals are constructed and tasks and activities focusing on these skills are generated. See Appendix 4.2 for additional specific skills addressed at Stage 2.

Stage 3: Group stability, relationships, and connections

The stage of *Group stability, relationships, and connections* emphasizes the real power of interactive group process. The focus here is on tapping into the established and now ongoing stability that comes from the familiarity achieved between group members on rules, boundaries, and managing positive/negative interactions. Group members identify with other group members and with the group leader as strong alliances develop, but these relationships will vary between group members depending on the issue and the emotions connected.

Modes of communication are established, facilitated by the group leader, with significant emphasis placed on the development, enhancement, and reinforcement of positive modes and the diminishment and extinguishing of negative modes and styles of interaction. During this stage, the group must learn to directly and openly address and manage conflict and hostility when it arises between group members and to learn appropriate conflict resolution strategies.

At this stage, group members are expected to employ skills and strategies learned at previous stages to manage and deal with issues and concerns as they arise. A process of circular feedback is employed. When an issue arises and is managed by the group, this is then discussed and debriefed. When a similar issue arises at a later time, subsequent discussions and debriefings make explicit connections to the previous issues and manner of resolution, connecting the two and developing a series of possible solutions. The next time a similar issue arises, the group has been adequately primed to discuss and connect previous problem-solving techniques to the current issue and to develop new solutions as needed. This pattern of circular feedback appears to be particularly effective with very verbal and articulate high-functioning ASD groups.

Stage 3 provides a level of group stability and an opportunity to use meaningful and deepening relationships in the group to solve issues. Connections in relationships are emphasized and connections of group experiences to real-world experiences, outside of group, are targeted and highlighted. As a group enters Stage 3, the opportunities for corrective group experiences occur with increasing frequency and the group leader must remain vigilant to pointing out, reinforcing, and using these situations to increase group awareness and insight.

Setting group goals for Stage 3

The group goals for Stage 3 *Group stability, relationships, and connections* will often include:

General

- the group will take increasing control

- corrective experiences are provided and emphasized

Specific

- group members will help each other acknowledge and manage stress and anxiety when observed

- increased awareness and attention to the needs of others through feedback, support, and problem solving

- emphasis on flexible shifts requiring cooperative and interactive choices, problem solving, and decision making

- the group will manage conflict and hostility as it arises

- modes of communication are defined and refined

- group acceptance and respect will emerge and solidify

- the group will emphasize creating and maintaining memories of specific group situations and interchanges.

At this stage, the group is systematically encouraged to become more active in structuring the individual sessions based on a consensus of group needs. The group is positioned to initiate discussions, allocate time, resolve conflicts, respect and take care of one another, and continue to move forward on the discussed and articulated goals. The group leader increases the emphasis on his role as group facilitator and decreases emphasis on the role of decision maker for the group.

During Stage 3, the group goals focus on facilitating a gradual shift in the arrangement of power and control. The group as a whole will be required to discuss and understand the responsibility of taking on increasing power, authority, and control in decision making and conflict resolution. By placing the emphasis on goals requiring communication enhancement, management of conflict and hostility, and acceptance of each group member as part of the group as a whole, the group is forced to address and sort out what is effective and constructive interaction and what is not, in attempting to meet these goals.

Setting the Stage 3 group structure

The specific environment for Stage 3 relates to providing opportunities for the group to take control of managing issues, conflicts, communication, and aspects of decision making. The group setting is intended to encourage the taking on of this responsibility to manage the interactions and decisions on activity selection, time management, discussion, and free time and by emphasizing tasks and activities which gradually allow the group as a whole to assert itself as a decision-making force for its own benefit. The group leader gently moves the group through this stage, taking less and less of a controlling posture, and more and more that of an encouraging and supportive facilitator. By the end of Stage 3, the group leader smoothly moves back and forth from a facilitator to a consultant role. With the increased responsibility taken on by the group as a whole, individuals speaking only for themselves have relatively little power unless they can garner group support. At this stage, even more vocal and assertive members are influenced and controlled by the joint efforts of the group with support by the group leader.

At Stage 3, the group also plays a significant role in influencing the type and intensity of stress and anxiety that emerges both for individuals and for the group as a whole. For example, when a decision is made by the group to engage in a certain activity, an individual dissenter may experience increased stress and anxiety. At this stage, the group should have some awareness of the types of situations that trigger stress and tension in each of the group members and is encouraged to react to these events with responses that help the individual manage and control his level of stress and tension more effectively. At this stage, the group begins to demonstrate focused efforts to help one another manage and control stress and anxiety, to be sufficiently attentive to each member's needs, and to join in making cooperative, flexible plans and decisions regarding what is in the group's best interests.

Specific skills to be addressed at Stage 3

Since Stage 3 relates to group stability, meaningful relationships, and solid connections, the specific skills addressed relate to maintenance of relationships in the "relationship zone," staying on topic and following changes in topic, cooperation, compromise, learning and understanding what makes a good friend, and giving and receiving compliments.

If individuals within the group share common areas of interest or individual goals relating to any of these Stage 3 skills, then group goals are constructed and tasks and activities focusing on these skills are generated. See Appendix 4.3 for additional specific skills addressed at Stage 3.

Stage 4: Group adaptations and perspective taking

The fourth stage of *Group adaptations and perspective taking* relates to the group's capacity to adapt flexibly to a broad range of issues, behaviors, and emotional reactions that may arise. This will include the ongoing positive and negative issues that arise each session as well as adjustments in time management, modes of communication, decision making, and the evaluation of the needs of the group. As the issues or the group needs change or shift, the group must develop the capacity at this stage to adjust and adapt using the group interactions as the basis for the types of adaptations necessary.

During this stage, there is increasing emphasis on the goals of flexibility and the capacity to shift and on theory of mind—that is, the capacity to think about and experience what another person might be thinking or feeling ("putting yourself in the other person's shoes"). This emphasizes the need to understand situations and interactions, to recognize, experience, and feel the need for empathy toward others, and to respond accordingly.

Setting group goals for Stage 4

The group goals for Stage 4 *Group adaptations and perspective taking* will often include:

General

- making necessary adaptations and adjustments
- responding with flexibility and the capacity to shift and change

Specific

- considering and using alternative approaches and views in decision making

- using assertiveness appropriately

- using feedback constructively

- repairing "breaks" in relationships

- living and surviving with disappointment

- experiencing empathy and responding appropriately.

At this stage, the group learns to manage and direct itself through the ups and downs of managing and resolving conflict, of repairing breaks in relationships, and of having to consider multiple points of view and alternative ways of thinking. The emphasis at this stage is on letting the group take increasing control, make decisions, resolve conflicts, adapt to change, and flexibly manage unknown or unpredictable situations.

The Stage 4 goals are constructed to ensure practice in self-management and self-direction by requiring honest and respectful interactions, appropriate confrontation, discussion of alternative solutions to problems, and unanimous agreement in decision making. Significant emphasis at Stage 4 is given to goals that foster flexibility, openness, and resiliency when faced with difficult, perplexing, and hard-to-solve problems. Activities are specifically constructed with these goals in mind.

Within Stage 4, the goals related to core variables, such as stress and anxiety control and management, joint attention, perspective taking, or relatedness, are now integrated within the discussions and interactions of the group and the weekly tasks and activities selected by the group. At this stage of group development, it is expected that group members have attained adequate levels of self-awareness and knowledge of their own stress and anxiety triggers both personally and occurring within the group context, can recognize and focus on the need for attention directed to the other group members across a variety of situations, and are able to tolerate the frequent shifts in group process that require flexibility and transition. At Stage 4, the group goals reflect this progression from self-regulation through relatedness being thoroughly embedded within each group session. Group goals at this stage continue to emphasize flexibility and transitions as this remains a critical variable for the continuing development of group process variables and skills at the higher stages.

Setting the Stage 4 group structure

At this stage, the group demonstrates its capacity to appropriately take control and assert the competencies and the skills learned in previous stages. The group leader begins this stage in the role of facilitator and by the end of Stage 4 functions primarily as a consultant and observer to the group. The environment fostered is one of trust, support, flexibility, and encouragement of appropriate risk taking. At this stage, the structure provided emphasizes the need and capacity to adjust and adapt flexibly to changing sets of information, interactions, and circumstances, with growing confidence that the group can manage unpredictable situations that they confront. As well, stress- and anxiety-producing personal and interpersonal situations can be managed effectively with techniques for stress and anxiety management initiated on demand or prompted by peer pressure.

Specific skills to be addressed at Stage 4

Since Stage 4 relates to group adaptations and perspective taking, the specific skills addressed at Stage 4 relate to adjusting flexibly to change, moving easily from one topic to another, agreeing to another's point of view, and negotiating or giving in to another's demands.

Stage 4 skills include recognizing and interpreting nonverbal and conceptual cues, assertiveness, managing conflict and confrontation, giving and receiving criticism, using humor, role playing, recognizing and using emotions in interactions, sympathy and empathy, and perspective taking.

If individuals within the group share common areas of interest or individual goals relating to any of these Stage 4 skills, then group goals are constructed and tasks and activities focusing on these skills are generated. See Appendix 4.4 for additional specific skills addressed at Stage 4.

Stage 5: Terminations, loss, and endings

Stage 5 *Terminations, loss, and endings* relates to endings, losses, significant transitions, and goodbyes that occur within or related to the group or group members. Attempts are made to understand the thoughts, emotions, and behaviors that these events stir up and the effects that they have on the interactions between group peers as well as on others outside of the group. This stage focuses on recognizing what these experiences are like, how to tell when they occur, and what effects they have on individuals. Typically, Stage 5 *Terminations, loss, and endings* begins when the end of group is announced or discussed with the end clearly in mind. In most of these groups, this begins 3–5 sessions prior to the last group session. It often includes heavily emotional discussions as endings stir up significant, often unresolved emotional content related to loss, transitions, and endings. Strong emphasis is placed on the need for the group leaders to prepare for this stage by constructing specific Stage 4 goals that facilitate the move into Stage 5 termination. A structure and environment can then be put into place that will manage and support the unpredictable emotional content and allow careful and systematic movement into Stage 5.

Setting group goals for Stage 5

The group goals for Stage 5 *Terminations, loss, and endings* will often include:

General

- addressing termination, loss, transition, change, and goodbyes

Specific

- recognizing termination feelings
- recognizing termination behaviors
- managing termination feelings and behaviors
- creating memories
- maintaining memories
- planning for goodbye
- saying goodbye.

The goals for Stage 5 *Terminations, loss, and endings* focus on addressing and managing thoughts, emotions, and behaviors related to change, transitions, losses, and endings. Following the introduction of termination, the group members are encouraged and helped to create goals specific to endings. Here, as in previous stages, the creating of individual goals should connect and relate to the overall group goals. The group members at Stage 5 should be able to agree on the appropriate construction of group goals and how these goals can be achieved within their group. Individual goals may more flexibly fit the individual group members' needs, and here too information and feedback from parent and teacher sources should be included as well as the group leader's observations of each individual's management of change, transition, loss, and endings within the group setting (i.e. as it relates to the individual's using other group members for support, security, etc.).

Setting the Stage 5 group structure

The Stage 5 group structure continues the themes of fostering emotional safety and security, redefining confidentiality and privacy issues, requiring openness and honesty between group members, encouraging the sharing of thoughts, feelings, and emotions, and tolerating flexibility in allowing for alternative ways of thinking and behaving. Over the course of moving through stages of group development, the group structure has very gradually reduced the amount of overall structure provided to the group in order to allow increased flexibility to develop and for the practice and use of learned skills around control, assertion, flexibility, and self-management to take place. The group as a whole is encouraged to self-direct discussions of issues related to endings as they arise. The group is expected to share relevant termination thoughts and emotions and to use peers to process and understand these experiences. The group leader, as in previous stages, actively becomes less directive, more facilitative, and consultative, to the extent that the group can manage and tolerate.

Specific skills to be addressed at Stage 5

Since Stage 5 is about terminations, loss, and goodbyes, the specific skills addressed at Stage 5 relate to those thoughts, emotions, and behaviors related to endings of meaningful things in group members' lives. These include saying goodbye, recognizing the loss associated with goodbyes, and creating a memory to preserve the relationship.

If individuals within the group share common areas of interest or individual goals relating to any of these Stage 5 skills, then group goals are constructed and tasks and activities focusing on these skills are generated. See Appendix 4.5 for additional specific skills addressed at Stage 5.

Specific skills related to stages of group development

Throughout the five stages of group development, primary consideration within the SCEP model is given at every stage to each of the seven core variables and their role in social and relationship development. In providing training and practice in the development of specific skills, an ongoing awareness of the effects of these core variables on the individual's capacity to learn and use skills is maintained. Training and practice of specific skills are constantly adjusted and modified based on the individual and group response to these underlying variables. The SCEP program attempts to follow a logical sequence paralleling normal social development and providing training and practice for social skills in a progressive and sequential manner.

Part IV
Social Competence Enhancement Program (SCEP) Tasks and Activities

with Cheryl Desautels

Part IV of this book contains sets of strategies that are based on the conceptual frameworks laid out in Parts I–III. Specific tasks and activities are described and how they relate to core areas and related deficits ("core variables") in ways that a group leader/clinician can systematically apply in the implementation of a group intervention program such as SCEP. Tasks and activities are indexed according to stage of group development and according to the "core variable" needing to be addressed, allowing the group leader to make decisions on tasks and activities most useful and appropriate for the particular group they are working with, the particular variable that needs to be addressed, and the particular spontaneous group issues that arise. Tasks and activities are cross-referenced by stage of development and core variable to make selection of the appropriate task or activity more fluid and group leader-friendly.

Cheryl Desautels

Cheryl Desautels holds a M.A. in Counseling and has over eight years of experience working with children who exhibit social communication challenges including those with ASD, ADHD, NLD, mood disorders, and learning disorders. She has worked with children and teens in private and public schools, non-profit organizations, camp programs, and in residential treatment settings. Cheryl's interests include developing specialized activities to support social competence curriculum and facilitating social and emotional growth through creative, instructional, and therapeutic approaches. She has also presented workshops to assist parents and caregivers in understanding the complexity of social interactions and developing the knowledge, skills, and tools necessary to help their children improve both emotional and social competences.

Chapter 17

SCEP Individual and Group Goals for Tasks and Activities by Stages of Group Development

This chapter provides comprehensive individual and group goals related to each stage of group development. Based on the stage of group development for the specific group, the group leader defines the specific individual goals for each group member and the overall group goals. Typically, groups will begin at Stage 1 *Group formation and orientation*, and systematically move through stages (1 through 5) until Stage 5 *Terminations, loss and endings* is reached. Specific group tasks and activities are selected as the group moves through the stages from those provided here or can be uniquely created by the group leader based on the determination of goals and stage of group development.

Stage 1: Group formation and orientation

The first stage observed is one of *Group formation and orientation*, a process where the group comes together for initial sessions and begins to get to know one another as individuals and as a group. These initial group sessions are used to observe how the children react, respond, and interact with one another and to encourage engaging in conversation, sharing of interests, and establishing connections.

Group goals at Stage 1 provide an overall focus on the common and shared experiences and needs of all group members as they emerge and are intended to provide structure about what is expected and what is and is not tolerated (i.e. setting and defining rules and boundaries), about what information, behaviors, and thoughts fit within the group setting, and about shared feelings, thoughts, and experiences common to all group members when beginning in a new situation.

Specific skills focused upon relate to the overall group goals of fostering and developing cohesion, connections, and relationships within the group. These include learning about one another (sharing information, asking questions, attending to others, exploring for common interests, etc.), learning about how the group can work together, acknowledging common issues (anxiety in relationships, needs for flexibility, etc.), and creating a group plan.

Stage 1 individual goals by core variable
a. Self-regulation (self-management, self-awareness, insight, impulse and behavior control)

1. Child will attend to and follow directions (attention, self-control).

2. Child will wait turn (flexibility, attention, self-control).

3. Child will identify individual goals.

4. Child will participate in creating group goals (perspective taking).

b. Emotion competence (recognition, labeling, expressing, understanding, and regulation)

1. Child will recognize and label own basic emotions.

2. Child will begin process of learning to express appropriately own basic emotions.

3. Child will identify and label own triggers to strong emotions.

c. Stress and anxiety control and management

1. Child will identify own basic strategies to manage strong emotions/ stress.

2. Child will respond positively to adult help in managing strong emotions.

d. Attention (focused, sustained, selective, flexible)/joint attention

1. Child will identify and label body parts involved in active listening (eyes, ears, whole body).
2. Child will identify reasons for attending.
3. Child will increase focused attention on others and group activities and stay with the group.
4. Child will recognize and identify reciprocal behaviors of others.

e. Flexibility, change, and transition

1. Child will transition from one task/activity to another independently.
2. Child will tolerate participating in tasks/activities chosen by others (non-preferred).
3. Child will tolerate participation in non-preferred tasks/activities.
4. Child will take turns in conversations.
5. Child will take turns in tasks/activities.

f. Perspective taking/theory of mind (awareness of others, sensitivity to others, sympathy, empathy)

1. Child will identify how own behaviors affect others.
2. Child will recognize that others "think" about him and have feelings about him related to observed behaviors.

g. Relatedness (emotional connections, physical connections)

1. Child will respond to a peer's or adult's greeting.
2. Child will greet other members.
3. Child will identify strategies to initiate friendships (share, question, comment).
4. Child will introduce self each time meeting someone new.

b. Communication (expressive language, receptive language)

1. Child will respond to peer and adult questions.

2. Child will say hellos and goodbyes when seeing someone familiar.

3. Child will use other members' names in greetings and closings.

4. Child will ask an introductory question upon entering a conversation.

5. Child will engage in multiple sequential segments of related conversation.

Stage 1 group goals by core variable

a. Self-regulation (self-management, self-awareness, insight, impulse and behavior control)

1. Group members will remain together as a group (at a table, rug).

2. Group members will acknowledge group expectations (leader-generated), rules schedule.

3. Group members will recognize and acknowledge the need for self-regulation and agree to manage and direct own thoughts, emotions, and behaviors.

b. Emotion competence (recognition, labeling, expressing, understanding, and regulation)

1. Group members will share feelings with the group.

2. Group members will acknowledge sharing of feelings by other group members.

c. Stress and anxiety control and management

1. The group will acknowledge stress of beginning participation in a group.

2. The group will identify tasks/activities/interactions which create stress.

3. The group will identify potential group strategies to manage stress.

d. *Attention (focused, sustained, selective, flexible)/joint attention*

1. The group will recognize and acknowledge the need for attention and joint attention capacities in interpersonal interactions.

2. The group will identify and label active listening strategies.

e. *Flexibility, change, and transition*

1. The group will transition from one activity to another.

2. The group will engage in appropriate turn taking in conversation.

3. The group will engage in appropriate turn taking in tasks/activities.

f. *Perspective taking/theory of mind*

1. The group will identify how certain behaviors affect the whole group.

2. The group will recognize that each group member "thinks" and "feels" differently.

3. The group recognizes that group decisions can be made even though each group member may think and feel differently from others.

g. *Relatedness (emotional connections, physical connections)*

1. Group members will learn about each other's common interests.

2. The group will acknowledge shared interests.

3. Group members will request information from other group members.

h. *Communication (expressive language, receptive language)*

1. Group members will listen to other group members' questions.

2. The group will engage in sustained, ongoing, interactive conversation among all group members.

Stage 2: Group cohesion

The second stage of *Group cohesion* relates to the group's capacity to form a bond as a group and to use that bond as a force to hold the group together as it begins to deal with increasingly more stressful issues. Information learned from Stage 1 sessions about the group's strengths and weaknesses, particularly in core areas and related core variables, such as stress/anxiety, attention, and flexibility/transitions, will inform the construction of Stage 2 goals as the group moves forward.

At Stage 2, group goals foster interaction, an increased awareness of individual strengths and weaknesses, and an increased understanding of the group as a whole. Individual goals work on specific aspects of a group member's thinking or behavior that might interfere with effective group participation and involvement. These are replaced with more effective group interactive techniques. Group goals provide the opportunity for interaction, while individual goals focus on the specific needs of the individual to make interactions successful. For example, a Stage 2 group goal may focus on group decision making, while individual goals may focus on a member being more positive, using cooperation strategies, or complying with the majority.

Specific skills focused upon relate to the overall group goals of acknowledging, managing, and coping with the stress and anxiety that arises as individuals take risks to share personal information, joining others in an attempt to gain support and feedback, expressing needs that may be embarrassing, and recognizing intimacy and affiliation needs. These skills include asking for and receiving help from peers, taking turns, competing, and initiating conversations and activities.

Stage 2 individual goals by core variable
a. Self-regulation (self-management, self-awareness, insight, impulse and behavior control)

1. Child will identify own behaviors.
2. Child will identify friendship behavior.
3. Child will identify annoying behavior.
4. Child will learn how to filter thoughts.
5. Child will understand the purpose of filtering thoughts.
6. Child will identify situations where thoughts must be filtered.
7. Child will respect the boundaries of peers and adults.

b. Emotion competence (recognition, labeling, expressing, understanding, and regulation)

1. Child will identify and label the emotions of others.

2. Child will identify and label the emotion triggers of others.

3. Child will identify and label a range of feelings of others.

c. Stress and anxiety control and management

1. Child will learn strategies to manage stress and anxiety.

2. Child will implement strategies for stress and anxiety management as needed.

3. Child will learn strategies to manage strong emotions/stress.

4. Child will use strategies to manage strong emotions/stress (deep breathing, movement, etc.).

5. Child will acknowledge, manage, and cope with stress and anxiety from the group.

6. Child will acknowledge how support from peers can reduce stress and anxiety.

d. Attention (focused, sustained, selective, flexible)/joint attention

1. Child will increase sustained attention with others.

2. Child will invite peers to engage in shared tasks/activities or play.

3. Child will join in tasks/activities or play at peer's request.

e. Flexibility, change, and transition

1. Child will follow group-established rules.

2. Child will make flexible choices within the group.

3. Child will comply with the majority.

f. Perspective taking/theory of mind

1. Child will recognize and acknowledge that others have their own thoughts and beliefs that govern their own behaviors.

2. Child will recognize and acknowledge that others have needs.

3. Child will identify the needs of others.

4. Child will recognize and acknowledge that our own interpersonal (e.g. friendly) behaviors have an effect on others (e.g. hellos and goodbyes).

5. Child will recognize and acknowledge the effects of asking others for help.

6. Child will recognize and acknowledge the effects of giving others help.

g. *Relatedness (emotional connections, physical connections)*

1. Child will recognize and identify the purpose of maintaining a topic of conversation.

2. Child will identify the purpose of taking turns.

3. Child will recognize and identify the need and purpose for remembering information about others.

4. Child will recognize and identify strengths in peers.

5. Child will recognize and identify challenges in peers.

6. Child will recognize the need to ask questions of peers.

7. Child will use information learned about peer group members to ask relevant questions.

h. *Communication (expressive language, receptive language)*

1. Child will initiate a conversation or activity with a peer group member.

2. Child will engage in interactive conversation with a peer group member.

3. Child will remain on topic to conclusion of discussion.

4. Child will transition to other topic appropriately.

5. Child will recognize and acknowledge nonverbal communications (body, face, tone).

6. Child will use nonverbal communications appropriately and consistently.

7. Child will initiate a discussion of a comfortable topic with a peer (share).

Stage 2 group goals by core variable

a. Self-regulation (self-management, self-awareness, insight, impulse and behavior control)

1. Group members will discuss and set group goals.

2. Group members will recognize and acknowledge their role in the group.

3. Group members will recognize and acknowledge a positive contribution to the group.

b. Emotion competence (recognition, labeling, expressing, understanding, and regulation)

1. Group members will recognize, identify, and label their own emotions.

2. Group members will recognize, identify, and label the emotions of other group members.

3. Group members will recognize, identify, and label the emotion triggers of other group members.

c. Stress and anxiety control and management

1. Group members will recognize and acknowledge their own stress and anxiety experiences.

2. Group members will recognize and discuss the stress and anxiety of transitioning into group.

3. Group members will practice strategies to manage stress and tension.

d. Attention (focused, sustained, selective, flexible) / joint attention

1. Group members will increase sustained attention with others.

2. Group members will engage peers in reciprocal tasks/activities or play.

3. Group members will initiate and engage in group tasks/activities.

e. Flexibility, change, and transition

1. The group will follow group-established rules.

2. The group will recognize and follow turn-taking rules in conversations.

3. The group will recognize and follow turn-taking rules in tasks/ activities.

f. Perspective taking/theory of mind

1. The group will recognize and acknowledge each member's "place" in the group.

2. The group will recognize and identify the purpose of asking others for help and information.

3. The group will recognize and acknowledge the positive effects of asking others for help and information.

g. Relatedness (emotional connections, physical connections)

1. Group members will recognize and acknowledge similarities in self with other group members.

2. Group members will spontaneously ask information gathering and week-to-week connecting questions of other group members.

3. Group members will ask questions of one another about wishes/ desires/choices for task/activity before decision making.

h. Communication (expressive and receptive language)

1. Group members will ask information gathering questions of one another.

2. Group members will collect information from peers through questions and information sharing.

3. Group members will use information gathered from one another to ask follow-up questions.

Stage 3: Group stability, relationships, and connections

The third stage of *Group stability, relationships, and connections* emphasizes the power of interactive group process. The focus here is on tapping into the established and now ongoing stability that comes from the familiarity achieved between group members on rules, boundaries, and managing positive/negative interactions. Group members identify with other group members and with the group leader, and strong alliances develop, but at this stage these will vary between group members depending on the issue and the emotions aroused.

At Stage 3, the group is gradually encouraged to become more active in structuring the individual sessions based on a consensus and approval of group needs. The group is positioned to initiate discussions, allocate time, resolve conflicts, respect and take care of one another, and continue to move forward on the discussed and articulated goals. The group leader increases the emphasis on his role as group facilitator and decreases emphasis on the role of decision maker for the group. The Stage 3 group goals focus on facilitating a gradual shift in the arrangement of power and control. The group as a whole is required to discuss and understand the responsibility of taking on increasing power and authority in control, decision making, and conflict resolution.

Emphasis is placed on goals requiring communication enhancement within the group, group management of conflict and hostility when it arises, and total acceptance of each group member within the group as a whole. Specific skills which address these issues are focused upon and include learning about nonverbal communication, working cooperatively, giving and getting feedback/criticism, emotion regulation, and anxiety management.

Stage 3 individual goals by core variable

a. Self-regulation (self-management, self-awareness, insight, impulse and behavior control)

1. Child will recognize and identify own strengths and challenges.

2. Child will increasingly self-initiate cooperative and interactive behaviors.

3. Child will self-initiate requests for adult support.

4. Child will self-initiate requests for peer group member support and feedback.

b. Emotion competence (recognition, labeling, expressing, understanding, and regulation)

1. Child will independently use strategies to manage strong emotions.

2. Child will recognize and identify connections between feelings/ emotions to causes/thoughts and responses/behaviors.

c. Stress and anxiety control and management

1. Child will maintain emotional regulation by utilizing stress and anxiety management strategies.

2. Child will use strategies at appropriate times to manage stress and anxiety.

d. Attention (focused, sustained, selective, flexible)/joint attention

1. Child will attend and respond to nonverbal communications of other group members.

e. Flexibility, change, and transition

1. Child will accept and positively comment on the opinions of others.

2. Child will engage in non-preferred topics of conversation and tasks/ activities.

3. Child will give feedback and criticism.

4. Child will accept feedback and criticism.

f. Perspective taking/theory of mind

1. Child will recognize and identify the purpose and effects of helping others.

2. Child will recognize when to refrain from engaging another group member.

3. Child will recognize and understand the positive effects of filtering thoughts.

4. Child will identify and employ appropriate social faking.

g. Relatedness (emotional connections, physical connections)

1. Child will express his own opinions or thoughts at the appropriate times.

2. Child will respond positively to help from peers when attempting to manage conflicts or problems.

3. Child will use information about others in relationship building.

4. Child will recognize and identify different types of relationships.

5. Child will recognize and identify the purpose and effects of sharing information about himself.

6. Child will develop alliances within the group.

7. Child will recognize when to ask a peer for advice.

8. Child will ask a peer for advice on topic of self-interest.

9. Child will ask follow-up questions related to topics from previous groups.

10. Child will ask appropriate personal questions.

11. Child will share personal information.

12. Child will request input/advice from peer group members.

h. Communication (expressive language, receptive language)

1. Child will recognize and identify humor.

2. Child will recognize and identify sarcasm.

3. Child will recognize and identify criticism.

4. Child will recognize and be aware of his own verbal communications.

5. Child will recognize and be aware of his own nonverbal communications.

6. Child will identify acceptable topics of conversation within levels of relationships.

7. Child will identify and use strategies to initiate friendships (e.g. compliments, statements of encouragement).

Stage 3 group goals by core variable

a. Self-regulation (self-management, self-awareness, insight, impulse and behavior control)

1. Group members will acknowledge each other's individual goals.

2. Group members will acknowledge group goals and review as needed.

3. Group members will include all members' input in group decision making.

b. Emotion competence (recognition, labeling, expressing, understanding, and regulation)

1. The group will self-initiate the use of strategies to manage strong emotions.

2. The group will link feelings/emotions to causes/thoughts and responses/behaviors.

c. Stress and anxiety control and management

1. The group will spontaneously apply learned strategies for stress and anxiety management.

2. The group will differentiate strategies for stress and anxiety management and apply appropriately in stress situations.

d. Attention (focused, sustained, selective, flexible)/joint attention

1. The group will recognize and attend to nonverbal signs of communication of others.

e. Flexibility, change, and transition

1. Group members will consider and include the opinions of other group members.

2. The group will purposely engage in non-preferred topics of conversation and tasks/activities.

f. Perspective taking/theory of mind

1. The group will recognize and identify the purpose and effects of helping others.

2. Group members will recognize when to refrain from engaging another group member.

3. The group will identify and employ appropriate social faking.

g. Relatedness (emotional connections, physical connections)

1. The group will formulate and express group opinions.

2. The group will manage conflicts or problems in positive ways.

3. Group members will use knowledge and information about one another in decision making.

4. The group will recognize and identify different types of relationships within the group.

5. The group will recognize and identify alliances and how they contribute/detract from decision making, conflict resolution, and task/activity completion.

h. Communication (expressive language, receptive language)

1. The group will recognize and identify humor.

2. The group will recognize and identify sarcasm.

3. The group will recognize and identify criticism.

4. The group will recognize and identify humor vs. sarcasm vs. criticism.

5. The group will recognize and be aware of personal signs of verbal and nonverbal communication.

6. The group will recognize and identify acceptable topics of conversation within levels of relationships.

7. The group will recognize and identify strategies to initiate friendships (e.g. compliments, statements of encouragement).

Stage 4: Group adaptations and perspective taking

The fourth stage of *Group adaptations and perspective taking* relates to the group's capacity to adapt flexibly to the ongoing positive and negative issues that arise each session, adjusting time management, modes of communication, decision making, and responses to the needs of the group. As the issues change or as the group needs shift, the group must develop the capacity at this stage to adjust and adapt quickly, using the group interactions to decide the types of adaptations required.

At this stage the group learns to manage and direct itself through the ups and downs of managing and resolving conflict, of repairing breaks in relationships, and of having to consider multiple points of view and alternative ways of thinking. The emphasis at this stage is on letting the group take increasing control, make decisions, resolve conflicts, adapt to change, and flexibly manage unknown or unpredictable situations.

At Stage 4, increasing emphasis is placed on goals relating to flexibility, openness, resiliency when faced with difficult, perplexing, and hard-to-solve problems, on the ability to shift, and on theory of mind—that is, the capacity to think about and experience what another person might be thinking or feeling ("putting yourself in the other person's shoes"). The Stage 4 goals are constructed to ensure a focus on and practice in self-management and self-direction by requiring honest and respectful interactions, appropriate confrontation, discussion of alternative solutions to problems, and unanimous agreement in decision making. Activities are specifically constructed with these goals in mind. Specific skills addressed at Stage 4 include negotiating compromise, recognizing and using criticism, seeing things through another person's eyes, apologizing, and getting "unstuck."

Stage 4 individual goals by core variable

a. Self-regulation (self-management, self-awareness, insight, impulse and behavior control)

1. Child will consistently filter thoughts in a full range of different situations.

2. Child will recognize and identify his own challenges.

3. Child will tolerate and understand others' opinions different from his own.

b. Emotion competence (recognition, labeling, expressing, understanding, and regulation)

1. Child will recognize and identify emotions and feelings in others when exhibited through nonverbal and verbal cues.

2. Child will acknowledge "feelings" about group participation.

3. Child will assist group members in the management and regulation of strong emotions.

c. Stress and anxiety control and management

1. Child will assist group members in the management of intragroup conflicts and problems.

2. Child will assist group members in the management of extragroup conflicts and problems.

d. Attention (focused, sustained, selective, flexible)/joint attention

1. Child will monitor responses of other group members toward their own behaviors.

2. Child will identify and discuss responses of others outside of group toward their own behaviors.

e. Flexibility, change, and transition

1. Child will recognize and identify the purpose and effects of compromising with group members.

2. Child will identify and manage unpredictable situations.

3. Child will adapt to changes within the group.

4. Child will make non-preferred choices for the benefit of the group.

5. Child will use alliances built within the group flexibly to address group and personal issues.

f. Perspective taking/theory of mind

1. Child will recognize and identify his role in establishing and maintaining relationships.

2. Child will consistently and appropriately filter thoughts so as to benefit the group.

3. Child will understand and appreciate multiple points of views.

g. *Relatedness (emotional connections, physical connections)*

1. Child will recognize and identify the purpose and effects of cooperating with group members.

2. Child will recognize and identify the purpose and effects of cooperating with others outside of group.

3. Child will share personal information/feelings with others for the purpose of connecting with others.

4. Child will recognize and identify strategies which maintain friendships (apologizing, forgiving).

5. Child will repair damaged relationships within group.

6. Child will help a peer on a personal topic raised by peer.

7. Child will sustain appropriate interactive conversation throughout group.

8. Child will recognize and express comfort as a participating group member.

9. Child will request help from the group with a personal issue or problem.

10. Child will recognize and identify strategies which negatively impact friendships or connections within group.

h. *Communication (expressive language, receptive language)*

1. Child will use humor appropriately.

2. Child will use sarcasm appropriately.

3. Child will use criticism appropriately.

4. Child will differentiate humor vs. sarcasm vs. criticism.

5. Child will use communication skills to manage conflicts.

6. Child will use communication skills to express positive support for group members.

Stage 4 group goals by core variable

a. Self-regulation (self-management, self-awareness, insight, impulse and behavior control)

1. The group will tolerate disagreements as part of group functioning.

2. Group members will tolerate all opinions even when disagreeing with group opinion.

3. The group will resolve disagreements regarding group decisions.

b. Emotion competence (recognition, labeling, expressing, understanding, and regulation)

1. Group members will recognize and identify emotions and feelings in other group members by observing nonverbal and verbal cues.

2. The group will respond appropriately and spontaneously to group members' expression of emotions.

c. Stress and anxiety control and management

1. The group will identify strategies to assist peers in the management of conflicts and problems.

2. The group will implement strategies to assist peers in the management of intragroup conflicts and problems.

3. The group will implement strategies to assist peers in the management of extragroup conflicts and problems.

d. Attention (focused, sustained, selective, flexible)/joint attention

1. The group will recognize, identify, and acknowledge group members' attention to one another.

2. Group members will monitor responses of others towards their own behavior.

3. Group members will recognize, identify, and acknowledge nonverbal behaviors of others that affect their own behavior, thinking, and emotions.

e. Flexibility, change, and transition

1. The group will identify the purpose and effects of compromising with others.

2. Group members will solicit the opinions of other group members.

f. Perspective taking/theory of mind

1. Group members will recognize and acknowledge their role in establishing and maintaining relationships within the group.

2. Group members will recognize and acknowledge their role in establishing and maintaining relationships with others outside of group.

3. Group members will recognize and acknowledge the role of others in establishing and maintaining relationships with others outside the group.

g. Relatedness (emotional connections, physical connections)

1. The group will identify the purpose and effects of cooperating within the group.

2. Group members will recognize and identify the importance of sharing personal information and feelings as a way of connecting with other group members.

3. The group will identify and discuss strategies which develop and maintain friendships (apologizing, forgiving).

4. The group will implement strategies which develop and maintain friendships and relationships.

h. Communication (expressive language, receptive language)

1. The group will use humor, sarcasm, and criticism in appropriate situations.

2. Group members will accept feedback on their use of humor, sarcasm, and criticism and its appropriateness to the situation.

Stage 5: Terminations, loss, and endings

Stage 5, *Terminations, loss, and endings*, relates to endings, losses, significant transitions, and goodbyes. Attempts are made to understand the thoughts, feelings, and emotions that these events stir up and the effects that they have on interactions with peers and others. This stage focuses on recognizing what these experiences are like, how to tell when they occur, and what effect they have on each group member. Related to group termination, this stage typically begins when the end of group is announced or discussed with the end clearly in mind, and it often includes heavily emotional discussions as endings stir up significant, often unresolved emotional content related to loss, transitions, and endings.

The goals for Stage 5 *Terminations, loss, and endings* all focus on addressing and managing thoughts, feelings, and emotions related to change, transitions, losses, and endings. Following the introduction of group termination, the group members are encouraged and helped to create goals specific to endings and the holding on to memories. At Stage 5, the group members should be capable of agreeing on the appropriate construction of group goals and how these goals can be achieved within their group. Specific skills addressed at Stage 5 include expressing termination emotions, understanding endings, and saving the memories.

Stage 5 individual goals by core variable

a. Self-regulation (self-management, self-awareness, insight, impulse and behavior control)

1.   Child will recognize potentially disorganizing, anxiety-provoking influences that termination experiences evoke.

2.   Child will manage positive termination experiences in developmentally appropriate ways.

3.   Child will manage negative termination experiences in developmentally appropriate ways.

b. Emotion competence (recognition, labeling, expressing, understanding, and regulation)

1.   Child will recognize and identify emotions related to termination, losses, and endings.

2. Child will recognize and identify emotional responses with others related to termination, losses, and endings.

3. Child will recognize and respond to the emotional state of others.

c. Stress and anxiety control and management

1. Child will recognize and identify stress and anxiety related to termination, loss, and ending experiences and relationships.

2. Child will recognize and identify stress and anxiety related to specific experiences of group termination.

3. Child will identify and implement successful techniques for stress and anxiety control and management when termination, loss, and ending stresses emerge.

d. Attention (focused, sustained, selective, flexible)/joint attention

1. Child will remain focused and attentive to self-generated termination, loss, and ending issues.

2. Child will direct focus and attention to management of termination, loss, and ending issues raised by other group members.

3. Child will recognize and identify how other group members manage termination, loss, and ending issues.

e. Flexibility, change, and transition

1. Child will recognize and identify the unpredictable nature of termination, loss, and ending experiences.

2. Child will respond flexibly with strategies to address termination, loss, and ending issues.

f. Perspective taking/theory of mind

1. Child will recognize other group members' termination, loss, and ending issues.

2. Child will respond with sensitivity and understanding to other group members' termination, loss, and ending experiences.

3. Child will recognize and identify that each group member has a personal and unique reaction to termination, losses, and endings.

g. Relatedness (emotional connections, physical connections)

1. Child will recall and identify memories from the group experience.

2. Child will identify and share experiences of being a group member.

3. Child will acknowledge positive and negative elements of the group experience.

4. Child will acknowledge the importance of saying goodbye to this group.

5. Child will acknowledge the importance of addressing termination, loss, and ending issues.

6. Child will generalize termination, loss, and ending experiences in group to similar experiences outside of group.

h. Communication (expressive language, receptive language)

1. Child will communicate own termination, loss, and ending experiences effectively.

2. Child will effectively express understanding of other group members' termination, loss, and ending experiences.

Stage 5 group goals by core variable

a. Self-regulation (self-management, self-awareness, insight, impulse and behavior control)

1. The group will manage, control, and regulate the range of thoughts, feelings, and behaviors stirred up by termination, losses, and endings.

2. The group will participate collaboratively and cooperatively in termination, loss, and ending issues of the group.

b. Emotion competence (recognition, labeling, expressing, understanding, and regulation)

1. Group members will share emotional responses with others related to termination, losses, and endings.

2. Group members will respond to the emotional state of others related to termination, loss, and ending issues.

c. Stress and anxiety control and management

1. The group will recognize and acknowledge each member's own emotional responses to termination, loss, and ending issues.

2. The group will recognize and acknowledge each member's own emotional responses to terminating relationships.

3. The group will implement appropriate strategies for stress and anxiety control and management as needed to address effectively termination, loss, and ending issues.

d. Attention (focused, sustained, selective, flexible) / joint attention

1. The group will attend to termination, loss, and ending issues raised by group members.

2. The group will recognize and acknowledge stress and difficulties of group members related to termination, losses, and endings.

e. Flexibility, change, and transition

1. The group will respond flexibly to group members' needs around termination, loss, and ending issues.

2. The group will facilitate the effective management by group members of termination, loss, and ending issues.

f. Perspective taking / theory of mind

1. Group members will recognize and acknowledge others' reactions and experiences related to termination, losses, and endings.

2. Group members will recognize and identify similarities and differences between their own and other group members' experiences of termination, losses, and endings.

3. Group members will generalize their own and other group members' experiences of termination, losses, and endings.

g. Relatedness (emotional connections, physical connections)

1. The group will recall and identify memories from the group experience.

2. The group will encourage and facilitate the appropriate expression of thoughts, feelings, and behaviors by all group members.

h. Communication (expressive language, receptive language)

1. The group will express termination, loss, and ending thoughts, feelings, and behaviors appropriately as a group.

2. The group will explore, discuss, and identify a range of different ways to express termination, loss, and ending issues appropriately.

Index of tasks and activities by stage of group development

Chapter 18

SCEP Individual and Group Goals for Tasks and Activities by Core Areas of Development and Related Deficits in ASD

This chapter provides comprehensive individual and group goals related to each core area and related deficits in ASD. Based on the stage of group development and core area and related deficit to be focused upon for the specific group, the group leader defines the specific individual goals for each group member and the overall goals. Typically, groups will begin at Stage 1 *Group formation and orientation*, and systematically move through each core area and related deficit, beginning with self-regulation through relatedness, as needed. As the group leader moves the group through each stage, core areas are generally selected based on the individual and group goals established for each group as a whole. Specific group tasks and activities are selected from those provided here or can be uniquely created by the group leader based on the determination of goals, stage of group development, and core and related deficit.

Core variable: Self-regulation

Initial tasks encourage group members to assume certain degrees of personal control over physical interactions (e.g. boundaries), motor involvement, cognitive awareness, and emotional regulation. This control is expected to increase as the group learns and masters appropriate control and management strategies within the group and in group social interactions. While the tasks and activities themselves may vary, the underlying goals and objectives of self-regulation should be maintained.

Core variable: Emotion competence

Emotion tasks and activities involving this core variable (emotion recognition, labeling, expression, understanding, and regulation) typically follow a developmental progression in their use and presentation. Initial tasks and activities address only a few basic, simple emotions with more difficult and complex emotions added gradually in a systematic fashion as the group learns and masters their appropriate use through activities presented in group social interactions. For example, with pictorial emotion recognition tasks, simpler tasks begin with line drawings of emotions, followed upon mastery by more detailed caricature drawings, followed by pictures of real people. With verbal information, tasks are initially presented with simpler emotion vocabulary words that are gradually increased in complexity and difficulty level depending on the cognitive and developmental level of the group, individual and group goals, and specific stage of group development. While the tasks and activities within this core variable may vary, the underlying goals and objectives of emotion recognition, labeling, and understanding should be maintained.

Core variable: Stress and anxiety control and management

Individuals with ASD often experience heightened arousal levels in response to internal and external triggers, usually stress-related. When these situations are not managed or coped with effectively, they result in increased stress and often anxiety, which can potentially spin out of control. Goals for this core variable focus on the recognition and awareness of the triggers for these heightened levels of arousal, on learning ways to control and manage them effectively, and on implementation of effective techniques for stress and anxiety control and management on demand.

Several programs address the increased arousal levels inherent in stress by working to control and reduce the effects that they generate. Several of those found most effective and feasible to implement with individuals with ASD are described here for use within the SCEP program.

Initial tasks emphasize the learning and practice of basic techniques for stress and anxiety management for use in group social interactions. While the tasks and activities themselves may vary, the underlying goals and objectives of stress and anxiety control and management should be maintained.

Core variable: Attention (focused, sustained, selective, flexible)

These tasks emphasize focused, sustained, selective, and flexible attention by group members on specific tasks, activities, or topics presented while maintaining motor control, cognitive awareness, and emotional regulation within the group and in group social interactions. While the tasks and activities themselves may vary, the underlying goals and objectives of attention should be maintained.

Core variable: Joint attention

Joint attention involves the ability to engage another individual in a reciprocal interaction which includes aspects of focused, sustained, selective, and flexible attention. It involves cognitive functions (attention), social functions (awareness and engagement), communication (conversation), and self-regulation (managing and controlling the individual's own half of the interaction). The goals for joint attention focus on the recognition and awareness of others and their behaviors and experiencing and responding to others. While the tasks and activities themselves may vary, the underlying goals and objectives of joint attention should be maintained.

Core variable: Flexibility, change, and transition

Inflexibility/rigidity is one of the defining characteristics of ASD and one that significantly interferes with age-appropriate social development. Conversely, the ability to respond flexibly and adaptively to cognitive, social, and behavioral information is key to successful social interaction and requires the accurate processing of information, the generation of a response appropriate to the situation, the implementation of the response, and flexible and socially responsive adaptations as an interaction progresses.

The goals for the core variable flexibility, change, and transition, involve learning and practicing how to respond and shift flexibly as the topic/task/expectation or another individual shifts or changes, recognizing and using the nonverbal communications of others, and working together cooperatively in a group situation (taking turns, sharing, tolerating others' opinions, managing criticism, etc.). While the tasks and activities themselves may vary, the underlying goals and objectives of flexibility, change, and transition, should be maintained.

Core variable: Perspective taking

Perspective taking as a core variable requires an understanding that, as individuals, we exist as separate from others. It also requires an understanding that those others also exist as separate from us with their own thoughts, feelings, beliefs, and behaviors. Further adding to this complexity, perspective taking also requires an understanding that the thoughts, feelings, and behaviors of those other individuals may affect our own thoughts, feelings, and behaviors. Finally, those thoughts, feelings, and behaviors of other individuals can also be affected by our own thoughts, feelings, and behaviors.

Social situations are inherently influenced and affected by the thoughts, feelings, and behaviors of all those involved, including an individual group member's understanding or beliefs about what or how other individuals in the group think, believe, or feel about each other (the other individuals involved). To simplify, this translates into situations such as Jon asking, "What does Ben think about what Will just said?" or Jim thinking, "Carl looks angry at Josh for what he just did to Matt." As such, the goals of tasks and activities focusing on the core variable perspective taking target both an understanding of one's own thoughts, feelings, and behaviors and how they affect social interactions and on how awareness and understanding of others' thoughts, feelings, and behaviors can affect one's own social responses in both positive and negative ways.

Initial tasks and activities emphasize the recognition of one's own thoughts, feelings, and behaviors and of how they affect a social interaction and of when others' thoughts, feelings, and behaviors are different from one's own and of how these affect the nature and course of the social interaction. While the tasks and activities themselves may vary, the underlying goals and objectives of perspective taking should be maintained.

Core variable: Relatedness

Relatedness is the capacity to connect with another individual or group on multiple levels, including within all core areas, cognitive, social, emotional, behavioral, communication, sensory, motor, and self-regulation. It may bring with it experiences of calmness, intimacy, excitement, security, and comfort. However, for individuals who have difficulty processing experiences on any (or all) of these levels, such as the individual with ASD, the experiences can be confusing, disorienting, scary, threatening, or overwhelming.

Becoming part of a group and connecting with others around common goals and experiences can provide an understanding of how relatedness and connectedness enrich our lives and how one can develop and learn ways to foster this process. This requires an understanding of our own thoughts, feelings, and behaviors and how they are experienced by others, with the goal of changing those aspects of ourselves that prohibit or interfere with the relatedness and connectedness with others that we may seek.

Initial tasks and activities focus on the experience of being part of a group and what thoughts, feelings, and behaviors affect this process, on the development of interactions which foster relatedness and connectedness, and of how to focus on others as a way to make them feel better about their relationship (their relatedness and connectedness) with us.

Core variable: Pragmatic communication

Pragmatic communication is the capacity to use semantic language for the purpose of engaging in a language-based, social interaction with another person or group. Pragmatic communication involves the ability to understand and use language on a level that goes beyond mere mechanics and word usage. It includes the intent, purpose, and meaning of the spoken word and of all the unspoken characteristics conveyed in a reciprocal social interchange. While basic language skills are necessary, they are not required, nor are they sufficient to communicate effectively. Effective communication involves the effective use of a combination of spoken language and messages together with pragmatic forms of communication, such as gestures, body language, visual signs and signals, and other forms of nonverbal communications.

Those forms of pragmatic communication used in social, interactive, group-based situations are considered of most importance within the SCEP approach and are addressed within this core variable and the related tasks/activities.

Core variable: General

These tasks/activities do not apply to any one specific core variable, but cut across several related issues and focus primarily on stage-related issues. They are intended to develop and solidify stage-related aspects of group development. Most activities, even those with no specific core variable focus, will address some aspect of core variable issues, but those presented here are meant to have a primary stage focus with only a secondary core variable focus. General tasks/ activities are usually a good place to start at the outset of a group or when a new stage is introduced.

Index of tasks and activities by core variable

SCEP Tasks and Activities Related to Stages of Group Development and to Core Areas of Development and Related Deficits in ASD

This chapter provides specific group tasks and activities that relate to stages of group development and to core areas and related deficits in ASD as they emerge in groupwork with children with ASD. Dozens of group tasks and activities are provided, each specific to a particular stage of group development and to a core area and related deficit in ASD. Typically, the group leader follows the developmental progression from Stages 1 through 5, focusing on the core areas and related deficits as needed and as defined by group members' individual goals and by the overall goals of the group as a whole.

My group book

Stage
1: Group formation and orientation

Core variable
General

Group goal
- Group members will recognize, acknowledge, and record experiences as part of a group.

Objectives
- Group members will engage other group members in awareness, attention, and discussion of what it means to be part of a group.

- Group members will record and save their experiences as they evolve as part of a group.

Task/activity description
Pre-group preparation
Book-making materials are made available.

Group task
The group leader discusses and explains the group book-making project and begins by having each child design and decorate a cover for their own individual group book. Over subsequent groups, each group member will draw pictures, write stories, and insert completed projects and other information which characterize and represent different aspects and stages of their group experience. The group book is intended to represent an ongoing record of each group member's group experiences, including tasks and activities completed during group, reminders of social competencies and social skills worked on and mastered, recollections of shared experiences, and markers of moving through progressive group stages.

Each group may designate a part of each group session (e.g. one group per month) to use for recording and saving group experiences in a group book. Younger children tend to enjoy the "arts and crafts" and book-making of the experience, while older children may choose to employ digital book-making techniques, such as constructing and saving on a DVD or computer flash drive, or to videorecord their group experiences. The emphasis throughout is placed on "group" and shared experiences as individuals record and save what is most important to them.

Discussion

Following each task/activity saved in the group book, the group discusses and processes the importance of the activity for the individual and for the group as a whole, its connection to group goals, its relationship to the specific stage of group development, and the utility of the particular skill addressed.

My favorites

Stage
1: Group formation and orientation

Core variable
Self-regulation

Group goal
- Group members will manage and direct self in the service of joining a group of peers.

Objective
- Group members will learn about and manage their own feelings, thinking style, and behaviors in order to become viable members of a group.

Task/activity description
Group task

The group leader discusses and explains the task/activity to be completed by all group members and provides the materials necessary. Each group member creates their own list, card, or book of their favorite things. They list as many items as they can with help and prompting from the group leader. This could include favorite person, food, breakfast item, dessert, snack, fruit, drink, color, book, author, movie, actor, song, singer, TV program, teacher, school activity, school subject, piece of clothing, toy, stuffed animal, game, friend, relative, place to visit, vacation, memory, time of day, relaxation spot, relaxation activity, etc.

Following the creation of each group member's favorites list (card, book), the group leader directs a discussion and sharing of the items selected by each child, with emphasis placed on the child's thinking about those items selected.

Discussion

This task encourages group members first to address issues of self, self-control, self-awareness, self-management, and self-interest, and to consider their own interests, thoughts, and feelings in the context of a group setting where they also hear about other group members' interests, thoughts, and feelings.

The group leader draws attention to similarities and differences, with emphasis on the diversity of interests among group members. Group members are encouraged to save these items (list, card, book, etc.) in their own individual group folder or to include them in their group book.

Faces

Stage

1: Group formation and orientation

Core variable

Emotion competence

Group goal

- Group members will experience themselves as a part of group through shared experiences.

Objectives

- Group members will engage other group members in awareness, attention, and discussion of recognizable similarities and differences among peers.

- Group members will recognize, develop, and emphasize the importance of the recognition of facial features in social interactions.

Task/activity description

Pre-group preparation

Head-and-shoulders pictures of each group member and leader are taken in advance of the activity. Each picture is enlarged and reproduced in color (4 × 6 or 8 × 10 inches are best), then laminated if desired.

Group task

The group leader discusses and explains the task/activity, its purposes, and its goals. Each child is then given the picture of a peer member and in turn asked to report one prominent feature of the child whose picture he has with responses recorded on a flipchart or whiteboard. As features are collected, group members are prompted to focus on eyes, mouth, forehead, eyebrows, etc. and to comment on similarities and differences between and among group members and group leader.

Discussion

As the information is collected, attention is drawn to similarities and differences between members so as to foster a sense of uniqueness within the context of group togetherness. The extent and complexity of the discussion should take into account the cognitive, communication, sensory, social, and emotional abilities within the group and requires the group leader to monitor and adjust the direction of the discussion based on group abilities.

Today I feel...

Stage

1: Group formation and orientation

Core variable

Emotion competence

Group goal

- Group members will label and express, to the group, emotions they are experiencing while participating in the group.

Objectives

- Group members will share with each other how they are feeling while sitting in the group.

- Group members will attend to and acknowledge each other's emotions/feelings.

- Group members will identify similar emotions between members.

- Group members will identify how certain emotions may affect others in the group, group activity choices, or order of activities.

Task/activity description

Pre-group preparation

Ten or more pictures of emotions, either drawings or photographs, are displayed on a small poster. Names of emotions may be provided for each emotion. The poster may be laminated if desired. Sample emotions may include: mad, sad, happy, fine, excited, bored, worried, sick, tired, and hungry.

Group task

During the introduction and sharing time at the beginning of the session, the children will take turns holding the card/poster, and recognizing, identifying, labeling, and expressing what emotions they are experiencing as the group begins.

Discussion

During the sharing of feelings, members are encouraged to share or express multiple feelings. Discussions about the causes and sources of these feelings are encouraged and explored. Depending upon the level of the group, the group leader may facilitate discussions on how a member's feelings may affect others in the group or how those feelings relate to activity choices, group interactions, decision making, etc., that must be considered. Members who are not able to share are encouraged to make "smart" guesses about the feelings of others based on available information (i.e. body language).

Members may also begin to express feelings which are not found on the "Today I feel…" poster. Additional emotions are added to the poster as the group broadens and expands its emotional vocabulary.

Today you feel...

Stage
1: Group formation and orientation

Core variables
Emotion competence
Perspective taking

Group goal

- Group members will label and express, to the group, their understanding of what emotions other group members may be experiencing.

Objectives

- Group members will share with each other what they think other group members are feeling while in the group.

- Group members will attend to and acknowledge each other's emotions/feelings.

- Group members will identify emotions they observe in other group members.

- Group members will identify how certain emotions observed in other group members may affect others in the group, group activity choices, or the order of activities.

Task/activity description
Pre-group preparation
Ten or more pictures of emotions, either drawings or photographs, are displayed on a small poster. Names of emotions may be provided for each emotion. The poster may be laminated if desired. Sample emotions may include: mad, sad, happy, fine, excited, bored, worried, sick, tired, and hungry.

Group task
During the introduction and sharing time at the beginning of the session, the children will take turns holding the card/poster, and recognizing, identifying, labeling, and expressing what emotions they think other group members may be experiencing at that time.

Discussion

During the sharing time, members are asked in turn to share or express feelings that they think other group members may be experiencing. Those group members are then asked to verify and comment upon the emotions attributed to them and why they think those named emotions were considered. Depending upon the level of the group, the group leader may facilitate more extensive discussions of emotions and feelings and how they affect others in the groups, how feelings relate to activity choices, group interactions, decision making, etc.

Members may describe and express perceived emotions of others which are not found on the "Today you feel…" poster. Additional emotions are added to the poster as the group broadens and expands its emotional vocabulary.

Things that stress me out

Stage
1: Group formation and orientation

Core variable
Stress and anxiety control and management

Group goal
- Group members will identify, label, and express, to the group, their stress triggers.

Objectives
- Group members will share with each other the activities, places, and people that operate as stress triggers.

- Group members acknowledge and attend to each other's stress triggers.

- Group members will identify similar triggers between members.

- Group members will identify how certain triggers may affect the group and group activity choices.

Task/activity description
Pre-group preparation
The group leader creates and prepares multiple sets of "stress trigger cards," one set for each group member or pair of members. Also, blank cards are available for members to write in triggers not found in the set of cards. Stressors may include specific academic tasks, social tasks, sensory input, environmental structure, and age-appropriate (or not) expectations.

Group task
Following a brief introduction about stress triggers by the group leader, a set of cards is given to each member, or pair of members, for them to sort through and identify their own specific triggers. Depending upon the group, members may be asked to share their selected cards with other members of the group, or their specific triggers may remain anonymous while the group leader collects and leads a discussion of everyone's triggers.

Discussion

Cards are collected by the group leader and reviewed on a whiteboard or flipchart in order for the group to recognize and identify the varying stress triggers. Group members can take turns identifying the trigger cards they select in order to learn more about each other. The group leader makes a point of identifying similar as well as different triggers between members if not noted by the members themselves. This activity encourages members to identify similarities and differences among group members related to stress and stress triggers. The group leader may choose to explore how certain triggers affect the group and its ability to engage interpersonally in group tasks and activities.

What's new?

Stage
1: Group formation and orientation

Core variables
Focused attention
Flexible attention
Flexibility, change, and transition

Group goal
- Group members will establish and maintain focus on a single topic while flexibly shifting attributes of that topic.

Objectives
- Group members will establish and maintain focused attention on a task/activity/topic while key attributes of that task/activity/topic change rapidly.

- Group members will shift attention effectively and flexibly from one group member to the next in turn and from one attribute to another within the task/activity/topic.

Task/activity description
Group task

The group leader discusses and explains the task/activity, its purpose, and its goals. Each group member in turn must provide a comment about themselves that relates and connects the comment given by the previous group member about themselves.

An order is initially selected for turn taking. The group member who goes first selects a comment about himself (e.g. a detail, a favorite, an association). When the first group member finishes, the next group member follows in turn with a *related* detail, favorite, or association of their own. The only rule here is that the detail, comment, or association must be related in some way to what the previous group member has reported (e.g. "I had a pizza for lunch"…"I had a peanut butter sandwich"…"I had grapes for a snack"…"I like to play outside after snack"…"I like to watch TV"…etc.).

As turns proceed and as comments are given and because each comment relies on the previous statement and its interpretation, the comments often become silly, humor-laden, and outrageous, a process that tends to foster connectedness and cohesion and to keep group members interested and motivated. Group leaders serve to focus and refocus group members as needed to keep the group on task.

Discussion
This task/activity focuses simultaneously on two core variables—attention (focused and flexible) and flexibility, change, and transition—within each stage. It requires attention to the task as it flows from one group member to the next and each member must respond based on previous statements, particularly related to those made by the group member just preceding him.

It requires flexibility and shifts in thinking as each group member must add new but related information to that given previously. During each member's turn, the information contributed will add a new twist and unexpected and unknown turn and will require shifts in each group member's thinking. When the next group member's turn arrives, he must attend, process, formulate, and respond, providing connections and continuity as he passes the task to the next group member.

Guess what I'm thinking

Stage
1: Group formation and orientation

Core variables
Joint attention
Perspective taking

Group goal

- Group members will develop awareness of how others have thoughts different from their own.

Objectives

- Group members will develop awareness that other people in the group have thoughts that are different from their own.

- Group members will develop an understanding of how to use the information they have about others to make informed choices (i.e. smart guesses) about the thoughts, feelings, and needs of other group members.

- Group members will recognize and identify similar thoughts and feelings among members.

Task/activity description

Group task

Following a sharing activity or discussion, members are asked to see if they can make a "smart guess" as to what another person in the group might be thinking. Following their guess, the group leader will ask why they think that is what the person is thinking. Members are encouraged to reflect on previous knowledge about the person they are trying to make a guess about.

With preparation, this activity may also be done with a collection of pictures of people in various situations (i.e. found in magazines). Children can be asked individually to write a thought or speech bubble for each person in the picture. The group leader can then collect and share with the group everyone's responses, followed by a discussion about why they might be "smart" or "wacky" guesses.

Discussion

Group members are encouraged to understand perspective taking related to how others in the group have thoughts different from their own. Group members will be encouraged to construct social connections that are then used to make social inferences. Most important in this task/activity is how group members go about making their guesses. Smart guesses build on information that the individual already has and that can be linked realistically or logically with new information obtained. "Wacky" guesses are based on limited information and seem odd.

This activity also encourages group members to attend to each other as they share information, knowing that they will later use this information to make smart guesses and informed choices.

Our list of group favorites

Stage
2: Group cohesion

Core variables
Self-regulation
Perspective taking

Group goal

- Group members will consider and think of themselves as an integral part of a peer group.

Objective

- Group members will construct ways in which they view themselves as similar and different from other group members.

Task/activity description
Pre-group preparation
Group members will use items constructed during Stage 1 tasks/activities, such as *My group book* and *My favorites*. These lists, cards, or books, created by each group member to foster group awareness, will be used to enhance Stage 2 group cohesion and connectedness.

Group task
Group begins with group members sharing items from their list, card, or book of their favorite things with other group members. The group leader records these items as shared by each group member on a whiteboard or flipchart, noting those items that are mentioned by more than one group member and by whom, emphasizing points of similarity and difference. Help and prompting is provided as needed by the group leader to draw these issues out.

Following the creation of this group list of members' favorites on a whiteboard or flipchart, the group leader directs a discussion of similarities and differences of the items recorded with emphasis placed on the group's thinking about those items selected.

Discussion

This task encourages group members first to address issues of self, self-awareness, self-management, and self-interest, and then to consider their interests, thoughts, and feelings in the context of a group setting where they also hear and learn about others' interests, thoughts, and feelings, making connections about individual and group similarities and differences.

Face puzzles

Stage
2: Group cohesion

Core variable
Emotion competence

Group goals

- Group members will recognize and acknowledge group similarities and differences in their recognition, identification, and labeling of emotions as part of a unique and special group experience.

- Group members work with peers in problem-solving activities, together with emphasis on the recognition of facial features.

Objectives

- Group members will engage in awareness and discussion of easily recognizable facial similarities and differences between group members.

- Group members will foster increased awareness, attention, and regulation of facial features of other members.

Task/activity description

Pre-group preparation
Head-and-shoulders pictures of each group member and leader are taken in advance of the activity. Each picture is enlarged and reproduced in color (4 × 6 or 8 × 10 inches are best), then laminated if desired. Each picture is then cut into random puzzle pieces (e.g. 6–8 pieces for 6–8-year-olds, 10–20 pieces for 9–12-year-olds) and placed in an envelope with the child's name on it.

Group task
In group, the children are paired and given an envelope of puzzle pieces of different children to work together on assembling. Within each pair of children, puzzle pieces are divided equally and the children are instructed to assemble the puzzles to completion, noting to each other how they accomplish this task.

Discussion

Following assembly of the puzzles, the group discusses what strategies work best to assemble the face puzzles successfully, with attention drawn to background, colors, specific facial features, familiarity, etc. Information is recorded on a flipchart or whiteboard, with attention drawn to best working-together and cooperation strategies, problem-solving techniques, strategies for focusing, attention to unique cues, etc.

The content and complexity of the group process and discussion in this activity will vary depending on the stage, with progressive and more complex expectations placed on the group as it moves through stages.

Our group

Stage
2: Group cohesion

Core variables
Emotion competence
Stress and anxiety control and management
Perspective taking
Relatedness

Group goals
- Group members will recognize and identify critical elements related to being part of a group.

- Group members will recognize and identify characteristics of group membership.

- Group members will differentiate individual vs. group characteristics.

Objectives
- Group members will recognize and acknowledge each other's presence and participation in the group.

- Group members will identify and label emotions related to group participation.

- Group members will identify points of stress and tension related to group participation.

- Group members will implement at least one stress/anxiety management strategy to address stress or tension.

- Group members will participate actively in bringing group members into the group.

Task/activity description

Pre-group preparation
This activity may also follow *What's a group?* or can stand alone. This activity is used only when all the members of the group are present.

Group task
The group leader selects a short and easy story, craft, or puzzle which requires all group members to participate. The group completes the task with an emphasis on group togetherness. Following completion of the task, the group leader brings all the members to the center of the room, with everyone in close proximity to one another. Members are asked to share what it is like to be together as a group. Words such as "friendship," "team," "group," and "togetherness" are prompted if they do not arise spontaneously.

Next, the group leader asks one group member to leave the group and stand approximately ten feet away. The leader questions the group about how it feels to have one member outside or not connected to the rest of the members. Also, the member who is outside the group is asked to share what it feels like to be outside of the group. A discussion of the emotions, thoughts, and experiences that are shared is encouraged and facilitated. The group leader then encourages the group to "enthusiastically" invite or call back the member so that the group is whole again. The group concludes with an all-group "high five" as recognition of the group efforts to come together as a group.

Discussion
This task emphasizes group togetherness and cohesion, while recognizing the emotions, thoughts, and experiences related to this process. When appropriate, aspects of stress and tension are acknowledged and labeled, and strategies for stress and anxiety control and management are invoked and practiced. Group discussions center on being part of a group and on related thoughts, feelings, and behaviors, and potential stress and tension points.

Helping the group when others are upset

Stage
2: Group cohesion

Core variable
Stress and anxiety control and management

Group goal
- Group members will recognize and identify how the group can help when a member of the group is upset.

Objectives
- Group members will recognize and identify helpful behaviors when a group member is upset.

- Group members will recognize and identify behaviors that are not helpful when a group member is upset.

- Group members will learn that they have control only of their own behaviors or feelings and not of those of others.

Task/activity description
Pre-group preparation
The group leader preselects an assortment of positive management strategies for a group member who becomes upset. Examples of strategies might include: stop, wait, count to ten; three deep breaths; get an adult; walk away; or leave them alone. The group leader then assembles sets of pictures, verbal cues, written scripts, or other materials related to managing upset behaviors or feelings.

Group task
The group leader will facilitate a group discussion on how one person's stress (being upset) can affect both other individuals and the group as a whole. Strategies that are helpful and not helpful to the group when someone is upset are explored. Various media (pictures, cards, words, written scripts, etc.) are used

to support and reinforce the ideas of the group members. Using different media as necessary, members are then encouraged to express and share experiences that have been successful or not successful when they themselves or another group member has gotten upset in a group.

Discussion
The Discussion provides an opportunity for group members to share the effects that others' behavior and feelings have on the group as well as on each individual. The activity provides group members with a range of alternative management strategies for consideration in managing their own feelings of stress and anxiety which arise when someone in the group is upset.

My stress reducers

Stage
2: Group cohesion

Core variable
Stress and anxiety control and management

Group goals

- Individual group members will recognize and identify effective strategies currently used to manage stress and share these with the group.

- Group members will recognize and identify similarities and differences among effective stress-management strategies used by group members.

Objectives

- Group members will share with each other strategies and activities that help them reduce stress.

- Group members will attend to, acknowledge, and support each other's stress reducers.

- Group members will identify and discuss effective strategies that may be used to manage or reduce stress between members within the group.

Task/activity description

Pre-group preparation

The group leader creates multiple sets of "stress reducer cards," one set for each group member or pair of members. Also available are blank cards for members to write in strategies or activities not found in the set of cards. Strategies may include both positive and negative strategies to manage stress.

Group task

Following a brief introduction about stress-reducing strategies, the group leader gives a set of cards to each member or pair of members. Using the cards they receive, individual members or pairs of members sort through and identify ways they manage their own stress. Discussions between group members are encouraged and facilitated. Depending upon the group, members share their selected cards with the group, or they may remain anonymous with the group leader reading each member's strategies. The group leader lists each group member's preferences and a discussion of similarities and differences, effectiveness and non-effectiveness, etc. may follow.

Discussion
This activity highlights the similarities and differences in strategies that group members use to manage and control stress. Members practice sharing information regarding their own stress-management techniques and learning those that others use. The group leader highlights the differences between effective stress-reducing strategies and non-effective strategies and how different strategies may apply only to specific locations or to specific situations. The introduction of new strategies for use by group members may also occur.

What's new? 2

Stage
2: Group cohesion

Core variables
Focused attention
Flexible attention
Flexibility, change, and transition

Group goal
- Group members will establish and maintain group focus on a single topic while flexibly shifting attributes of that topic.

Objectives
- Group members will establish and maintain focused attention on a task/activity/topic while key attributes of that task/activity/topic change rapidly.

- Group members will shift attention effectively and flexibly from one group member to the next in turn and from one attribute to another within the task/activity/topic.

Task/activity description
Group task
Each group member in turn must provide a comment about themselves that relates and connects the comment given by the previous group member about himself.

An order is initially selected for turn taking. The group member who goes first selects a comment about the person whose turn it is next. The group member may provide a known detail, a favorite, or an association. When the first group member finishes, the next group member must say something *related* about the person whose turn is next. The group member whose turn it is must come up with a detail, favorite, or association, about the person whose turn is next (in turn), but it must be related to what the person before that group member reported (e.g. "A. likes *Star Wars*"…"B. likes legos"…"C. got a new bike"…"D. got a new coat," etc.).

As turns proceed and as comments are given and because each comment relies on the previous statement and its interpretation, the comments often become silly, humor-laden, and outrageous, a process that tends to foster connectedness and cohesion and to keep group members interested and motivated. Group leaders serve to focus and refocus as needed to keep the group on task and connected.

Discussion

This task/activity focuses simultaneously on two core variables—attention (focused and flexible) and flexibility, change, and transition—within each stage. It requires attention to the task as it flows from one group member to the next and each member must respond based on previous statements, particularly related to those made by the group member just preceding him.

It requires flexibility and shifts in thinking as each group member must add new but related information to that given previously. During each member's turn, the information contributed will add a new twist and unexpected and unknown turn and will require shifts in each group member's thinking. When the next group member's turn arrives, he must attend, process, formulate, and respond, providing connections and continuity as he passes the task to the next group member.

The mirror game

Stage
2: Group cohesion

Core variable
Joint attention

Group goal
- Group members will experience joint attention with others in the group.

Objectives
- Group members will experience joint attention.

- Group members will explore the roles of leading (speaking) and following (listening).

Task/activity description
Group task

The group is divided into pairs which can be switched as the activity progresses. Each person sits facing the other. One member of each pair is chosen to be the leader first, followed by a switch with other members also given a chance to be leader. The leader of the pair is instructed to move his face or arms and hands slowly as if in front of a mirror. The other member (the mirror member) must try his best to follow every movement of the leader. After a few minutes "leader" and "mirror" reverse roles. The group leader then facilitates the forming of new pairs so that all group members have the opportunity to work with each other.

A variation of this activity is similar to that of "Simon says," where only one leader is chosen and the other group members function as mirrors. The group members can then discuss the different experiences, working in a pair or as a whole group. Which was easier, more fun, and why? How does this game relate to holding a conversation?

Discussion

The discussion, facilitated by the group leader, can be broadened to explain the roles of each person as a speaker or listener. The members can discuss which was more challenging for them—the leader or follower role—and why. Language such as "focused attention" and "joint attention" may be introduced to help members identify this specific skill as a critical aspect in conversations and in friendship and relationship building.

What's a group?

Stage
2: Group cohesion

Core variables
Perspective taking
Relatedness

Group goals

- Group members will recognize and identify elements of the group experience.

- Group members will recognize and identify when they are functioning as an effective group.

- Group members will recognize and identify what a group looks like.

- Group members will recognize and identify when we are together, but not a group.

- Group members will recognize and identify when a cluster of individuals are not functioning as a group.

Objectives

- Group members will identify individual behaviors that allow them to be part of a group.

- Group members will identify when other members are functioning as part of the group.

- Group members will identify when other members are not functioning as part of the group.

- Group members will identify when they themselves are functioning as part of the group.

- Group members will identify when they themselves are not functioning as part of the group.

- Group members will learn how being part of a group is perceived by others.

Task/activity description

Group task

The group leader chooses a story in which multiple characters interact together and reads the story to the group. This activity may be simplified by making all the characters the same species (e.g. all frogs, all birds, all fish) or a traditional "people" story may be used, particularly for older children. Following the story activity, a craft activity is developed where each group member will create one of the characters referenced in the story. When members have finished, the group leader collects all the characters and asks the members to close their eyes. The leader arranges all the character descriptions in a group formation on a magnetic board or on the floor. Members then open their eyes and respond to the way the characters are placed. Many children respond that they look as if they are a family, a class, or a group. Again, the leader asks everyone to close their eyes, this time moving one character far away from the others. The leader has the group members open their eyes and report how the characters are now placed. Children may respond that the separated character is lonely, being bullied, being scapegoated/made fun of, or not chosen by the group. Now, the children close their eyes again, and all the characters are moved far away from each other. Members are asked once more to say what they think about the characters based on the way they are placed.

This activity may then be repeated with members holding their own characters. In turn, the members themselves are asked by the leader to separate themselves from the group. Subsequently, the other members ask them to return and join the group. This is followed by a discussion of what this experience is like both for the separated group member and for the rest of the group.

Discussion

The group leader facilitates discussion related to belonging to a group and how this makes a group member feel, how they may look as part of a group (happy, friendly), and how the group and the individual members look to others outside the group. How does the group look when someone is separated from the group, isolated, or by themselves? When someone is separated, do they look as if they are part of a group, or do they look as friendly to others as when they are acting as a group member? Emphasis is placed on how their group *looks* (i.e. is perceived by the group members and by others outside the group).

Yours and my favorite "person"

Stage
3: Group stability, relationships, and connections

Core variables
Self-regulation
Perspective taking

Group goal

- Group members will make group decisions in the selection, direction, and construction of group activities.

Objectives

- Group members will work cooperatively and collaboratively on a joint group task that involves individual contributions to a collective task.

- Group members will build a "person" that shares common attributes and similarities of group members.

Task/activity description

Pre-group preparation

Large sheets or rolls of manila or construction paper (e.g. 3 × 6 feet or larger) are made available.

Group task

This task involves the construction of a "person" using manila or construction paper, markers, stick-on materials, etc.

Group members are divided into pairs to work together. With each pair referring to their personal description card and favorites card, list, or book, the pair constructs and creates a single "person," making decisions on hair color, eye color, clothing, preferences, and other favorites. Each pair of group members will produce a life-size picture/drawing that is a compilation of both individuals' similarities, preferences, and favorites.

Discussion

This task encourages group members to work closely with a peer on understanding each other's favorites and intertwining them with their own. This task encourages group members to consider their own interests, thoughts, and feelings together with others' interests, thoughts, and feelings. It is designed to encourage increased identification with the group and discussion of similarities.

Gift giving and receiving

Stage
3: Group stability, relationships, and connections

Core variables
Emotion competence
Flexibility, change, and transition
Perspective taking
Pragmatic communication

Group goal
- Group members will recognize and identify the reasons for the use of "social faking."

Objectives
- Group members will attend to nonverbal communication of other group members.

- Group members will learn, use, and understand social faking as appropriate social etiquette.

- Group members will practice the skill of giving and accepting a gift.

Task/activity description

Pre-group preparation
The group leader collects a number of small gift boxes and cuts small cards to fit into the boxes. On each of the cards, the group leader writes the names of a typically preferred gift item (e.g. toy, game, candy, money) or a non-preferred gift item (e.g. socks, plain T-shirt, plate, pencils). For young children and/or non-readers, pictures of these items can be used in addition to words.

Group task
The group leader discusses with the group members the steps of the activity. Each group member will have a turn at being the "gift receiver" while the other group members are the "gift givers." The group leader places the various "gifts" into each of the boxes, shows the group members the different cards,

and how the cards will be switched around each time the group has a new gift receiver. Taking turns, the gift givers present their gifts to the gift receivers who opens the gifts using appropriate social faking to show appreciation for their gift, even if it was a non-preferred gift. The gift givers also use and practice appropriate gift-giving etiquette.

Discussion

This activity targets a number of social challenges, including focusing on nonverbal communication, on emotional management, on social etiquette, and on interpersonal connections. Some of the questions addressed include: How can you tell if someone likes or does not like the gift they receive? What emotions do you experience when you get a gift that you don't really like? How do you manage not to get upset when you receive a gift you don't want or like? Why is it important that, as a gift receiver, you say that you like the gift even if you do not like it? How does it feel when you give a gift that someone likes? How does it feel when you give a gift that someone clearly does not like or does not want?

Preferences

Stage
3: Group stability, relationships, and connections

Core variables
Emotion competence
Flexibility, change, and transition
Relatedness

Group goal

- Group members will recognize and identify the thoughts and feelings related to making choices.

Objectives

- Group members will identify and acknowledge their preferences as choices.

- Group members recognize and acknowledge that thoughts and feelings are connected to their preferences and choices.

- Group members will recognize and acknowledge that their personal preferences can affect others.

Task/activity description
Pre-group preparation
The group leader cuts a variety of colored sheets of paper into 4 × 12 inch cards, two cards for each color. On each same-colored pair of cards, the group leader writes two different items that fit within a specific category (e.g. cat/dog, spaghetti/pizza, summer/winter). Approximately 12–20 pairs of cards are typically used.

Group task
The group leader explains to the group members that the goal of this game is to make a preferred choice between the two options. This is called our "preference." An explanation of the difference between preference and favorite may be necessary, depending on the ability level of the group. The leader calls out the two choices, placing the cards on different sides of the room. Group

members then select from the two choices and move to the card/side which they "prefer" most. They continue to do this until all the pairs of cards are used.

Discussion

During the game, the group leader highlights the similarities or differences between members' preferences. Following the game, the leader facilitates a discussion on how this was a simple or difficult activity. For example, is it hard when you are not given a choice that is your favorite or most preferred? Was there a time when you got upset over not getting something the way you wanted it to be? How does an individual's flexibility or inflexibility affect a group? How should the group respond to an individual's inflexibility?

What's new? 3

Stage

3: Group stability, relationships, and connections

Core variables

Focused attention

Flexible attention

Flexibility, change, and transition

Group goal

- Group members will establish and maintain group focus on a single topic while flexibly shifting attributes of that topic.

Objectives

- Group members will establish and maintain focused attention on a task/activity/topic while key attributes of that task/activity/topic change rapidly.

- Group members will shift attention effectively and flexibly from one group member to the next and from one attribute to another within the task/activity/topic.

Task/activity description

Group task

Each group member in turn must provide a sentence that relates and connects the sentence given by the previous group member. An order is initially selected for turn taking. The group member who goes first selects a topic and begins with an opening statement about the topic selected. As soon as the first group member finishes his statement, the next group member must add a related statement to what the first group member provided. This task proceeds until all group members have had at least one turn (most groups prefer to keep the task going until the topic and related statements have been exhausted by the group).

As turns proceed and as statements are given and because each statement relies on the previous statement and its interpretation, the topic themes often become silly, humor-laden, and outrageous, a process that tends to foster connectedness and cohesion and to keep group members interested and motivated.

Discussion

This task/activity focuses simultaneously on two core variables—attention (focused and flexible) and flexibility, change, and transition—within each stage. It requires attention to the task as it flows from one group member to the next and each member must respond based on previous statements, particularly related to those made by the group member just preceding him.

It requires flexibility and shifts in thinking as each group member must add new but related information to that given previously. During each member's turn, the information contributed will add a new twist and unexpected and unknown turn and will require shifts in each group member's thinking. When the next group member's turn arrives, he must attend, process, formulate, and respond, providing connections and continuity as he passes the task to the next group member.

Circles of people we know

Stage
3: Group stability, relationships, and connections

Core variables
Flexibility, change, and transition
Pragmatic communication

Group goal

- Group members will work together to discuss how they interact and communicate with the people they know.

Objectives

- Group members will identify topics of conversation which are appropriate for the various types of people they know.

- Group members will work together to make uniform decisions.

- Group members will discuss with each other their ideas of who they share what with and why.

Task/activity description

Pre-group preparation

The group leader creates a large target poster, with five concentric rings. The center ring is labeled "Family," the next ring "Close friends," the next ring "Friends," the next ring "Acquaintances," and the final outer ring "Strangers." A list of topics of conversation that would be appropriate for the different categories of people we meet is constructed. These topics are put on small cards which will be attached by glue, tape, or magnets to the target by the group members.

Group task

The group leader discusses with the group how different topics of conversation occur with different people, depending upon how well we know them. The group leader reviews the different categories of people on the target. Each group member is given a number of conversation topic cards. In turn, each member will make a choice of where to place his topic card. The group member then checks with the group about the level of agreement with his choice. The person whose turn it was can make a decision to change the position if persuaded by his peers. Turns continue until all the topic cards are attached to the target.

Discussion

This activity encourages thought and discussion about connections and relationships with others and their relative importance to us. In considering the correct placement of the cards, group members are encouraged to seek out each other's support and input, including adjustment and compromise when necessary, to complete the activity. This activity also explores how some topics of conversations are socially acceptable and comfortable with certain individuals and socially unacceptable and uncomfortable with others.

Our favorite "person"

Stage
4: Group adaptations and perspective taking

Core variable
Self-regulation

Group goal
- Group members will make group decisions in the selection, direction, and construction of group activities.

Objectives
- Group members will work cooperatively and collaboratively on a joint group task that involves individual contributions to a collective task.

- Group members will build a "person" that shares common attributes and similarities of group members.

Task/activity description
Pre-group preparation
Large sheets or rolls of manila or construction paper (e.g. 3 × 6 feet or larger) are made available.

Group task
This task involves the construction of a "person" using manila or construction paper, markers, stick-on materials, etc.

With each child referring to his own personal description card and favorites card, list, or book, the group leader collects information on hair color, eye color, skin tone, clothing and color preferences, height, weight, etc. This information is then used to create a "group person," who is a compilation of the group members' personal qualities. The emphasis is on personal qualities and similarities and differences. The group leader draws or constructs a head, body, clothing, etc., with features drawn from group similarities and differences. The depiction is intended to introduce the idea of a caricature of a real person and of a collective representation of a "group person."

Discussion

This task encourages group members to consider their own interests, thoughts, and feelings together with others' interests, thoughts, and feelings. It is designed to encourage increased identification with the group and discussion of similarities.

Different faces

Stage
4: Group adaptations and perspective taking

Core variables
Self-regulation
Perspective taking

Group goal
- Group members will adapt flexibly to different views within the group process.

Objective
- Group members will share and consider multiple individual views and ways of thinking and to incorporate these into "group" views and perspectives.

Task/activity description
Group task
Each group member is given the same picture of a person to look at and study. They are asked to think about and write down what they think, including what the person looks like, what the person is thinking, what the person is feeling, etc. After being given time to complete this activity, the group leader asks group members in turn to share with the rest of the group what they thought and recorded. The information from each child is recorded on a flipchart or whiteboard for all to see.

The group leader then leads a discussion of how the same picture can invoke a range of different views and responses. The group leader fosters the view of awareness and acceptance of others' views even though they may not agree with their own. Consideration and acceptance of others having different views is the focus of this task.

Discussion
The purpose of this task is for group members to acknowledge others as having different views from their own to the same experience and to make sense of this discrepant occurrence. Each child must consider multiple different views to the same stimulus and process these within the context of the group relationships.

Yours and my favorite "person" together

Stage

4: Group adaptations and perspective taking

Core variables

Self-regulation

Flexibility, change, and transition

Perspective taking

Group goal

- Group members will develop and foster interpersonal modes of communication, adapt decision making based on group needs, and respond flexibly within the group.

Objectives

- Group members will share and consider multiple individual views and ways of thinking and incorporate these into group views and perspectives.

- Group members will manage and resolve disagreements and conflicts within the group.

Task/activity description

Pre-group preparation

Large sheets or rolls of manila or construction paper (e.g. 3 × 6 feet or larger) are made available. This task involves the construction of a "person" using manila or construction paper, markers, stick-on materials, etc.

Group task

Group members are divided into pairs to work together. Using information recorded on their favorites card, list, or book, group members create their own individual favorite person, consisting of appropriate facial, coloring, clothing, and other characteristics. When completed, each child in a working pair then exchanges his "person" with the other child in his pair. Each child then makes changes, additions, and reconstructions of his choice to the drawing by the other child.

The emphasis is placed on tolerating others' views and ideas imposed on us (our constructions and ways of thinking), considering our own personal (emotional), interpersonal (social), and behavioral reactions to this, flexibly shifting our own points of view and ways of thinking, and learning to manage and to accommodate to this input.

Discussion

This task forces group members to consider and accept the views and input of their peer-group members in situations that are personal and potentially emotion-arousing and that require flexible shifting in our own ways of thinking and working with peers. This activity is designed to push the envelope of collaborative thinking, sensitive decision making, and working together, as well as learning how to manage and resolve disagreement and conflict within a relationship.

Dealing with a loss

Stage
4: Group adaptations and perspective taking
5: Terminations, loss, and endings

Core variables
Emotion competence
Stress and anxiety control and management
Perspective taking
Relatedness

Group goals

- Group members will consider the thoughts and feelings of another group member who has experienced a loss.

- Group members will generate appropriate thoughtful and affective responses to a group member who has suffered a loss.

- Group members will connect their own experiences of losses to those of the group member currently experiencing a loss.

Objectives

- Group members will recognize and discuss the loss experience of another group member.

- Group members will appropriately relate thoughts, label emotions, and connect behaviors related to their own experiences of loss.

- Group members will appropriately relate thoughts, label emotions, and connect behaviors related to those of the group member currently experiencing a loss.

- Group members will tolerate, support, and encourage the sharing of thoughts, emotions, and behaviors of another group member relating to a loss experience.

- Group members will support and empathize with the thoughts, emotions, and behaviors of the group member currently experiencing a loss.

Task/activity description

The experience of loss is a frequent occurrence during the course of ongoing groups. The group leader must nurture and encourage the connections and relationships with group members and parents so that information regarding any experience of termination, losses, and endings is shared as soon as possible after it occurs, that permission is granted to discuss the experience, and that a plan for managing the experience within the group can be constructed immediately. This task/activity focuses on the management of the significant loss (e.g. the death of a family member, relative, or friend), other family issue (e.g. parents' divorce, mental health issue), or environmental trauma (e.g. fire, hurricane, flood).

Pre-group preparation

The group leader recognizes and prepares for the fact that addressing losses evokes stress, a wide range of emotions, and a fixed pattern of coping and managing. In this task, group members will be requested to think about a time when they experienced an important and meaningful loss, what they thought about it, how they felt about it, what they did about it, and what others did for them that helped support them and manage more effectively.

The group leader prepares three decks of cards: an assortment of cards that note common experiences of loss for children, an assortment of cards that depict common and effective management strategies for significant loss, and a pile of blank cards with pencils and markers.

Group task

With the group members seated in a circle (around a table or on the floor), the group leader places one "loss" card (favorite toy broke, a pet ran away, best friend moved, grandfather died, parents divorced, etc.) at a time in front of the group and encourages and supports each group member to respond and relate to the card/experience, either with a description of the particular card or of a related personal experience that the card triggers. The group goes through this set of loss cards.

With the loss cards in front of the group, the leader then introduces the "coping/managing" cards (replaced the toy, adopted another dog, exchanged addresses with the friend who moved, visited the cemetery where grandfather is buried, saved a picture, visit surviving grandparent frequently, journaled about the loss, etc.) and supports and encourages the group members to relate to each and to describe whether they have used this coping/managing strategy in the past and how it worked.

With the loss and coping/managing cards in front of the group, group members are encouraged to generate additional coping/managing cards that they can think of that may be used and/or are personal to them. A discussion of how these coping and managing strategies were useful is encouraged and supported. The group member currently experiencing a loss is asked to relate to each and consider his use for them personally.

Discussion

This task/activity can be completed in one group session but is often continued over several group sessions, both because of the ongoing nature of this issue and because the issue requires ongoing thinking, consideration, and processing within a variety of core areas of functioning (cognitive, emotional, social, behavior, communication) and core variables (stress and anxiety control and management, emotion competence, joint attention, perspective taking, relatedness). It is of great importance for the group leader to be sensitive and responsive to each group member's experience, reactions, and comfort level of loss experiences, particularly the intensity which the experiences generate. Often, this task/activity generates such thought and emotion that the group may need to return frequently to these issues for processing, resolution, and debriefing in order to integrate and understand their importance to all involved.

Freeze: What's the message?

Stage
4: Group adaptations and perspective taking

Core variables
Stress and anxiety control and management
Joint attention
Perspective taking
Relatedness
Pragmatic communication

Group goals

- Group members will attend to the emotional needs of other group members.

- Group members will attend to the emotional needs of other group members, particularly when these needs are not explicitly expressed.

Objectives

- Group members will identify nonverbal signs of anxiety or stress from group members.

- Group members will respond appropriately to nonverbal signs of anxiety or stress from group members.

- Group members will discuss and understand how attention to the nonverbal communications of others affects their responses.

Task/activity description
Pre-group preparation
The group leader prepares group members for this activity by discussing with them the use of the word "stop" or "freeze" to momentarily pause the conversation or activity in order to make some guesses about how a group member is feeling and why.

Group task

While the group participates in various activities, the group leader attends to the nonverbal communications of all the members. When nonverbal communication occurs, the group leader asks the members to momentarily "stop" or "freeze." Members are first asked to observe the person and to guess his emotion(s) and then are asked if they can identify the trigger or cause of the emotions. Emotions and feelings charts (i.e. pictorial characteristics of emotions) may be used when appropriate, particularly for younger children who may recognize an emotion but have difficulty labeling or expressing it verbally. Feedback on how accurate the members' guesses are is given by the person whose nonverbal communications were observed and commented upon. Further discussions may include how the members feel when their nonverbal signals are noticed, identified, and understood by their peers. The question "How important is reading or paying attention to nonverbal communication in developing or maintaining peer relationships?" can be discussed. "Who do you know that does this well?" and "How does this person make you feel?" may also be discussed.

Discussion

This task addresses nonverbal communications directly and forces group members to think about and consider both sides of the communication, from the observer's perspective as well as from the perspective of the person whose nonverbal communication is observed. Discussions within the group allow for clarification and consideration of alternative views of how the situation was observed and played out.

Solve this!

Stage

4: Group adaptations and perspective taking

Core variables

Stress and anxiety control and management
Flexibility, change, and transition
Relatedness
Pragmatic communication

Group goal

• Group members will work together cooperatively to solve a problem.

Objectives

• Group members will participate as constructive and helpful participants.

• Group members will work through conflicts and challenges in a positive way in order to have a successful experience regardless of the outcome of the activity.

Task/activity description

Pre-group preparation

The group leader identifies tasks/activities for the group to solve based on levels of difficulty. The less difficult activities tend to be best for younger or less cohesive groups, while more difficult tasks/activities are best suited for older or more cohesive groups. Examples of tasks/activities chosen include puzzles, word searches, number/math puzzles, mazes, and strategy games.

Group task

As a group or in teams or pairs, members are given a task/activity to solve. Additional challenges include not allowing members to use words, one or more members being blindfolded, or members being placed back to back so that they can talk to each other and see the activity but not each other (unable to use any visual forms of communication). Members can be given a set time limit to complete the task/activity with an understanding that this is not about competition. Positive reinforcement is provided with an emphasis on participation rather than "winning." A discussion with members takes place about how they reward each other and themselves for managing the task, including the stress of not completing the activity, not winning the activity, or failing to find a solution.

Discussion

The group leader facilitates a discussion about what aspects of the task/ activity made working together easier or more difficult, helpful or obstructive, cooperative or divisive, etc. (e.g. the task/activity, their partner, other members in the group, lack of sufficient information to solve the problem). A discussion of what was specifically helpful/stressful and what strategies were helpful/not helpful for managing the specific stress is encouraged.

What's new? 4

Stage

4: Group adaptations and perspective taking

Core variables

Focused attention
Flexible attention
Flexibility, change, and transition
Perspective taking

Group goal

- Group members will establish and maintain group focus on a single topic while flexibly shifting attributes of that topic and considering other perspectives and points of view on the topic.

Objectives

- Group members will establish and maintain focused attention on a task/activity/topic while key attributes of that task/activity/topic change rapidly.

- Group members will shift attention effectively and flexibly from one group member to the next in turn and from one attribute to another within the task/activity/topic.

- Group members will consider and recognize the perspectives and points of view as presented by other group members.

Task/activity description

Group task

Each group member in turn must provide a sentence that relates and connects the sentence given by the previous group member.

An order is initially selected for turn taking. The group member who goes first provides the opening to a story that each group member in turn will add to. The group goal is to complete a story that will include multiple details relevant to the whole group. The first group member provides the initial story line or theme provided in a sentence or two; then the next group member must provide several additional *related* and *connected* thoughts or details that add and contribute to the story being created. This could include a made-up story, a fantasy theme, a real-life event, or a personal event (e.g. a vacation trip, amusement park ride, school event). When the next group member finishes his statements, the next group member takes over and so forth. This task proceeds until all group members have had at least one turn (most groups prefer to keep the task going until the story is complete to the group members' satisfaction).

As turns proceed and as sentences, thoughts, and details are given and because each statement relies on the previous information and its interpretation, the stories often become silly, humor-laden, and outrageous, a process that tends to foster connectedness and cohesion, and to keep group members interested and motivated.

Discussion

The intent of this task/activity is to focus simultaneously on two core variables—attention (focused and flexible) and flexibility, change, and transition—within this stage while encouraging and fostering an emphasis on perspective taking through consideration of multiple points of view. This requires attention to the content of the task and to the meaning the speaker gives his thoughts, details, and story additions as they flow from one group member to the next. Each member must respond appropriately based on previous information, particularly related to details given by the group member just preceding him.

This task focuses on flexibility and shifts in thinking as each group member must add new but related information to that given previously and attempts to capitalize upon group members' knowledge of one another by employing information that has been learned as the group has proceeded. During each member's turn, the information contributed will add a new twist and unexpected and unknown turn and require shifts in each group member's thinking. When the next group member's turn arrives, he must attend, process, formulate, and respond, providing connections and continuity and considering the perspective and points of view previously provided, and then pass the task to the next group member.

What's my role?

Stage
4: Group adaptations and perspective taking

Core variables
Flexibility, change, and transition
Perspective taking
Pragmatic communication

Group goal
- Group members will recognize the role they take as group participants.

Objectives
- Group members will identify their strengths as group participants.

- Group members will recognize the roles which others play as group participants.

Task/activity description
Pre-group preparation
The group leader will make cards with identifiable roles that people take when participating in a group project. Examples may include "director," "scribe," "mediator," and "ideas person." The leader should consider the group members as these cards are created and ensure that at least one card is matched to each of the members of the group.

Group task
For a group to work successfully, there are different roles that are typically filled by the group members. Group members are asked to think about their own strengths and what role(s) they can play or prefer to play in group activities or projects. The group leader also encourages each member to think about the other members and the roles those members may play, identifying the positive traits of their peers. The group leader may also ask parents to identify what role they believe their child may play in a group, later sharing this with the group members. The group leader highlights the positive traits members

exhibit when they participate in a group and looks for similarities among group members to emphasize.

The group leader then distributes role cards to each member. The group leader may choose specific activities for the group to complete, such as a sequenced task (puzzle making), a game ("Sorry"), free choice activity (baking), or do the normal task/activity planned for that day. For this task/activity, the actual group task/activity completed will vary depending on the stage of group development and core variable focused on. During whatever activity that follows, group members must follow the prescribed role assigned to them, acting and responding in ways that are consistent with the role given.

Regardless of the specific task/activity, the group members understand that they are to stay within their role throughout the task/activity. Descriptions, such as playing, pretending, acting, and performing, may be used to help group members understand how to stay in role while completing another activity that would normally have them participating as themselves (without a role taken on).

The group leader may follow this with a discussion in which group members are asked to assess their own performance with the roles they were assigned or voluntarily assumed. The discussion may include whether one's role can change depending upon who else is in the group, whether that role should change, and whether one group member's role changes when another group member changes his role.

Discussion

This task/activity encourages group members to think about and consider their role in a group on several levels, including roles that are assigned externally, roles that are decided and assumed willingly, roles that evolve over time as the group changes, and roles that members are forced to take as other group members alter their roles. Specific tasks/activities are designed for each particular group based on the needs of the group.

My goodbye picture

Stage
5: Terminations, loss, and endings

Core variable
Self-regulation

Group goal

- Group members will think about, process, and manage effectively thoughts, feelings, and behaviors related to termination, losses, and endings.

Objective

- Group members will share and experience thoughts, feelings, and behaviors related to termination, losses, and endings.

Task/activity description

Group task

In preparation for this task/activity, the group leader initiates and facilitates a discussion of terminations, losses, and goodbyes. Group members are then instructed to create a drawing or picture that captures a loss or goodbye moment important to them. Each child works individually and is encouraged to create a real or imagined pictorial representation of a termination, loss, or ending, adding as much detail as he wishes.

After completing the drawing, each child shares his picture with the group and tells a story about its meaning to him. The group leader then facilitates a discussion of termination, loss, and endings and relates this to the loss events experienced by the group during the year (e.g. member leaving group) or loss shared by one group member but connected to by all (e.g. death of pet).

Discussion

The group leader facilitates a discussion around the intense feelings, sad thoughts, and difficult behaviors that emerge when termination, loss, and ending issues are stirred up. Discussion and practice of stress-management techniques to confront and manage these experiences are reinforced and connected to the group process.

Our group goodbye book

Stage
5: Terminations, loss, and endings

Core variable
Self-regulation

Group goal
- Group members will address and consider the group experience in processing and managing thoughts, feelings, and behaviors related to termination, losses, and endings.

Objective
- Group members will share and experience thoughts, feelings, and behaviors related to loss and endings specifically connected to this group.

Task/activity description
Group task

The group leader encourages thinking and discussion of how the group as a whole will experience the ending of the group. Other experiences of group loss may also be addressed in this way (e.g. a group member leaving the group, a loss/ending experience shared by a group member that relates to the "whole group" issues). The group members then attempt to construct a set of group memories related to loss/goodbye experiences of the group over the course of the year. The group leader collects these stories and themes from group members, which may be in the form of pictures or stories from group books or recollected experiences, and summarizes the group's experience around a representative moment of "group loss" or "group ending" (e.g. member leaving group) or loss shared by one group member but connected to by all (e.g. death of pet).

These termination or loss memories/experiences can be collected by the group leader in pictorial, written, or other forms and are used to create a "memories book" (goodbye book, endings book, collage, etc.). The format (book, list, drawings, DVDs, etc.) is dictated by the age and developmental, cognitive, and emotional level that the group has achieved.

Discussion

The group leader facilitates a discussion about the broad range of experiences that the group has gone through since it began and relates these to the intense feelings, sad thoughts, and difficult behaviors as well as feelings of hyperstimulation, intense anxiety, and distractibility that emerge when these issues are stirred up. Discussion and practice of stress-management techniques are addressed in order to confront and manage related experiences connected to this group process.

Last day countdown

Stage
5: Group terminations, loss, and endings

Core variables
Emotion competence
Flexibility, change, and transition
Relatedness

Group goal
- Group members will use the countdown process to prepare for termination of the group.

Objectives
- Group members will identify emotions that arise around termination, losses, and endings.

- Group members will recognize and identify that anticipating and acknowledging upcoming change encourages the addressing of related feelings which may otherwise not be addressed.

Task/activity description
Group task
The group leader presents to the group the number of group sessions remaining and writes the numbers (e.g. 4, 3, 2, 1) on a large sheet of paper. The paper is clearly displayed in a prominent spot so that the members will take notice during each of the remaining group sessions. If members do not spontaneously notice or acknowledge the countdown sheet, the group leader prompts them to address the issue. A discussion about change, transitions, and endings can then occur, identifying endings that are planned, such as the end of the school year and their own group, and situations that are surprises, such as trip cancellations, snow days off school, or becoming sick, when no or little preparation is available.

The group leader encourages and facilitates discussion and sharing of different feelings that arise when we think about change and transitions related to termination, losses, and endings. The group leader also encourages the group members to acknowledge and address how thinking about the group termination now affects experiences of what we do and how we interact with one another, but does not and should not stop the termination, loss, or ending from occurring.

Discussion
The group leader facilitates discussion around issues of termination, losses, and endings and the changes and transitions that result from these situations. Questions relevant and important to termination, losses, and endings, both specific to the group and general to all related experiences, are considered such as why it is important to think ahead about changes and endings, why we avoid them, and how we feel when a big change happens without warning. As termination, loss, and ending feelings are stirred up for the group members, the group leader may use a scale of emotions to discuss the varying responses to the same event.

Chapter 5: The end

Stage
5: Terminations, loss, and endings

Core variables
Focused attention
Flexible attention
Flexibility, change, and transition
Perspective taking

Group goal
- Group members will maintain a group focus on terminations, losses, and endings related to the group while shifting flexibly through multiple related endings.

Objectives
- Group members will address group losses and endings while maintaining continuous attention to the task/activity as it shifts frequently and rapidly through details and descriptions of related group loss and endings.

- Group members will acknowledge and understand how other group members understand and experience group loss and endings.

Task/activity description
Pre-group preparation
The group task/activity at this stage makes use of many of the tasks/activities used at previous stages for the core variables of focused attention, flexibility, change, and transition, and perspective taking. This task, however, will be one that allows the group members to develop themes meaningful to the group that relate specifically to group terminations, losses, and endings. These tasks may include the completion of the whole group "book" and the creation and development of pictures, stories, or movies related to loss and endings that require the group to respond and react frequently and rapidly in related sequence to the themes addressed.

Group task

The group members decide on an order for turn taking and are instructed that this task relates specifically to terminations, losses, and endings. The group member who goes first chooses a thought, topic, story, picture, or movie which addresses the theme of loss or endings and provides a beginning or starting point for the group. If a story, then the group member provides the opening few sentences; if a movie, then the group member provides an initial few scenes; if a picture, then the group member draws the first few details. He then turns it over to the next group member who provides related and connected material to the group loss and ending material already provided. Each group member takes a turn and must provide information that relates and connects the information given by the previous group member.

As the task/activity proceeds, the Stage 5 theme of loss and endings is addressed in story, picture, or movie format. As the task/activity proceeds and moves in sequence from one group member to the next, the group must maintain focused attention to the task, must shift and adjust flexibly as the task moves along and changes, must contribute related information in sequence, and must manage simultaneously the related cognitive and emotional information of terminations, losses, and endings.

Discussion

This task/activity addresses three core variables simultaneously—attention (focused and flexible), flexibility, change, and transition, and perspective taking—while emphasizing Stage 5 termination, loss, and ending issues. The specific termination of this particular group is one major focus, but these tasks/activities are also used to focus on other terminations, losses, and endings as they arise within the group. These tasks/activities occur within the context of focused and flexible attention, flexibility, change, and transition, and perspective taking, and they require frequent shifts and changes in thinking and information presented, as many different perspectives must be considered and addressed.

Group timeline

Stage
5: Terminations, loss, and endings

Core variable
Relatedness

Group goal

- Group members will review their group experiences in order to remember and collect their group memories and to find connections in their favorites.

Objectives

- Group members will identify and chart the different activities explored throughout the year.

- Group members will share and discuss with each other as a group their favorite memories of group activities.

Task/activity description
Pre-group preparation
A whiteboard or flipchart may be used to visualize the concept of a timeline to the group. If necessary, the group leader discusses and explains how to construct a chronological "timeline."

Group task
The group begins by reporting group tasks/activities recalled and remembered, beginning at the start of group, which are recorded by the group leader or a designated group member. When a list is generated, these tasks/activities are placed in chronological order along a timeline, starting with the first group task/activity (first session) and ending with the last group task/activity (last session). In the end, the group will have created and constructed a timeline of group tasks/activities recalled and remembered, which encourage reflection, discussion, and processing experienced by the group as a whole.

Discussion

This task/activity focuses on the whole group experience, beginning to end, as it relates to all core variables embedded within the range of tasks/activities presented. In the termination sessions, the group leader uses this timeline of the group to return to certain core variables (e.g. emotion competence, stress and anxiety management) for further discussion, emphasis, or reinforcement. Ultimately, the goal is to provide the group with opportunities to experience and process terminations, losses, and endings occurring within the group in appropriate ways and to generalize these experiences to other similar situations.

Ways we say goodbye

Stage
5: Terminations, loss, and endings

Core variable
Pragmatic communication

Group goal
- Group members will appropriately and effectively communicate thoughts, feelings, and behaviors related to termination, loss, and endings.

Objectives
- Group members will identify the different ways in which terminations, losses, and endings are managed.

- Group members will share with each other their different experiences in endings.

Task/activity description
Pre-group preparation

This group task/activity focuses on the different ways that individuals say goodbye to one another and on how our choices are dependent upon the nature of the relationships with the individuals with whom we are interacting, including family, relatives, close friends, acquaintances, classmates, others less well known, or strangers.

Group task

The group leader facilitates a discussion with the group members about the different ways that one can say goodbye, considering a variety and range of experiences, such as those that occur in different situations, with different people, using different words, with individuals of different ages, etc. Examples include: words—bye, see ya later, I'll miss you; body language—wave, hug, hand shake, kiss; activities—party, gifts, cards, sign a year book, exchange phone numbers or addresses, give pictures or books.

On a whiteboard or flipchart, the group leader places group members' ideas under different communication modalities, such as "words," "body language/actions," and "activities." The group generates as many ideas as possible, encouraging the group members to include a variety of different ways we say goodbye to the different kinds of people we know and the different situations that we may be involved in. The group leader may raise questions such as "Do we say goodbye to a close friend or family member the same way we do to an acquaintance?" and "Do we say goodbye differently if we are going to see the person later in the day/the next day/the next week/the next year/maybe even never again?"

Discussion
The group must remain flexible and prepared to deal with and address a broad range of thoughts, feelings, and behaviors that may emerge relating to termination, loss, and ending experiences. The group leader may discuss how goodbyes are often determined by how well we know or like the person or group as well as whether we will see them again (refer to activity *Circles of people we know*). Following this discussion, the group leader may ask the group to generate ideas about how they would like to say goodbye to each other. Termination, loss, and ending tasks/activities may then be constructed based on group input.

Favorites

Stages
1–5

This activity is appropriate to use at each stage of group development, 1 through 5, with modifications that fit individual goals, the specific stage, and the group goals. The group leader (or the group as indicated) adapts and modifies the task/activity depending on the specific stage addressed.

Core variable
General

Group goal
- Group members will create connections with other group members that will endure and allow members to challenge one another as they move through stages of group development.

Objectives
- Stage 1: Group members will learn about one another and establish connections to one another.

- Stage 2: Group members will use information learned about one another to initiate and maintain conversations and to maintain connections with one another.

- Stage 3: Group members will recognize and appreciate similarities and differences among group members and will understand the relationship between individual connections and connections as a group.

- Stage 4: Group members will use information learned about one another to create, solidify, and maintain meaningful individual relationships and group connections.

- Stage 5: Group members will understand, manage, and maintain relationships when moving through transition, termination, loss, ending, and transition experiences.

Task/activity description
Pre-group preparation
This activity can be completed in a variety of different formats. The group leader chooses the best format for the age and developmental level and stage of the particular group. The different formats include a card, a poster, or a book. Manila card, poster board, and book-making materials are made available.

Activity 1: Group task
Each child receives a "favorites card" (8.5 × 11 and 9 × 12 manila stock work best), with a list of "favorites" running down along the left-hand side. These can include favorite color, animal, food, dessert, movie, book, activity, breakfast item, TV show, game, etc.

Each child fills out a card for himself, listing his favorites for each item. Upon completion, the group leader directs a discussion of each item and the similar and different responses group members have given, encouraging a discussion of reasons for their choices and soliciting comments on their choices.

Activity 2: Group task
Each child receives a "favorites card" (8.5 × 11 and 9 × 12 manila stock work best), with a list of "favorites" running down along the left-hand side. These can include favorite color, animal, food, dessert, movie, book, activity, breakfast item, TV show, game, etc.

Each child fills out a card for another group member with the child's name placed at the top. The group leader directs a discussion of favorites and each item is taken in turn. As each child responds with his favorite, the child who has that child's favorites card records his response. At the end of this segment, each child reports on the favorites for the child whose card he completed. After the favorites are reviewed for all the children, the group leader directs a discussion of the similarities and differences, pointing out when children agree or disagree on particular items. A discussion of the reasons for individual choices is encouraged and comments on each other's choices are solicited.

These cards are saved, added to, and elaborated upon when used during different stage-related activities. The complexity of the tasks and expectations increase as the group moves through progressive stages.

Discussion
At Stage 1, this activity is used to encourage an awareness of similarities, an acceptance of differences, and an understanding of how our preferences (likes/dislikes) intersect with those of other group members.

At Stage 2, this activity is used to demonstrate our uniqueness as individuals with our favorites lists representing a set of individual preferences that are then shared with others.

At Stage 3, this activity is used to draw the group members together with an emphasis on common experiences. A discussion of the reasons behind their choices and the need to work with others at points of intersection is encouraged.

At Stage 4, this activity is used to emphasize acceptance of an individual's preferences when different from our own, but never at the expense of our relationships with our peers.

At Stage 5, this activity is used as a means to link the termination, loss, or ending/goodbye process to each group member. Favorite endings, bedtime stories at age five, and transitional objects, for example, allow the group to discuss their thoughts and feelings about past endings, losses, and goodbyes. Group members discuss their favorite activities, favorite snacks, favorite game, favorite joke, and so on, and these are added to their existing favorites list which can be taken with them at the end of group.

How am I feeling?

Stages
1–5

This activity is appropriate to use at each stage of group development, 1 through 5, with modifications that fit individual goals, the specific stage, and the group goals. The group leader (or the group as indicated) adapts and modifies the task/activity depending on the specific stage addressed.

Core variable
Emotion competence

Group goal

- Group members will address and explore different feelings and emotions.

Objectives

- Group members will learn about the range of emotions and feelings that can be experienced.

- Group members will label emotions and feelings appropriately.

- Group members will discuss and understand different situations where emotions and feelings emerge.

Task/activity description
Group task

Each child in turn is given a picture of a different facial expression and then asked to name an emotion or feeling that best fits the picture. This can be done by asking the child to verbally provide an emotion label that best fits the picture, to select the most appropriate emotion from an array of emotion pictures provided, or to select from a list of verbal labels provided.

The group leader facilitates a discussion of that description and encourages input and alternative suggestions from others, which are also discussed. Several sequences of this task are gone through, with all group members having several opportunities to recognize and label different emotional depictions, to discuss their choices and the descriptions of others, and to understand the reasoning for the different descriptions given.

Discussion
The group leader directs a discussion about the facial expressions, the children's descriptions of them, and the connections to feeling states that occur. This task gives group members the opportunity to explore their own emotional labeling capacities and to hear how other group members approach this task. It provides group members with multiple opportunities to address, recognize, label, and understand different emotions as well as learning when and how to use them appropriately. The group leader facilitates a discussion around feelings, thoughts, and behaviors related to emotions and feelings. Discussion and practice of stress-management techniques to handle these experiences can be employed as needed to help manage and enhance the emotional experiences within the group process.

Emotions matching

Emotions concentration

Emotions bingo

Stages
1–5

This activity is appropriate to use at each stage of group development, 1 through 5, with modifications that fit individual goals, the specific stage, and the group goals. The group leader (or the group as indicated) adapts and modifies the task/activity depending on the specific stage addressed.

Core variables
Emotion competence
Specific area
Emotion recognition

Group goal
- Group members will develop and enhance appropriate emotion recognition capacities.

Objectives
- Group members will increase awareness and obtain practice in the recognition of an increasing array of emotions.
- Group members will learn about the range of emotions and feelings that can be experienced.

Task/activity description

Group task 1

Matching pairs of cards (e.g. 2 × 2 or 3 × 3 inches), each containing the facial expression of a basic emotion, are constructed (usually beginning with a deck of 6–10 emotion cards that is enlarged to 20–30 as emotion recognition skills are mastered). Each card consists of a facial expression with the appropriate emotion label printed under the face. One set of cards is placed on the table face up in front of the group members, while a second identical set is placed face down in front of the group members. Each child in turn turns over a card and places that card on the appropriate matching card while verbalizing the emotion depicted.

Group task 2

The same matching pairs of emotion cards, each with a facial expression and the appropriate emotion label underneath it, are used in an emotions matching game of Concentration where all the cards are placed face down on the table. As in Concentration, each group member in turn turns over two cards and, if they match, places them in a match pile. If they do not match, then both cards are turned back over face down and the next group member takes a turn. The game proceeds until all the pairs are found and matched.

Group task 3

Several large bingo cards are constructed (e.g. 8.5 × 11 or 11 × 14 inches) with several rows and columns (e.g. 3 × 3 or 4 × 3 or 4 × 4) containing different pictorial depictions of different emotions. Each individual item contains a facial expression of a basic emotion with the appropriate emotion label printed underneath the expression. As in any form of bingo, each card contains a different and random array of the emotions being used. Individual emotion cards (picture and label) (e.g. 2 × 2 or 3 × 3) are also constructed to match the emotions being used on the large bingo cards and placed in a stack for the bingo caller.

Each child is given a small box of chips. The group leader or group member designated as caller or each group member in turn draws an emotion card from the stack, shows the group the card, and verbalizes the emotion depicted and labeled. Each child scans his own bingo card and places a chip on the appropriate emotion if found on his card. The child who gets a complete row or column of emotions first raises his hand and the arrays are reviewed. The number of rows and columns can be increased on the large bingo cards (first 3 × 3 or 3 × 4, then 4 × 4 or 4 × 5, and so forth) as the group learns to recognize (label, understand) emotions and as the group masters the recognition (labeling, understanding) task.

Discussion: Tasks 1, 2, and 3
These tasks increase the group members' exposure to a broad range of emotions experienced by individuals, particularly within group social interactions. Following the completion of the activity, the group leader facilitates a discussion of emotions and how we recognize them in others. The group members are encouraged to share their thoughts and feelings about the process of the recognition of facial characteristics, to generate examples of how this task/activity relates to real-life situations, and to consider how the recognition, labeling, and understanding of facial expressions might be useful to them.

Emotions naming

Stage
1–5

This activity is appropriate to use at each stage of group development, 1 through 5, with modifications that fit individual goals, the specific stage, and the group goals. The group leader (or the group as indicated) adapts and modifies the task/activity depending on the specific stage addressed.

Core variables
Emotion competence
Specific area
Emotion labeling

Group goal
- Group members will develop and enhance appropriate emotion-labeling capacities.

Objectives
- Group members will increase awareness and obtain practice in the labeling of an increasing array of emotions.

- Group members will learn about the range of emotions and feelings that can be labeled.

Task/activity description
Group task 1
Pairs of emotion cards (e.g. 2 × 2 or 3 × 3 inches) are again used, but this time they are not matching sets. One set of cards is constructed containing only facial expressions of basic emotions (again usually beginning with a deck of 6–10 emotion cards that is enlarged to 20–30 as emotion-labeling skills are mastered) with no emotion label printed under the face. A second set of cards is constructed containing only the appropriate word label to match each emotion card. The set of cards containing only the facial expression is placed on the table face up in front of the group members, while the second set containing only the emotion word label is placed face down in front of the group members. Each child in turn turns over a card and places that card on the

appropriate matching card while verbalizing the emotion depicted and pairing it with the appropriate facial expression.

Group task 2

The same two sets of emotion cards—one with only a facial expression with no emotion label and the second with only the emotion word label—are used in an emotions labeling game of Concentration. All the cards are placed face down on the table as in Concentration. In turn, each group member turns over two cards and attempts to match a facial expression card with the appropriate emotion word label. If they match, the child places them in a match pile. If they do not match, then both cards are turned back over face down and the next group member takes a turn. The game proceeds until all the pairs are found and matched.

Group task 3

Several large bingo cards are constructed (e.g. 8.5 × 11 or 11 × 14 inches) with several rows and columns (e.g. 3 × 3 or 4 × 3 or 4 × 4), containing different pictorial depictions of different emotions. Each individual item contains only a facial expression of a basic emotion. As in any form of bingo, each card contains a different and random array of the emotions being used. Individual emotion-labeling cards (e.g. 2 × 2 or 3 × 3 inches) containing only the emotion word label are constructed to match the facial expression of emotions used on the large bingo cards and placed in a stack for the bingo caller.

Each child is given a small box of chips. The group leader or group member designated as caller or each group member in turn draws an emotion word label card from the stack, shows the group the card, and verbalizes the emotion depicted and labeled. Each child scans his own bingo card for the appropriate matching facial expression and places a chip on the appropriate emotion if found on his card. The child who gets a complete row or column of emotions first raises his hand and the arrays are reviewed. The number of rows and columns can be increased on the large bingo cards (first 3 × 3 or 3 × 4, then 4 × 4 or 4 × 5, and so forth) as the group learns to recognize (label, understand) emotions and as the group masters the recognition (labeling, understanding) task.

Discussion: Tasks 1, 2, and 3

These tasks increase the group members' capacity to label and use a broad range of emotions experienced by individuals, particularly within group social interactions. Following completion of the activity, the group leader facilitates a discussion of emotions, how we recognize and label them, and how we use them in social interaction with others. The group members are encouraged to share their thoughts and feelings about the process of the recognition and labeling of different emotional characteristics (e.g. facial expressions, voice inflexion, voice volume and tone, body language), to generate examples of how this task/activity relates to real-life situations, and to consider how the recognition, labeling, and understanding of emotions, including facial expressions, might be useful to them.

Emotions sentence completion

Stages
1–5

This activity is appropriate to use at each stage of group development, 1 through 5, with modifications that fit individual goals, the specific stage, and the group goals. The group leader (or the group as indicated) adapts and modifies the task/activity depending on the specific stage addressed.

Core variables
Emotion competence
Specific area
Emotion understanding

Group goal
- Group members will develop and enhance their understanding of appropriate emotions.

Objectives
- Group members will increase awareness and understanding of an array of emotions.

- Group members will learn about the range of emotions and feelings that can be experienced.

- Group members will understand different situations where emotions emerge and how they can be used.

Task/activity description
Group task
Individual cards are constructed, each containing a facial expression depicting an emotion. Underneath each picture is a short sentence stem, such as "I felt happy when I _____" or "I was most excited when I _____." Cards are shuffled and each child in turn takes a card and must complete the sentence stem using appropriate "emotions language." As the group masters this task, more and varied emotion cards are added.

Also, as the group masters this task, cards are constructed containing only the short sentence stem with no facial expression to aid the child. In this variation, the child must recognize the appropriate emotion to be communicated only from the written/verbal communication contained in the sentence stem.

Next, as the group masters this task, emotion cards are constructed with sentence stems requesting a response involving another person, such as "I think Julie was nervous when she _____" or "I saw James get confused when _____."

Discussion

These tasks increase the group members' ability to recognize, label, and understand a broad range of emotions experienced by individuals, particularly within group social interactions. Following the completion of the activity, the group leader facilitates a discussion of emotions, how we recognize them, how we label and use them, and how we understand them in group social interactions with others. The group members are encouraged to share their thoughts and feelings about the process of the recognition of facial characteristics, to generate examples of how this task/activity relates to real-life situations, and to consider how the recognition, labeling, and understanding of facial expressions might be useful to them.

Progressive muscle relaxation

Stages
1–5

This activity is appropriate to use at each stage of group development, 1 through 5, with modifications that fit individual goals, the specific stage, and the group goals. The group leader (or the group as indicated) adapts and modifies the task/activity depending on the specific stage addressed.

Core variables
Stress and anxiety control and management
Specific area
Relaxation

Group goal
- Group members will recognize, identify, and manage heightened arousal levels.

Objective
- Group members will learn, practice, and master muscle relaxation strategies.

Task/activity description
Pre-group preparation
Plush or inflatable chairs, beanbag chairs, exercise mats, or other comfortable sitting or reclining aids may be provided. The group leader provides a brief introduction and description of the activity and of the beginning of the relaxation process. This is accomplished by reducing irrelevant sensory input, such as lowering the lights, separating the members into chairs or mats, lowering the volume of one's voice, providing soothing background music, prohibiting conversation, or having the group members close their eyes.

Group task
Each group member is asked to find a relaxing spot and physical position to locate themselves and to separate themselves from other group members within the room. They are guided to settle into the relaxation position that

best suits the task of relaxation. The group leader begins with some calming activity, such as a "singing bowl," calming music, deep breathing, or a brief visualization, to set the tone and create the mood.

The group leader then takes the members through a series of progressive relaxation exercises focusing on the main large and small muscle groups of the body, beginning progressively with the hands and fingers, then arms, shoulders, neck, head, upper torso, lower torso, legs, and feet. Instructions focus on tensing the muscles in each muscle group for 5–10 seconds, then releasing the tension to experience the "relaxation effect," and focusing on the differences between tense and relaxed muscle sensations.

Discussion

The group leader provides help and direction in understanding the physiological reactions occurring within progressive muscle relaxation and encourages discussions of how this relaxation task can be used to manage and control heightened arousal, stress, tension, and anxiety created by stress triggers that are experienced. Verbal cues are created by each member to use when self-initiating strategies for stress and anxiety control and management.

Variations of these tasks are also described in Bourne (2005), Cautela and Groden (1978), and Cotugno (2009).

The Relaxation Response

Stages
1–5

This activity is appropriate to use at each stage of group development, 1 through 5, with modifications that fit individual goals, the specific stage, and the group goals. The group leader (or the group as indicated) adapts and modifies the task/activity depending on the specific stage addressed.

Core variables
Stress and anxiety control and management
    Specific area
Relaxation

Group goals

- Group members will recognize, identify, and manage heightened arousal levels.

- Group members will develop and fine-tune their own set of relaxation techniques.

- Group members will discuss and understand their own unique relaxation techniques and how they work in a group situation.

Objectives

- Group members will learn, practice, and master the Relaxation Response technique.

- Group members will identify when and how to use this technique.

- Group members will recognize and understand its use as a group relaxation technique.

- Group members will understand the need to help their fellow group members use relaxation techniques when appropriate.

Task/activity description

Pre-group preparation

Plush or inflatable chairs, beanbag chairs, exercise mats, or other comfortable sitting or reclining aids may be provided. The group leader provides a brief introduction and description of the activity and of the beginning of the relaxation process. This is accomplished by reducing irrelevant sensory input, such as lowering the lights, separating the members into chairs or mats, lowering the volume of one's voice, providing soothing background music, prohibiting conversation, or having the group members close their eyes.

Group task

Each group member is asked to find a relaxing spot and physical position to locate themselves and to separate themselves from other group members within the room. They are guided to settle into the relaxation position that is best suited for the task of relaxation. The group leader begins with some calming activity, such as a "singing bowl," calming music, deep breathing, or a brief visualization, to set the tone and create the mood.

The group leader then instructs the group to close their eyes and to begin to relax all muscles deeply, beginning with the feet and progressing up to the face. Group members are instructed to become aware of their breathing, breathing slowly in and out through their nose. Each member is instructed to choose a "relaxation word" (e.g. one, calm, quiet, relax) to repeat with each slow breath in and out. Breathing is slow, calm, and paced and continues for several minutes until a state of calm relaxation—the Relaxation Response—is noticeable and achieved.

During this time, the group leader guides the group through a set of reminders about how to attain, notice, and maintain the Relaxation Response, the deep level of relaxation. The group leader may mention maintaining a passive attitude to allow relaxation to occur, how to manage and ignore distracting thoughts by returning to one's relaxation word, how to focus and refocus internally on relaxation, and how to register and recognize the associated feelings of relaxation.

In ending the relaxation phase, the group leader slowly, calmly, and deliberately transitions the group from the relaxation phase to the discussion phase or to the next group task.

Discussion

The discussion phase provides an opportunity for the group to discuss and process their own individual reactions to the Relaxation Response and to hear and benefit from other group members' reactions and responses. A group discussion also focuses on how this technique and variations of it can be used by the group as a whole to recognize states of distress and states of relaxation, to calm themselves when overstimulated, and to help other group members invoke relaxation when needed. Finally, there may be discussion of how the learned relaxation techniques can be used in other situations outside the group, such as at home, at school, and on the playground.

The group may also discuss how they will use the relaxation techniques within their group and may discuss and generate ideas for tasks and activities that directly relate to and use the Relaxation Response.

This relaxation task/activity is adapted from Benson (1975).

Autogenic Relaxation Training

Autogenic Relaxation Training is a relaxation method developed by Schulz in 1966 (Goldbeck and Schmid 2003) and focuses on achieving a state of physical relaxation by concentration on specific autosuggestions. This passive concentration on autosuggestions results in an autogenic shift and is intended to result in mental relaxation.

Stages
1–5

This activity is appropriate to use at each stage of group development, 1 through 5, with modifications that fit individual goals, the specific stage, and the group goals. The group leader (or the group as indicated) adapts and modifies the task/activity depending on the specific stage addressed.

Core variables
Stress and anxiety control and management
> Specific area
Relaxation

Group goals

- Group members will recognize, identify, and manage heightened arousal levels.

- Group members will develop and fine-tune their own set of relaxation techniques.

- Group members will discuss and understand how their own unique relaxation techniques work in a group situation.

Objectives

- Group members will learn and practice Autogenic Relaxation Training techniques.

- Group members will identify when and how to use these techniques.

- Group members will recognize and understand Autogenic Relaxation Training as a group relaxation technique.

- Group members will understand the need to help their fellow group members use relaxation techniques when appropriate.

Task/activity description

Pre-group preparation

Plush or inflatable chairs, beanbag chairs, exercise mats, or other comfortable sitting or reclining aids may be provided. The group leader provides a brief introduction and description of the activity and of the beginning of the relaxation process. This is accomplished by reducing irrelevant sensory input, such as lowering the lights, separating the members into chairs or mats, lowering the volume of one's voice, providing soothing background music, prohibiting conversation, or having the group members close their eyes.

Group task

Each group member is asked to find a relaxing spot and physical position to locate themselves and to separate themselves from other group members within the room. They are guided to settle into the relaxation position that is best suited for the task of relaxation. The group leader begins with some calming activity, such as a "singing bowl," calming music, deep breathing, or a brief visualization, to set the tone and create the mood.

The group leader then instructs the group members to close their eyes and to begin the Autogenic Relaxation process. The group is instructed through a series of exercises spread out over several sessions and includes attending to body sensations, concentrating on breathing and heart rate, passive concentration on deep breathing, and feelings of body comfort and relaxation. The group leader guides the group through a predetermined autosuggestion script spoken repeatedly by the group leader. The group members are instructed to hold the suggestions in their head and to use them to calm themselves during the performance of all other activities. Specific emphasis is maintained on the suggestions until they become automatic for the group members and are used readily when stressed. Group members are encouraged to notice the effects of autosuggestion on their activity and peer performance. The group leader instructs or reminds the group as it proceeds about maintaining a passive attitude to allow relaxation to occur and the suggestions to take hold.

Discussion

The discussion phase provides an opportunity for the group to discuss and process their own individual reactions to Autogenic Relaxation Training and to hear and benefit from other group members' reactions and responses. A group discussion also focuses on how this technique and variations of it can be used by the group as a whole to recognize states of distress and states of relaxation, to calm themselves when overstimulated, and to help other group members invoke relaxation when needed. Group members may also discuss how they will use the relaxation techniques within their group and may discuss and generate ideas for tasks and activities that directly relate to and use Autogenic Relaxation Training. Finally, there may be a discussion of how the learned relaxation techniques can be used in other situations outside the group, such as at home, at school, and on the playground.

Chapter 20

Child and Group Leader Roles within SCEP Groups

Roles that individual children may take within SCEP groups

"The General"

Typically, the individual who takes on the role of "the General" in a group situation is one who has high needs to be in control in most interpersonal situations. This often stems from a fear of losing control, a fear of being out of control, or a fear of having others in control (and not knowing what they will do or how they will act). This high need for control will also dictate the quality of this individual's interaction with others—that is, the General is in charge and he is likely to be intolerant of others who do not follow his orders, who argue or disagree with him, who try to assert their own views, who try to mediate for more moderate positions, or who side with others against him. In these situations, input or feedback from others, even from the group leader, is positioned so as to be of little value or useless.

In some situations, to ensure a position of control, the General will often appear to be "negotiating" with others, but in fact these are usually subtle or not-so-subtle forms of coercive techniques (e.g. "No, no, no, that won't work, we'll do it this way") intended to shift control back to the General. These positions are not genuine or reciprocal and reflect an artificial "negotiating stance" or a resorting to "bribes" if in danger of losing control, often with no intention of following through on his promises or his end of the bargain. "Look, let's do this and next time we'll do it your way." When the next time comes along, the General will anticipate the deal and likely undercut it with a series of alternative negotiations which are directed to keep the General in control and to render others' ideas or suggestions secondary to his will. In these situations, opposing views or information which disagree with his position must be recognized early and headed off before there can be any serious consideration of it or before it can take hold with one or more other group members.

The General may also use his position of control to "delegate"—that is, he may allow others to make decisions through his authorizing authority (but only if he allows it) of this temporary shift of control. In fact, it is, in reality, no shift in the control, but rather the General allowing a subordinate to share in his authority temporarily if followed through on the General's terms. Typically, if this appears to threaten the General's authority or control or appears to signal a shift away from his power and control, the General will initiate a battle to retain and win back the control of the group. Thus, others having any control or power must be contingent on the General's allowing it within his rules.

When there is another group member who will not back down from the General (and who may in fact be another General himself), then significant conflict, even chaos, is likely to break out. This arouses the General's fear of losing control represented by the other child's attempts to seize control and must be thwarted, overcome, or undermined, often with ferocity, so that the other child does not prevail and ultimately gain control, take the position of the General, and subsequently dominate and control the former General.

Suggested individual goals for the General are shown in Figure 20.1.

"The General"

Stage I
- The individual will learn to manage his stress and anxiety as it arises related to control issues.
- The individual will recognize but not hinder others' attempts to connect interpersonally within the group.
- The individual will view the "group" as an entity and force.

Stage 2

- The individual will interact with peers respectfully and with interest in others' views.
- The individual will respond positively to others' attempts to connect interpersonally.
- The individual will recognize and acknowledge other members' needs for control.

Stage 3

- The individual will consider alternative views presented in group.
- The individual will implement suggestions made by others on decision making or problem solving.
- The individual will not resist or hinder other members' attempts to assert self or control aspects of group.

Stage 4

- The individual will alter his own ways of thinking based on input from others.
- The individual will acknowledge and encourage the need for other group members to share in control issues (i.e. decision making).
- The individual will repair breaks in relationships that are self-created.
- The individual will request points of view from other group members for group consideration.

Stage 5

- The individual will acknowledge his role within the group as "part of the group."
- The individual will create termination memories about "the group."
- The individual will acknowledge and recognize the importance of the "group," not one individual being in charge or in control.

Figure 20.1 Suggested individual goals for "The General"

"The UN Observer"

Typically, the child who takes on the role of "the UN Observer" is one with low needs for control and who in fact avoids situations where he will have control or have to make decisions. He is best characterized as a passive observer, willing to get involved only when the situation presents no risks or dangers to himself. Usually, this posture stems from a fear of not being cared for or of abandonment—that is, taking no risks ensures that no rejection or abandonment will occur and, supposedly, that he will remain liked/loved, taken care of, and an accepted part of the group.

The UN Observer's primary purpose is to avoid taking risks interpersonally. To accomplish this in a group, he tries to anticipate what others want him to do and, in an attempt to keep others happy, he tries to be the compliant, easy-to-get-along-with peer. In order to avoid risks, the observer must take no strong or firm position, offer no opinions that deviate from the group norm, and take no clear sides in conflict. However, the avoidance of conflict is self-centered and self-protective, rather than for the purpose of keeping calm for the sake of the group.

The UN Observer may take a role of mediator, but this most often occurs only when forced to by opposing group members. The UN Observer, in this situation, will attempt to reflect or mirror both sides, but will rarely or overtly support one position or the other, letting the combatants do all the asserting and posturing for control. Needless to say, the UN Observer is reliant on others to take control, make decisions, and essentially dictate to him what he is to do. Ultimately, the UN Observer is forced to go along with the group norm or decision and to give up his own professed neutrality. This is solely in the service of allowing the UN Observer to remain passive and outside the realm of control. Only in this way can the UN Observer remain part of the group.

Although the UN Observer will avoid taking an active role in decision making, he is nevertheless likely to experience fairly high degrees of stress and anxiety. This relates to the uncertainty of his perceived role within the group and the possibility that the group could move quickly in one direction or another, leaving the UN Observer with no say or control over the outcome. The uncertainty of these situations appears to trigger high levels of stress and anxiety in the UN Observer. Despite the UN Observer's refusal to take positions or to express opinions within the group, his greatest fear appears to be that he will in some way be left out of the group (e.g. rejected, abandoned). Thus, the role of neutrality and passivity in the face of conflict is intended to make him appear valuable to either side of the conflict, willing to go along with either side, as long as the purpose is to eliminate the overt conflict, achieve a state of calm, and support the illusion of everyone getting along and agreeing.

In many situations, especially when recognizing the unpredictability of conflictual situations, the UN Observer will try to set the stage for calmness, serenity, and agreement (e.g. "Let's just do what we did last time"). The UN Observer's primary goal is to keep his own stress and anxiety in check by supporting the absence of conflict at best or the quick resolution of conflict at worst. For the UN Observer, the absence of conflict maintains a state of "cautious contentment." This relates to his passive position that relies on the direction of others and on others' decision making. The UN Observer generally tends to absolve himself through avoidance/denial of any responsibility for group behavior ("I didn't do anything, I just sat there and didn't say anything").

Suggested individual goals for the UN Observer are shown in Figure 20.2.

"The UN Observer"

Stage 1
- The individual will recognize stress and anxiety related to asserting self and speaking up.

Stage 2
- The individual will offer his own suggestions, points of view, or opinions on group topics.

Stage 3
- The individual will assert self to have own suggestions, points of view, or opinions considered.

Stage 4
- The individual will assert self to have own suggestions, points of view, or opinions implemented.

Stage 5
- The individual will acknowledge and reflect upon learning to be active and to assert self within the group.

Figure 20.2 Suggested individual goals for "The UN Observer"

"Forward Reconnaissance"

Typically, the individual who takes on the role of "Forward Reconnaissance" (Recon) tends to be an individual who is very cautious, careful, and deliberate, although not usually viewed as passive, in most interpersonal relations. This individual appears to have capacities for delay, for anticipation of events and circumstances, to be risk-avoidant, and to have moderate needs for control. This individual likes the role of figuring out possibilities and being in a position of presenting his thoughts and points of view to the other group members.

The Recon seems to get his needs for control met by the process of collecting, understanding, and conveying the information collected, then trying to influence the direction of the decision-making process. Though these individuals tend to be cautious and not individual risk takers, they can easily join in a group risk-taking activity and get their energy directly from the group if they view the group as valuing their role as Recon and information gatherer. They will value feedback from others if this process allows them to maintain the role of Recon (i.e. influence the decision/outcome), but they may also engage in manipulation of the flow of feedback if this process appears to be reducing or taking away control from them.

The Recon will often expend a fair amount of thinking about how different possibilities, alternatives, and choices may affect his own position as he lobbies for or attempts to direct a choice or decision. He will avoid getting in the middle of group conflicts, especially concerning control or power; however, he may mediate differences and disputes, but will rarely take firm positions or sides, often giving what sounds like or appears to be "objective" views or opinions about the "best" way of proceeding. The Recon typically is aware of all the possible minefields ahead in a situation and attempts to avoid them personally or navigate around them interpersonally. His investment is in avoiding risk, conflict, and battle, while still being part of the group process, and getting something done.

Suggested individual goals for the Recon are shown in Figure 20.3.

"The Recon"

Stage 1
- The individual will recognize stress and anxiety related to uncertainty and unpredictability.

Stage 2
- The individual will acknowledge the support and connectedness from being part of a group.

Stage 3
- The individual will tolerate personal stress and anxiety and interpersonal unpredictability and conflict.
- The individual will construct strategies to manage and cope with personal and interpersonal stress and anxiety to fit specific situations.

Stage 4

- The individual will allow problems and conflicts to emerge, to be "aired out," and to find solutions (i.e. the individual "trusts" the group to work it out).
- The individual will self-initiate appropriate strategies to manage personal and interpersonal stress and anxiety when it arises.

Stage 5

- The individual will acknowledge and reflect upon needs for predictability within the group.
- The individual will create memories related to uncertainty, variation, and unpredictability of this group (i.e. "I am OK with that").

Figure 20.3 Suggested individual goals for "Forward Reconnaissance" (Recon)

"The Mediator"

Typically, the role of "the Mediator" is taken by the individual with high needs for control, but who is conflict-avoidant. He will relish the opportunity to be in control when in the middle of a conflictual situation as long as he is not a combatant. His need typically is to take control of the situation by influencing and directing the combatants. Ultimately, the direction of the resolution of group conflict is highly influenced by the Mediator and often it is his own way of thinking or point of view that ultimately prevails.

The Mediator often attempts to occupy the space between conflicting sides. He may collect information, explain the options, alternatives, or possibilities, and appear to be actively seeking to find a middle ground. However, he is rarely satisfied with this role unless there is power and control attached to it and it appears valued by the other group members.

The Mediator gains sustenance and energy from the importance and power that this role conveys, particularly in moving the group forward and not allowing the group to get stuck. The Mediator usually does not seek out or encourage conflict, but is quick to jump into the role of Mediator and to direct solutions. Generally, the Mediator is a risk taker as long as this does not involve escalating conflict situations. Thus, all control struggles within the group, often between two Generals, are seen as opportunities for the Mediator to gain increased control by solving the emerging problem. The role of the Mediator allows the individual to be accepted and valued within the group.

Suggested individual goals for the Mediator are shown in Figure 20.4.

"The Mediator"

Stage 1
- The individual will recognize and tolerate the stress and anxiety of sitting, listening, and attending to others in the group.
- The individual will attend to others when needs are being communicated and expressed.

Stage 2
- The individual will acknowledge contributions of every member as part of the group.
- The individual will acknowledge and accept the central role of the group interactions.

Stage 3
- The individual will respect and accept the input of each group member as important.
- The individual will refrain from "taking charge" behaviors or attempts to "force decisions."
- The individual will acknowledge and accept the presence of conflict within the group.

Stage 4
- The individual will tolerate a range of different considerations, points of view, and opinions as part of the group process.
- The individual will tolerate other group members appropriately, assuming problem-solving and decision-making roles within the group.

Stage 5
- The individual will reflect upon and relate memories regarding the group's need for differences, uncertainty, and unpredictability.
- The individual will reflect upon and relate memories of how power and control is decided and delegated within the group and how problems and conflicts are resolved.

Figure 20.4 Suggested individual goals for "The Mediator"

Roles that the group leader may take within SCEP groups

"The Expert"

When the group leader assumes the role of "Expert" in the group, he is making a statement that "I am right, you are not!"—that is, "What I say is the norm for the group based on my sole judgment." This position leaves little room for group input, group disagreement, or group negotiation. The message conveyed is "I'm the only one who knows enough in this group to set rules, make decisions, give feedback, judge appropriateness, etc."

Often, the group leader approaches this role with his own high needs for control and is attempting to assert himself in the role as leader. Although there are a number of aspects to this role that serve positive group leadership, generally it tends to be a role that is overly rigid and restrictive with limited opportunities for the group members to gradually take on increased self-control and responsibility, to oppose structures in order to learn how to accommodate to them, and to observe models of flexible and supportive decision making and limit setting. Thus the group leader role of the Expert is best characterized as one of high control by the group leader, limited responsibility for the group members, and too narrow and rigid models for managing and responding to group issues and interactions.

Suggested goals for the group leader as Expert are shown in Figure 20.5.

"The Expert"

Stage 1
- The leader intervenes only when rules are broken, boundaries exceeded, or respect violated.

Stage 2
- Group members will be allowed to define aspects of their own group identity to the extent that they are capable.

Stage 3
- Group members will assume power and control in problem solving and decision making to the extent they can manage.

Stage 4
- The leader acknowledges and accepts his role as facilitator–consultant within the group.

Stage 5
- The leader will reflect on the group's capacity and successes in self-managing and self-directing tasks and activities.

Figure 20.5 Suggested goals for the group leader as "Expert"

"The Dictator"

The group leader role of "Dictator" is generally viewed as the counterpart to the authoritarian parent, but within the group setting. This is typically a role assumed by an adult who not only has high needs for control but who has an inability to recognize the impact of these control needs as they play out in a group or to use them constructively in the service of positive interactions and outcomes. This is one of the primary negative leader roles because it provides so few opportunities (often none) for the group to generate any movement on issues such as testing group rules, discussing and trying out different variations of group structures, group decision making, constructively altering the group dynamic, and providing feedback to the group leader and to other group members about different ways an issue or problem would be approached. The Dictator rules on the right or wrong way to address an issue, carry out a command, interact with a peer, etc. (i.e. "This is what you must do").

Since there is no flexibility tolerated by this therapist role, the modeling effect generally tends to be pervasively negative and claustrophobic to the group members who may need to explore and experiment with different ways of addressing or approaching tasks, situations, or problems in order to grow and develop interpersonally.

Suggested goals for the group leader as Dictator are shown in Figure 20.6.

"The Dictator"

Stage 1
- The leader will encourage the group members to consider and construct their own group rules defined by their own needs.

Stage 2
- The group leader will serve as guide and facilitator for task and activity selection.
- The leader will encourage the group members to design and construct their own task and activity selection schedule based on group goals.

Stage 3

- The leader will encourage and facilitate the group to construct and devise problem-solving and conflict-resolution strategies.

Stage 4

- The leader will allow the group to manage and resolve problems and conflicts as they arise in group.

Stage 5

- The group will reflect upon and recall effective self-directed and self-initiated problem-solving and conflict-resolution strategies.

Figure 20.6 Suggested goals for the group leader as "Dictator"

"The Role Model"

When the group leader assumes the role of "Role Model," he is making a statement to the group members that "You can follow my lead and do as I do without repercussion and with acceptance." It is a demonstration of how it can be done. "Try it, you'll like it." The group leader consciously acts out or demonstrates appropriate ways to interact and supportive things to say, using language and interactions that can be duplicated by the group members as is or reworked in their own language or style.

The group leader in the role of Role Model sees himself as one who, by demonstration, provides the words, the acts, and the interactions not by talking about them, requesting they occur, or dictating that they be done, but by showing group members, by using the exact words, and by using the exact tone, expression, and intonation to get the point across.

The group leader as Role Model typically exerts low needs for control as he relies on demonstration, repetition, and acceptance by the group. Rules are set and followed by demonstration and verbal walk-throughs, such as "I am sitting quietly waiting for everyone's attention…J. is ready and can begin." Those group members who comply by following the Role Model are provided with reinforcement and support, thus shaping the behavior to meet group norms. Reinforcement may be withheld from those who do not comply, but there are no negative consequences attached directly to the behaviors by the group leader.

The group leader as Role Model typically assumes a nonjudgmental posture to inappropriate behavior by providing a description or demonstration of the desired appropriate behavior. Rather than setting strict verbal limits such as

"We don't use that language here," the group leader provides the appropriate modeled behavior—"We are all talking at the same time and cannot hear each other" or "You're saying that J. hurt you and you're upset" or "We are excited and can't wait for vacation."

The group leader as Role Model establishes the rules and the behavioral norms by his modeling of the words, behavior, and interactions that provide an ongoing representation and demonstration of how appropriate interactions, verbalizations, and behaviors would sound and look. The group members are encouraged through reinforcement to take on these demonstrations and verbalizations as their own, as appropriate ways to communicate with each other.

"The Facilitator"

The group leader as "Facilitator" conveys an image of control, structure, consistency, and goal directedness. The interactions of the Facilitator to the group are initially highly structured and provide the group with a series of connections throughout the course of the group. Initially, the connections relate to stage-related issues, such as facilitating smooth and effective movement from one stage to the next. Other connections relate to the use of individual goals by each group member as they ally and connect with the group, followed by the discussion and development of group goals as they relate to individual issues.

The Facilitator provides the structure and consistency that encourages an inner sense of personal and group safety and security, allowing individuals and the group to relate to one another in honest, respectful, caring, and empathic ways. Peer-based, therapeutic interactions evolve naturally in this environment. The Facilitator conveys a sense of control only when needed, leaving the group to struggle with its own self-management issues, to test its own limits, and, when ready, to come up with its own mutually agreed-upon solutions and decisions. The Facilitator allows the group to develop within its capabilities, tailored to individual and group needs, providing structure, consistency, and limits only when necessary to keep the group moving forward. The Facilitator moves from directing interactions, tasks, and activities, to facilitating the group's positive, stage-based movement, to observing the self-directed, self-managed, peer-based interactions of a cohesive and connected group.

Examples of Areas of Interest

General

- Always anxious/nervous (stress/anxiety management).
- Never stops fidgeting (stress/anxiety management).
- Will not try new things (stress/anxiety management; flexibility).
- Needs lots of preparation (stress/anxiety management; flexibility).
- Does not listen or pay attention (attention).
- Cannot stick with things/never finishes things (sustained attention).
- Ignores other people (joint attention; relatedness; social-interpersonal; peer relationships).
- Avoids new things (flexibility).
- Always wants his own way (flexibility).
- Always has to win (flexibility; peer relationships; theory of mind).
- Always late/hard to leave (transitions).
- Has no friends (relatedness).
- Cannot converse with peers (relatedness).
- Isolates self (relatedness; sensory).
- Has temper tantrums (self-control).

- Will not acknowledge he is upset, scared, angry, etc. (self-awareness; emotional development).
- Will not say how he feels (self-awareness; emotional development)
- Wants friends (peer relationships).
- Says whatever he is thinking (theory of mind).

Specific

- Does not look people in the eye (joint attention).
- Never says hello (joint attention).
- Does not respond to name when called (attention).
- Cannot wait for his turn (attention; self-control).
- Blurts out (attention; self-control).
- Does not follow rules (flexibility).
- Cannot agree with others (flexibility).
- Will not let others touch his things (flexibility; sensory).
- Does not like loud noises, yelling, being touched, etc. (sensory).
- Touches everything (sensory).
- Has no awareness of others' feelings (theory of mind).

Examples of Individual Goals by Stage of Group Development

Stage 1

- I will introduce myself each time I meet someone new.
- I will say "hello" each time I see someone I know.
- I will ask an introductory question upon entering a conversation.
- I will initiate a discussion of a comfortable topic with a peer.

Stage 2

- I will ask how a peer is doing since last group.
- I will ask a question to a peer about something he mentioned at last group.
- I will ask a school-related question to a peer.
- I will ask a question relating to a peer's favorite hobby, activities, etc.

Stage 3

- I will ask a peer for advice on something that I am interested in.
- I will ask a follow-up question related to a topic of a previous group.
- I will ask a "personal" question.
- I will share "personal" information with more than one peer and request input/advice.

Stage 4

- I will ask to help a peer on a personal topic raised by the peer.
- I will maintain appropriate interactive conversation throughout the group session.
- I will feel comfortable as a fully participating group member.
- I will ask the group for help with a "personal" issue or problem.
- I will acknowledge "feelings" about group participation.

Stage 5

- I will share my experiences as a group member.
- I will identify and label "feelings" related to ending group.
- I will acknowledge a "positive" and a "negative" group experience.
- I will learn about how I say goodbye to this group.

Examples of Group Goals by Stage of Group Development

Stage 1

- The group will acknowledge the stress and anxiety of beginning a new group.
- The group will learn everyone's favorites (food, TV show, computer game, etc.).
- The group will learn about and acknowledge common interests.
- The group will self-initiate hellos, sharing, and activity suggestions.
- The group will discuss and understand the use of group rules and expectations.

Stage 2

- The group will self-initiate interactive discussions.
- The group will share individual choices for group decision making.
- The group will establish a "communication system" for the group.
- The group will acknowledge and understand the need for and use of "respect."

Stage 3

- The group will provide input/advice upon individual request.

- The group will consistently interact on all issues with "respect" for one another.

- The group will recognize issues of "conflict" as they arise.

- The group will recognize the needs of others and consider responses.

Stage 4

- The group will recognize and provide "help" to others spontaneously and without request.

- The group will resolve issues of group conflict.

- The group will spontaneously support one another when in need.

- The group will confront group members who deviate from group rules and expectations.

Stage 5

- The group will acknowledge, address, and support shared stress/ anxiety around ending group.

- The group will self-initiate discussions of "group memories."

- The group will self-initiate end of group activities (party, memory book, etc.).

- The group will acknowledge, discuss, and support each other's end of group "feelings."

- The group will discuss other non-group endings and relate them to this group experience.

Specific Skills Addressed at Stage 1

- Entering a group.
- Introductions of self.
- Initiating a conversation.
  - Eye contact.
  - Opening comments.
  - Facial expressions.
- Maintaining a conversation (conversational skills).
  - Active listening.
  - Active responding.
  - Asking related and pertinent questions.
  - Staying on topic.
  - Waiting.
- Expressing interest in others.
- Following directions.
- Exiting a group.
  - Ending a conversation.
  - Saying goodbye.

Specific Skills Addressed at Stage 2

- Initiating discussions using personal information and preferences.
- Soliciting personal information from others.
- Sharing personal information relevant to the topic or discussion.
- Taking turns in conversation.
- Taking turns in activities, tasks, or games.
- Acknowledging points/information that others contribute.
- Playing by the rules.
- Asking for help.
- Regulating the intensity and quality of one's interactions.
- Voice tone/voice volume.
- Facial expressions.
- Joint attention.
- Body language/body cues.

Specific Skills Addressed at Stage 3

- Understanding and respecting body space.
- Sharing (of things that matter to the individual).
- Cooperation.
- Helping one another.
- Compromise.
- Giving and receiving compliments.
- Giving encouragement.
- Expressing feelings.
- Assertiveness.
- Disagreeing.
- Being a good sport.
- Following changes in topic.
- Friendship.
  - Discussing and understanding what is a friend.
  - Discussing and understanding what is a friendship.
  - Discussing and understanding what is a good friend.
  - Discussing and understanding who is not a friend.
- Confronting teasing, putdowns, or bullying in a group.
- Understanding and using verbal interchanges.
  - Reading verbal signals.
  - Reading nonverbal signals.

Specific Skills Addressed at Stage 4

- Recognizing and interpreting nonverbal and conceptual cues.
- Assertiveness.
- Offering an opinion or suggestion.
- Giving and receiving criticism.
- Asking permission.
- Apologizing.
- Using humor.
- Role playing.
- Introduction of others.
- Recognizing and using emotions in interactions.
- Perspective taking.
- Sympathy and empathy.
- Managing conflict and confrontation.
  - Initiating discussion of conflict and confrontation.
  - Responding to conflict and confrontation.
- Discussing and resolving decision-making issues.
- Discussing and resolving problem-solving issues.

Specific Skills Addressed at Stage 5

- Recognizing the loss associated with goodbyes.

- Expressing the loss associated with goodbyes.

- Recognizing the feelings and emotions associated with goodbyes.

- Experiencing the feelings and emotions associated with goodbyes.

- Creating memories to preserve the relationships.

- Celebrating the loss, termination, or goodbyes.

- Saving the loss, termination, or goodbyes.

- Saying goodbyes.

List of Emotions for Emotion Recognition, Labeling, Understanding, and Regulation Tasks and Activities

Primary

- happy
- sad
- mad/angry
- confused
- excited
- worried

- calm/peaceful/ relaxed
- shocked/amazed
- proud/pleased/ satisfied
- bored
- lonely
- silly

- scared/frightened/ afraid
- frustrated
- determined
- surprised
- playful
- thoughtful/serious

Positive emotions

- happy
- relaxed
- fine
- pleased
- confident
- excited
- hopeful
- serious
- amazed

- calm
- interested
- optimistic
- satisfied
- curious
- enthusiastic
- silly
- ecstatic
- wondering

- peaceful
- relieved
- proud
- determined
- playful
- playful
- thoughtful
- loved
- affectionate

Negative emotions

- aggressive
- afraid
- sad
- mad
- confused
- upset
- worried
- pained
- annoyed
- cautious
- discouraged
- envious
- fearful
- hostile
- hysterical

- scared
- tired
- shocked
- angry
- bored
- lonely
- miserable
- regretful
- anxious
- depressed
- disgusted
- tense
- guilty
- humiliated
- jealous

- frightened
- unhappy
- frustrated
- nervous
- withdrawn
- suspicious
- stubborn
- alienated
- apathetic
- disappointed
- embarassed
- exhausted
- helpless
- hurt
- pessimistic

Glossary of Terms Used in SCEP

Anxiety

A specific state of overarousal triggered by an internal or external situation (i.e. the stressor), creating stress (i.e. the stress response) which cannot be managed, controlled, or coped with in any effective, adaptive ways.

Attention

This broad core variable contains five primary aspects of attention that operate along a developmental, hierarchical continuum. The five components of attention are:

> Focused attention—the ability of an individual to direct his attention to a desired task or activity on demand and to hold it there for some minimal amount of time.

> Sustained attention—the ability of an individual to hold and sustain attention to a desired task or activity over an extended period of time which is defined or decided either by the individual or by the task.

> Selective attention—the ability to differentiate types of stimuli to be focused on and to direct attention selectively and purposely to a task defined as relevant and important and simultaneously to withhold attention from other stimuli defined as irrelevant, unimportant, or distracting to the task currently focused on.

Flexible attention—the ability to shift attention flexibly and spontaneously from one task or activity to another task or activity without the prior task or activity disrupting focus or activity to the task or activity being shifted to.

Joint attention—a core variable related primarily to social and cognitive/executive functioning which involves the ability to recognize and respond to the requests, demands, or needs for attention necessitated by a reciprocal and mutual engagement or interaction with another person or group.

Cautious contentment

The seeking out or repeating of familiar, repetitive situations and activities for the purpose of maintaining a state of internal equilibrium and which may also invoke an internal state of calm and relaxation (Cotugno 2009). This state, however, is quite fragile and vulnerable to the intrusion and disruption caused by external rules, requests, demands, and expectations. Thus, the individual remains in a state of moderate arousal, vigilance, and alertness (and resistance) to external intrusion.

Cognitive restructuring

This involves the identification of maladaptive or distorted cognitions, the challenging of their underlying assumptions, and the correction, change, and replacement of those assumptions and cognitions with more adaptive, developmentally appropriate ways of thinking.

Coping

This involves the capacity of the individual to manage a heightened state of arousal or stress without compromising performance or functioning and without exceeding the available resources of the individual (Lazarus and Folkman 1984; Suldo *et. al* 2008).

Emotion competence

Emotion competence is a core variable which involves the ability to recognize and acknowledge appropriate and applicable emotions in both self and others and related to the situation at hand, to provide and use the appropriate labels and descriptions for these emotions, to understand how and why these particular emotions are used in a specific social-interpersonal situation, and to regulate these emotions in keeping with personal and social expectations of the situation.

Flexibility, change, and transition

This is a core variable related to cognitive/executive functioning which involves the capacity to cope with, manage, and adapt to changes, shifts, and transitions as they occur within an individual's personal and interpersonal environments (i.e. internal or external) and as they alter the demands and expectations placed on the individual.

Perspective taking

In its earliest form, this involves an individual recognizing and understanding that others have different thoughts and feelings from himself. At higher levels, this is the capacity for one individual to think/imagine/speculate on what another person may be thinking about him or others.

Relaxation

Relaxation is a state of calm. It can be induced by specific exercises or activities that reduce the intensity of physiological responses and reactions to environmental stimuli (e.g. arousal, stress, excitement, change) and is often the result of conscious and effective attempts to alleviate or diminish the effects of stress and its triggers. It is usually linked to the absence of stress.

Self-monitoring

This is the process of observing, recognizing, and identifying one's own thoughts, emotions, and behaviors and adjusting or altering them when necessary or in keeping with the situation one is involved in. The individual is then able to learn or apply strategies and techniques to address the thoughts, emotions, or behaviors for the purpose of increasing desirable outcomes or decreasing undesirable outcomes while maintaining ongoing control over this process.

Self-regulation

This is the total process of awareness, deliberation, control, management, adjustment/adaptation, regulation, and direction of one's thinking, feelings, behavior, or interactions in both a self-focused or an interpersonal process. Self-regulation includes the control and modulation of emotions, cognition/thinking, social interaction, behaviors, sensory experiences, communications, and motor movements, generally operating in combinaton and in a sequential pattern, resulting in deliberate and goal-directed behavior.

Social cognition

The ability of an individual to:

1. recognize and respond to central and peripheral social and emotional information (attention, joint attention)

2. recognize and correctly interpret verbal and nonverbal social and emotional information

3. understand social behaviors and their consequences in diverse social situations

4. understand others' cognitive and emotional states (i.e. empathy, theory of mind). (Crick and Dodge 1994).

Social competence

1. The ability of an individual to engage successfully in spontaneous social interactions within the constantly changing, dynamic nature of social situations.

2. Social competence consists of three critical elements, each necessary for successful social interaction, and includes:

    a. *the situation*—the ability to recognize and understand the social situation as it exists, as it unfolds, and as it develops, and moves forward

    b. *the interchange*—the ability to recognize and understand the involvement of self and others in a reciprocal social interchange, either as individuals or in a group

   c.   *the response*—the ability to formulate and implement an appropriate response to a specific situation with specific individuals.

3.   A multidimensional concept that includes the combinations of cognitive, social, emotional, and behavioral components that result in mutual and reciprocal social interactions.

Social skills

1.   Social skills are the repertoire of behaviors and the specific tools that the individual possesses or learns that appropriately fit the social situation being encountered, allowing an effective social interchange to take place. These skills allow the individual to initiate, maintain, manipulate, or solidify a social interaction, thereby creating a "social relationship."

2.   Social skills are complex sets of intersecting behaviors which allow an individual to engage in positive mutually reciprocal and beneficial social interactions.

Social skills training

Social skills training is the specific focus on the learning and acquisition of specific skills needed to accomplish a specific social task. These include the processes of teaching/learning, demonstrating, and practicing elements of the specific skill and obtaining feedback. This often occurs in a very structured, systematic, and step-wise progression of skill building.

Stress

A state of disequilibrium, triggered in an individual or group by a range of internally or externally generated stimuli which create a state of heightened arousal (Selye 1993), vigilance, or alertness to the source of the stimuli.

Stress and anxiety continuum

The representation of specific states or levels of arousal along a continuum which ranges from equilibrium to breakdown (Cotugno 2009).

Stress and anxiety control and management

A core variable related primarily to emotional functioning that includes the ability to recognize and identify stress- and anxiety-producing experiences and to invoke, on demand, appropriate techniques for stress and anxiety control and management to cope with the situation in adaptive, growth-fostering ways.

Stressor

A stressor is the specific internal or environmental event that produces or results in a stress response.

Systematic desensitization

This is an intervention that involves the reduction of anxiety by identifying and rank-ordering stimuli that elicit stress and anxiety. This is followed by exposure to the least anxiety-provoking stimulus with the intention of reducing or eliminating anxiety to that stimulus. Then, the next least anxiety-provoking stimulus is addressed and so forth until anxiety to that set of stimuli is reduced or eliminated (extinguished).

Visualization

This involves the creation and use of internally generated images (using pictures, words, memories, experiences, etc.) which are associated with different internal states (i.e. relaxation, competition, achievement, etc.). These images can then be used on demand to recreate or re-experience the associated internal states, such as relaxation, in order to cope with or manage a state of distress or discomfort.

The following terms are used in SCEP group situations to help group members recognize, confront, and solve particular stage-related situations or related core variable events.

Building a bridge

The group leader models and encourages the recognition, labeling, and connection of how one's own thoughts, feelings, and behaviors affect the thoughts, feelings, and behaviors of others in the group.

Chain reactions

It is often observed that, when one person does something (either positive or negative), others will repeat the same thing. In the group situation, attention is drawn to how one person's behaviors affect others in the group in a "chain reaction."

Check-ins

Time is allocated for the recognition, identification, acknowledgement, and understanding of the thoughts, emotions, and behaviors of all group members and how they affect the group as a whole.

Double-dip/triple-dip emotions

Group members are made aware or reminded that multiple emotions can be experienced simultaneously. At the same time or in the same situation, an individual can be both excited and worried, happy and sad, hurt and lonely, etc. Through emotion recognition, labeling and expression, and understanding, discussions explore and explain these double-dip and triple-dip emotions, address how they can be confusing and overwhelming, and provide strategies to manage these more effectively.

Emotion scales

Scales that quantify thoughts, emotions, or behaviors are helpful in the process of recognizing, identifying, understanding, and regulating those issues. Scales allow a discussion of the varying levels and degrees of emotional and behavioral response and reaction that can occur. Often targeted "thermometers" are used with gradations of 1 to 10 or 1 to 100.

Group choice/individual choice

The types of decisions made within the group are frequently reviewed and discussed in order to understand their effects on individuals and the group as a whole. Individual choices employ individual information and decision making without the input of others, while group choices require all members to think about others and to share and communicate with each other. The ways in which each type of choice impacts others' perceptions and responses are considered and discussed.

If–then questions

If–then questions help children identify cause and effect relationships, critical to problem solving.

Peer referencing

Group members are encouraged to become more aware of and to regulate their own behaviors and responses by "referencing" how others are responding or behaving toward them.

Positive reinforcement

Desired behaviors are increased with attention, recognition, encouragement, support, and reward. This is paired with the learning of strategies and problem-solving techniques to address problems, situations, or interactions.

Quiet thoughts

Not all thoughts need to be or should be expressed. A quiet thought is characterized as a thought that would be better off staying as a thought (not being expressed). These types of thoughts are reviewed and discussed with examples such as saying things that might hurt someone's feelings, something that might gross someone out, interrupting others, or disrupting an activity that is going on.

Relaxation strategies and techniques

A variety of strategies that aid group members in addressing the core variable stress and anxiety control and management are learned, practiced, and mastered to manage and cope with a range of stress-inducing situations and interactions. These strategies include progressive muscle relaxation, deep breathing, the Relaxation Response, Autogenic Relaxation Training, visualization, and positive self-talk.

Stuck thought

Often individuals with ASD are unable to let go of certain thoughts and get "stuck." Stuck thoughts are acknowledged, discussed, and problem-solved, particularly relating to their impact on others, including the group.

Thinking/wondering out loud

Group members are encouraged to verbalize and express their thoughts and feelings as a way to foster the recognition and understanding that each group member has separate and distinct thoughts, needs, and wishes.

Visual supports

Group members are provided with multiple and varied opportunities to visually experience information provided.

Whole body listening

Active listening often includes many parts of our body, in addition to the ears. Listening can be enhanced by the additional use of our eyes, mouth (words), hands and feet (gestures), and body language, in coordination with auditory processing. An emphasis is placed on "listening with care," where we are more interested in what the other person has to say and how they are saying it than what we want to say.

A Summary of SCEP

SCEP is a group-based, multidimensional, therapeutic, and skill-based intervention intended for use with individuals with ASD. It employs a peer-based, adult-facilitated group model within a cognitive-developmental framework using group therapy, cognitive-behavioral, and skill instruction techniques to address the social competence needs of individuals with ASD. Evaluation processes include a review of all relevant available information and an assessment of the individual's abilities and skills in specific core areas and related core variables in order to determine and elaborate areas of interest, individual goals for each child, and group goals once a group is assembled. Following review, interview, and evaluation, an individual is considered and placed in a group based on developmental level, age, ability/skill levels, and "best fit" match with similar peers.

SCEP is constructed around a five-stage model of group development, specific to individuals with ASD. Within each of the five stages of development, this program addresses specific aspects of social interaction and adaptive strategies to manage these effectively. At each stage, core areas and specific core variables are targeted (e.g. self-regulation, emotion competence, stress management, joint attention) and related skills for instruction are defined, elaborated, and practiced with a focus on the development of effective and age-appropriate strategies for peer interactions.

The types of specific interventions used are varied and dependent upon the stage of group development, the core variables involved, and the individual and group goals constructed. Generally, these include developmental leveling (experiences targeted to the developmental level of the group), self-management (individuals take responsibility for their behavior), peer mediation (peer-to-peer interactions), priming (complex tasks are broken into simple steps with preparation and training provided for new aspects of a task), and direct instruction (specific skills are selected, taught, and reinforced). Specific core variables in individuals with ASD—such as self-regulation, emotion competence, stress and anxiety management, joint attention, flexibility/ transitions, perspective taking, and relatedness—are addressed within each stage of group development, employing the most appropriate interventions for the structure and skill to be acquired and learned.

Social competence groups meet at least weekly for one hour, typically within a school year schedule, such as from September through June, for approximately 30 sessions, led by clinicians with training and expertise with children and youth with ASD and in group therapy interventions. Sessions are highly structured and consistent, consisting of four components:

1. an introductory period (greetings, sharing time)

2. group decision-making time

3. task/activity completion, addressing core variables, stage-specific issues, and group goals

4. snack time and group discussion of the activity, used for processing group dynamics, connecting to previous sessions and to the key core variables and specific skills, and a preview of the next session.

Activities used during group sessions are selected based on the following criteria:

1. current stage of group development

2. specific group goals related to the stage of group development

3. specific social competencies, core variables, and social skills related to group goals.

A Summary of the Stage Model of Group Development Used in the SCEP Approach for Individuals with ASD

The following stages are observed within the SCEP model employed with individuals with ASD:

Stage 1   Group formation and orientation

Stage 2   Group cohesion

Stage 3   Group stability, relationships, and connections

Stage 4   Group adaptations and perspective taking

Stage 5   Terminations, loss, and endings

The first stage observed is one of *Group formation and orientation*, a process in which the group comes together for initial sessions and begins to get to know one another as individuals and as a group. Group goals are constructed based on the common and shared needs as they emerge and are intended to provide structure about what is expected. Specific skills include learning about one another, learning about how the group can work together, acknowledging common issues, and creating a group plan.

The second stage of *Group cohesion* relates to the group's capacity to form a bond as a group and to use that bond as a force to hold the group together as it begins to deal with more stressful issues. Group goals foster interaction, while individual goals focus on the specific needs of the individual to make interactions successful. Specific skills include asking for and receiving help from peers, taking turns, competing, and initiating conversations and activities.

The third stage of *Group stability, relationships, and connections* emphasizes the power of interactive group process in which members identify with each other and with the group leader and strong alliances develop. Group goals focus on the shift in power and control, with the group assuming more authority in control, decision making, and conflict resolution. Specific skills include learning about nonverbal cues, working cooperatively, giving and getting feedback/criticism, emotion regulation, and anxiety management.

The fourth stage of *Group adaptations and perspective taking* relates to the group's capacity to adapt flexibly to issues that arise, adjusting modes of communication and decision making to the group needs. Goals focus on self-management and self-direction, respectful interactions, appropriate confrontation, alternative solutions to problems, and agreement in decision making. Specific skills include negotiating compromise, seeing things through another person's eyes, apologizing, and getting "unstuck."

The fifth stage of *Terminations, loss, and endings* relates to endings, losses, and goodbyes. Attempts are made to understand the thoughts, feelings, and emotions that these events stir up and the effects that they have on interactions with peers and others. The goals are specific to endings and the holding on to memories. Specific skills include expressing termination emotions, understanding endings, and saving the memories.

References

Adrien, J.L., Lenoir, P., Martineau, J., Perrot, A., Hameury, L., Larmande, C. *et al.* (1993) 'Blind ratings of early symptoms of autism based upon family home movies.' *Journal of the American Academy of Child and Adolescent Psychiatry 32* (3), 617–26.

Alexander, F.G. and Selesnick, S.T. (1966) *The History of Psychiatry.* New York: Harper and Row.

American Psychiatric Association (1980) *Diagnostic and Statistical Manual of Mental Disorders*, 3rd Edition. Washington, DC: American Psychiatric Association.

American Psychiatric Association (1987) *Diagnostic and Statistical Manual of Mental Disorders*, 3rd Edition Revised. Washington, DC: American Psychiatric Association.

American Psychiatric Association (1994) *Diagnostic and Statistical Manual of Mental Disorders*, 4th Edition. Washington, DC: American Psychiatric Association.

Asperger, H. (1979) 'Problems of infantile autism.' *Communication: Journal of the National Autistic Society, 13*, 45–52.

Asperger, H. (1991) [1944] 'Autistic Psychopathy in Childhood.' In U. Frith (ed.) *Autism and Asperger Syndrome.* Cambridge: Cambridge University Press.

Attwood, T. (2007) *The Complete Guide to Asperger's Syndrome.* London: Jessica Kingsley Publishers.

Axline, V. (1964) 'The Eight Basic Principles.' In M. Haworth (ed.) *Child Psychotherapy: Practice and Theory.* New York: Basic Books.

Barry, T.D., Klinger, L.G., Lee, J.M., Palardy, N., Gilmore, T. and Bodin, S.D. (2003) 'Examining the effectiveness of an outpatient clinic-based social skills group for high-functioning children with autism.' *Journal of Autism and Developmental Disorders 33* (6), 685–701.

Bauminger, N., Schulman, C. and Agam, G. (2003) 'Peer interaction and loneliness in high-functioning children with autism.' *Journal of Autism and Developmental Disorders 33* (5), 489–507.

Bellini, S. (2004) 'Social skills deficits and anxiety in high-functioning adolescents with autism spectrum disorders.' *Focus on Autism and Other Developmental Disabilities 19* (2), 78–86.

Bender, L. (1952) *Child Psychiatric Techniques.* Springfield, IL: Charles C. Thomas.

Benson, H. (1975) *The Relaxation Response.* New York: Scribner.

Benson, H. and Proctor, W. (2010) *Relaxation Revolution: Enhancing Your Personal Health Through the Science and Genetics of Mind Body Healing.* New York: Scribner.

Berger, H.J.C., van Spaendonck, K.P.M., Horstinck, M.W., Baylenhuij, E.L., Lammers, P.W. and Cools, A.R. (1993) 'Cognitive shifting as a predictor of progress in social understanding in high-functioning adolescents with autism: A prospective study.' *Journal of Autism and Developmental Disorders 23*, 341–59.

Bleuler, E. (1951) [1916] 'Lehrbuch der Psychiatrie.' In A.A. Brill (trans.) *Textbook of Psychiatry.* New York: Dover.

Bourne, E.J. (2005) *The Anxiety and Phobia Workbook*, 4th Edition. Oakland, CA: New Harbinger Publications.

Bowlby, J. (1952) *Maternal Care and Mental Health*. Geneva: World Health Organization.

Brown, B.B., Hedlinger, T. and Mieling, G. (1995) 'The power in universality of experience: A homogeneous group approach to social skills training for individuals with learning disabilities.' *The Journal for Specialists in Group Work 20*, 98–107.

Brown, W.H., Odom, S.L. and McConnell, S.R. (eds) (2008) *Social Competence of Young Children*. Baltimore, MD: Paul H. Brookes Publishing.

Caplan, G. (1955) *Emotional Problems of Early Childhood*. New York: Basic Books.

Cautela, J.R. and Groden, J. (1978) *Relaxation: A Comprehensive Manual for Adults, Children, and Children with Special Needs*. Champaign, IL: Research Press.

Center for Environmental Health, Environmental Epidemiology Program (2005) *Prevalence Estimates of Autism and Autism Spectrum Disorder in Massachusetts: Final Report*. Boston: Massachusetts Department of Public Health.

Centers for Disease Control and Prevention (2009) *Prevalence of Autism Spectrum Disorders: Autism and Developmental Disabilities Monitoring Network, United States, 2006*. Surveillance Summaries, December 18, 2009. *Morbidity and Mortality Weekly Report 58* (SS10), 1–20.

Charlop-Christy, M.H. and Kelso, S.E. (2003) 'Teaching children with autism conversational speech using a cue card/written script program.' *Education and Treatment of Children 26*, 108–28.

Ciesielski, K.T., Courchesne, E. and Elmasian, R. (1990) 'Effects of focused selective attention tasks on event-related potentials in autistic and normal individuals.' *Electroencephalography and Clinical Neurophysiology 75*, 207–20.

Cotugno, A.J. (2009) *Group Interventions for Children with Autism Spectrum Disorders*. London: Jessica Kingsley Publishers.

Coupland, N.J. (2001) 'Social phobia: Etiology, neurobiology and treatment.' *Journal of Clinical Psychiatry 62* (1), 25–35.

Courchesne, E. (1991) 'Neuroanatomic imaging in autism.' *Pediatrics 87* (5), 781–90.

Crick, N.R. and Dodge, K.A. (1994) 'A review and reformulation of social-information-processing mechanisms in children's social adjustment.' *Psychological Bulletin 115*, 74–101.

Davis, M., Eshelman, E.R. and McKay, M. (2000) *The Relaxation Response and Stress Reduction Workbook*, 5th Edition. Oakland, CA: New Harbinger Publications.

Dawson, G. (1991) 'A Psychobiological Perspective on the Early Socio-Emotional Development of Children with Autism.' In D. Cicchetti and S.L. Toth (eds) *Rochester Symposium on Developmental Psychopathology: Vol. 3. Models and Integrations*. Rochester, NY: University of Rochester Press.

Dawson, G. and Lewy, A. (1989) 'Arousal, Attention, and the Socio-Emotional Impairments of Individuals with Autism.' In G. Dawson (ed.) *Autism: Nature, Diagnosis, and Treatment*. New York: Guilford Press.

Dawson, G. Meltzoff, A.N., Osterling, J., Rinaldi, J. and Brown, E. (1998) 'Children with autism fail to orient to naturally occurring stimuli.' *Journal of Autism and Developmental Disorders 28*, 479–85.

Delis, D.C., Kaplan, E. and Kramer, J. (1999) *Delis–Kaplan Executive Function System Manual*. San Antonio, TX: Psychological Corporation.

DeMyer, M., Hingtgen, J. and Jackson, R. (1981) 'Infantile autism reviewed: A decade of research.' *Schizophrenia Bulletin 7*, 388–451.

Denham, S.A. (1998) *Emotional Development in Young Children*. New York: Guilford Press.

Denham, S.A., Blair, K.A., DeMulder, E., Levitas, J., Sawyer, K., Auerbach-Major, S. and Queenan, P. (2003) 'Preschool emotional competence: Pathway to social competence?' *Child Development 74* (1), 238–56.

Dettmer, S., Simpson, R.I., Myles, B.S. and Ganz, J.B. (2000) 'The use of visual supports to facilitate transitions of students with autism.' *Focus on Autism and Other Developmental Disabilities 15*, 163–9.

Ehlers, S. and Gillberg, C. (1993) 'The epidemiology of Asperger syndrome: A total population study.' *Journal of Child Psychology and Psychiatry 34* (8), 1327–50.

Ferguson, A., Ashbaugh, R., O'Reilly, S. and McLaughlin, T.F. (2004) 'Using prompt training and reinforcement to reduce transition times in a transitional kindergarten program for students with severe behavior disabilities.' *Child and Family Behavior Therapy 26*, 17–24.

Flannery, K.B. and Horner, R.H. (1994) 'The relationship between predictability and problem behavior for students with severe disabilities.' *Journal of Behavioral Education 4*, 157–76.

Fombonne, E. (2003) 'Epidemiological surveys of autism and other pervasive developmental disorders: An update.' *Journal of Autism and Developmental Disorders 33* (4), 365–82.

Frith, U. (1989) *Autism: Explaining the Enigma.* Oxford: Basil Blackwell.

Frith, U. (1991) 'Asperger and His Syndrome.' In U. Frith (ed.) *Autism and Asperger Syndrome.* Cambridge: Cambridge University Press.

Frith, U. and Baron-Cohen, S. (1987) 'Perception in Autistic Children.' In D.J. Cohen, A. Donnellan and R. Paul (eds) *Handbook of Autism and Pervasive Developmental Disorders.* New York: Wiley.

Ghaziuddin, M., Butler, E., Tsai, L. and Ghaziuddin, N. (1994) 'Is clumsiness a marker for Asperger syndrome?' *Journal of Intellectual Disability Research 38*, 519–27.

Ghaziuddin, M., Ghaziuddin, N. and Greden, J. (2002) 'Depression in persons with autism: Implications for research and clinical care.' *Journal of Autism and Developmental Disorders 32* (4), 299–306.

Ghaziuddin, M., Leininger, L. and Tsai, L. (1995) 'Brief report. Thought disorder in Asperger syndrome: Comparison with high-functioning autism.' *Journal of Autism and Developmental Disorders 25* (3), 311–17.

Gillberg, C. (1983) 'Perceptual, motor, and attentional deficits in Swedish primary school children: Some child psychiatric aspects.' *Journal of Child Psychology and Psychiatry 24*, 377–403.

Gillberg, C. (1991) 'Clinical and Neurobiological Aspects of Asperger Syndrome in Six Family Studies.' In U. Frith (ed.) *Autism and Asperger Syndrome.* Cambridge: Cambridge University Press.

Gillberg, C. and Gillberg, I.C. (1989) 'Asperger syndrome – some epidemiological considerations: A research note.' *Journal of Child Psychology and Psychiatry 30*, 631–8.

Gillott, A. (2007) 'Levels of anxiety and sources of stress in adults with autism.' *Journal of Intellectual Disabilities 11* (4), 359–70.

Gillott, A., Furniss, F. and Walter, A. (2001) 'Anxiety in high-functioning children with autism.' *Autism 5* (3), 277–86.

Goldbeck, L. and Schmid, K. (2003) 'Effectiveness of autogenic relaxation training on children and adolescents with behavioral and emotional problems.' *Journal of the Academy of Child and Adolescent Psychiatry 42* (9), 1046–54.

Gray, C. (1998) 'Social Stories 101.' *The Morning News 10* (1), 2–6.

Gray, C. (2000) *The New Social Stories Book.* Arlington, TX: Future Horizons.

Groden, J., Cautela, J., Prince, S. and Berryman, J. (1994) 'The Impact of Stress and Anxiety on Individuals with Autism and Developmental Disabilities.' In E. Schopler and G.B. Mesibov (eds) *Behavioral Issues in Autism: Current Issues in Autism.* New York: Plenum.

Gumpel, T. (1994) 'Social competence and social skills training for persons with mental retardation: An expansion of a behavioral paradigm.' *Education and Training in Mental Retardation and Developmental Disabilities 29* (3), 194–201.

Helmstetter, S. (1987) *The Self-Talk Solution.* New York: Pocket Books.

Jacobson, E. (1974) *Progressive Relaxation.* Chicago: University of Chicago Press.

Kadesjo, B., Gillberg, C. and Hagberg, B. (1999) 'Autism and Asperger syndrome in seven-year-old children: A total population study.' *Journal of Autism and Developmental Disorders 29*, 327–31.

Kanner, L. (1957) *Child Psychiatry*, 3rd Edition. Springfield, IL: Charles C. Thomas.

Kanner, L. (1958) *In Defense of Mothers*, 4th Edition. Springfield, IL: Charles C. Thomas.

Kanner, L. (1973) [1943] 'Autistic Disturbances of Affective Contact.' In L. Kanner (ed.) *Childhood Psychosis: Initial Studies and New Insights*. Washington, DC: V.H. Winston. (Original work published in *The Nervous Child*, 1943.)

Kanner, L. and Eisenberg, L. (1956) 'Early infantile autism.' *American Journal of Orthopsychiatry 26*, 55–65.

Kern, L. and Vorndran, C.M. (2000) 'Functional assessment and intervention for transition difficulties.' *Journal of the Association for Persons with Severe Handicaps 25*, 212–16.

Kim, J.A., Szatmari, P., Bryson, S.E., Streiner, D.L. and Wilson, F.J. (2000) 'The prevalence of anxiety and mood problems among children with autism and Asperger syndrome.' *Autism 4*, 117–32.

Kinsbourne, M. (1987) 'Cerebral Brainstem Relations in Infantile Autism.' In E. Schopler and G.B. Mesibov (eds) *Neurobiological Issues in Autism*. New York: Plenum Press.

Klein, G.S. (1970) *Perception, Motives, and Personality*. New York: Knopf.

Klein, M. (1954) 'Psychoanalysis of Children.' In E. Jones (ed.) and J. Strachey (trans.) *International Psychoanalytic Library*. London: Hogarth Press.

Klin, A., Jones, W., Schulz, R., Volkmar, F. and Cohen, D. (2002) 'Defining and quantifying the social phenotype in autism.' *American Journal of Psychiatry 159* (6), 895–908.

Klin, A. and Volkmar, F.R. (2000) 'Treatment and Intervention Guidelines for Individuals with Asperger's Syndrome.' In A. Klin, F.R. Volkmar and S.S. Sparrow (eds) *Asperger Syndrome*. New York: Guilford Press.

Koegel, R.L. and Frea, W.D. (1993) 'Treatment of social behavior in autism through the modification of pivotal social skills.' *Journal of Applied Behavior Analysis 26*, 369–77.

Kuusikko, S., Haapsamo, H., Jansson-Verkasalo, E., Hurtig, T., Mattila, M., Ebeling, H. *et al.* (2009) 'Emotion recognition in children and adolescents with autism spectrum disorders.' *Journal of Autism and Developmental Disorders 39*, 938–45.

Lazarus, R.S. and Folkman, S. (1984) *Stress, Appraisal, and Coping*. New York: Springer.

Leekham, S., Libby, S., Wing, L., Gould, J. and Gillberg, C. (2000) 'Comparison of ICD-10 and Gillberg's criteria for Asperger syndrome.' *Autism 4*, 11–28.

Leyfer, O.T., Folstein, S.E., Bacalman, S., Davis, N.O., Dinh, E., Morgan, J. *et al.* (2006) 'Comorbid psychiatric disorders in children with autism: Interview development and rates of disorders.' *Journal of Autism and Developmental Disorders 36* (7), 849–61.

Lezak, M.D. (1995) *Neuropsychological Assessment*, 3rd Edition. Oxford: Oxford University Press.

Lovaas, O.I., Koegel, R.L. and Schreibman, L. (1979) 'Stimulus overselectivity in autism: A review of research.' *Psychological Bulletin 86*, 1236–54.

Loveland, K.A. and Landry, S.H. (1986) 'Joint attention and language in autism and developmental language delay.' *Journal of Autism and Developmental Disorders 16*, 335–49.

Mahler, M.S. (1952) 'On Child Psychosis and Schizophrenia: Autistic and Symbiotic Child Psychosis.' *Psychoanalytic Study of the Child*, Vol. 7. New York: International Universities Press.

Mahler, M.S. (1968) *On Human Symbiosis and the Vicissitudes of Individuation. Vol. I: Infantile Psychosis*. New York: International Universities Press.

Maslow, A.H. (1954) *Motivation and Personality*. New York: Harper.

McCandless, B.R. (1967) *Children: Behavior and Development*, 2nd Edition. New York: Holt, Rinehart, & Winston.

McEvoy, R.E., Roger, S.J. and Pennington, B.F. (1993) 'Executive function and social communication deficits in young autistic children.' *Journal of Child Psychology and Psychiatry and Allied Disciplines 34*, 563–78.

Mirsky, A.F., Anthony, B.J., Duncan, C.C., Ahearn, M.B. and Kellam, S.G. (1991) 'Analysis of the elements of attention: A neuropsychological approach.' *Neuropsychology Review 2*, 109–45.

Mishna, F. and Muskat, B. (1998) 'Group therapy for boys with features of Asperger syndrome and concurrent learning disabilities: Finding a peer group.' *Journal of Child and Adolescent Group Therapy 8* (3), 97–114.

Moore, C. and Corkum, V. (1994) 'Social understanding at the end of the first year of life.' *Developmental Review 14*, 349–72.

Mundy, P., Sigman,M. and Kasari, C. (1993) 'The Theory of Mind and Joint Attention Deficits in Autism.' In S. Cohen, H. Tager-Flusberg and D. Cohen (eds.) *Understanding other Minds: Perspectives from Autism.* Oxford: Oxford University Press.

Mundy, P., Sigman, M. and Kasari, C. (1994) 'Joint attention, developmental level, and symptom presentation in autism.' *Development and Psychopathology 6*, 389–401.

Muris, P., Steerneman, P., Merckelbach, H., Holdrinet, I. and Meesters, C. (1998) 'Comorbid anxiety symptoms in children with pervasive developmental disorders.' *Journal of Anxiety Disorders 12*, 387–93.

National Foundation for Autism Research (2010) 'Early Warning Signs of Autism.' Retrieved from www.nfar.org/en/what-is-autism/autism-signs.html.

National Research Council (2001) *Educating Children with Autism.* Committee on Educational Interventions for Children with Autism. C. Lord and J.P. McGee (eds), Division of Behavioral and Social Sciences and Education. Washington, DC: National Academy Press.

Nevin, J.A. (1996) 'The momentum of compliance.' *Journal of Applied Behavior Analysis 29*, 535–47.

Odem, S.L. and McConnell, S.R. (1985) 'A performance-based conceptualization of social competence of handicapped preschool children: Implications for assessment.' *Topics in Early Childhood Special Education 4*, 1–19.

Ornitz, E.M. (1989) 'Autism at the Interface between Sensory and Information Processing.' In G. Dawson (ed.) *Autism: Nature, Diagnosis, and Treatment.* New York: Guilford Press.

Paul, R. and Wilson, K.P. (2009) 'Assessing Speech, Language, and Communication in Autism Spectrum Disorders.' In S. Goldstein, J.A. Naglieri and S. Ozonoff (eds) *Assessment of Autism Spectrum Disorders.* New York: Guilford Press.

Pierce, K.L., Glad, K. and Schreibman, L. (1997) 'Social perception in children with autism: An attentional deficit.' *Journal of Autism and Developmental Disorders 27* (3), 261–78.

Pierce, K.L. and Schreibman, L. (1995) 'Increasing complex social behaviors in children with autism: Effects of peer implemented pivotal response training,'. *Journal of Applied Behavior Analysis 28*, 285–95.

Pierce, K.L. and Schreibman, L. (1997) 'Using peer trainers to promote social behavior in autism: Are they effective at enhancing multiple social modalities?' *Focus on Autism and Other Developmental Disabilities 12*, 207–18.

Provost, B., Lopez, B.R. and Heimerl, S. (2007) 'A comparison of motor delays in young children: Autism spectrum disorder, developmental delay, and developmental concerns.' *Journal of Autism and Developmental Disorders 37* (2), 321–8.

Ray, K.P., Skinner, C.H. and Watson, T.S. (1999) 'Transferring stimulus control via momentum to increase compliance in a student with autism: A demonstration of collaborative consultation.' *School Psychology Review 28*, 622–8.

Repp, A.C. and Karsh, K.G. (1994) 'Hypothesis-based intervention for tantrum behaviors of persons with developmental disabilities in school settings.' *Journal of Applied Behavioral Analysis 27*, 21–31.

Rie, H.E. (1971) 'Historical Perspectives of Concepts in Child Psychopathology.' In H.E. Rie (ed.) *Perspectives in Child Psychopathology*. Chicago: Aldine-Atherton.

Ritvo, E.R. (2006) *Understanding the Nature of Autism and Asperger's Disorder*. London: Jessica Kingsley Publishers.

Romano, J.P. and Roll, D. (2000) 'Expanding the utility of behavioral momentum for youth with developmental disabilities.' *Behavioral Interventions 15*, 99–111.

Rose-Krasnor, L. (1997) 'The nature of social competence: A theoretical review.' *Social Development 6*, 111–35.

Rosenn, D. (2002) 'Is it Asperger's or ADHD?' *AANE News 10*, 3–5.

Saarni, C. (1990) 'Emotional Competence.' In R. Thompson (ed.) *Nebraska Symposium: Socioemotional Development*. Lincoln, NE: University of Nebraska Press.

Santangelo, S.L. and Tsatsanis, K. (2005) 'What is known about autism: Genes, brain, and behavior.' *American Journal of Pharmacogenomics 5*, 71–92.

Scattone, D., Tingstrom, D.H. and Wilczynski, S.M. (2006) 'Increasing appropriate social interactions of children with autism spectrum disorders using Social Stories.' *Focus on Autism and Other Developmental Disabilities 21* (4), 211–22.

Schatz, A.M., Weimer, A.K. and Trauner, D.A. (2002) 'Brief report: Attention differences in Asperger syndrome.' *Journal of Autism and Developmental Disorders 32* (4), 333–6.

Schmit, J., Alper, S., Raschke, D. and Ryndak, D. (2000) 'Effects of using a photographic cueing package during routine school transitions with a child who has autism.' *Mental Retardation 38*, 131–7.

Schreibman, L., Whalen, C. and Stahmer, A.C. (2000) 'The use of video priming to reduce disruptive transition behavior in children with autism.' *Journal of Positive Behavior Interventions 2*, 3–11.

Selye, H. (1993) 'History of the Stress Concept.' In L. Goldberger and S. Breznitz (eds) *Handbook of Stress: Theoretical and Clinical Aspects*, 2nd Edition. New York, NY: The Free Press.

Sheinkopf, S.J. (2005) 'Hot topics in autism: Cognitive deficits, cognitive style, and joint attention dysfunction.' *Rhode Island Medical Association 88* (5), 152–8.

Shores, R.L. (1987) 'Overview of research on social interaction: A historical and personal perspective.' *Behavior Disorders 12*, 233–41.

Sigman, M., Mundy, P., Sherman, T. and Ungerer, J. (1986) 'Social interactions of autistic, mentally retarded, and normal children and their caregivers.' *Journal of Child Psychology and Psychiatry 27*, 647–56.

Singer, G.H., Singer, J. and Horner, R.H. (1987) 'Using pretask requests to increase the probability of compliance for students with severe disabilities.' *Journal of the Association for Persons with Severe Handicaps 12*, 287–91.

Sterling-Turner, H.E. and Jordan, S.S. (2007) 'Interventions addressing transition difficulties for individuals with autism.' *Psychology in the Schools 44* (7), 681–90.

Stevens, S. and Gruzelier, J. (1984) 'Electrodermal activity to auditory stimuli in autistic, retarded, and normal children.' *Journal of Autism and Developmental Disorders 14*, 245–60.

Suldo, S.M., Shaunessy, E. and Hardesty, R. (2008) 'Relationships among stress, coping, and mental health in high-achieving high school students.' *Psychology in the Schools 45* (4), 273–90.

Szatmari, P. (1991) 'Asperger's syndrome: Diagnosis, treatment, and outcome.' *Psychiatric Clinics of North America 14*, 81–93.

Szatmari, P., Bremner, R. and Nagy, J. (1989) 'Diagnostic criteria for Asperger's syndrome: A review of clinical features.' *Canadian Journal of Psychiatry 34*, 554–60.

Tonge, B.J., Brereton, A.V., Gray, K.M. and Einfeld, S.L. (1999) 'Behavioural and emotional disturbance in high-functioning autism and Asperger syndrome.' *Autism 3*, 117–30.

Tonge, B. and Einfeld, S. (2003) 'Psychopathology and Intellectual Disability: The Australian Child to Adult Longitudinal Study.' In L.M. Glidden (ed.) *International Review of Research in Mental Retardation* (Vol. 26). San Diego, CA: Academic Press.

Tustin, R.D. (1995) 'The effects of advance notice of activity transitions on stereotypic behavior.' *Journal of Applied Behavior Analysis 28*, 91–2.

Vilensky, J.A., Damasio, A.R. and Maurer, R.G. (1981) 'Gait disturbances in patients with autistic disorder: A preliminary study.' *Archives of Neurology 38* (10), 646–9.

Volden, J. and Johnston, J. (1999) 'Cognitive scripts in autistic children and adolescents.' *Journal of Autism and Developmental Disorders 29* (3), 203–11.

Volkmar, F.R., Lord, C., Bailey, A., Schultz, R.T. and Klin, A. (2004) 'Autism and pervasive developmental disorders.' *Journal of Child Psychology and Psychiatry 41*, 135–70.

Wilczynski, S.M., Menousek, K., Hunter, M. and Mudgal, D. (2007) 'Individualized education programs for youth with autism spectrum disorders.' *Psychology in the Schools 44* (7), 653–66.

Wing, L. (1981) 'Asperger's syndrome: A clinical account.' *Psychological Medicine 11*, 115–30.

Wing, L. (1988) 'The Continuum of Autistic Characteristics.' In E. Schopler and G. Mesibov (eds) *Diagnosis and Assessment in Autism*. New York: Plenum.

Wing, L. (1991) 'The Relationship between Asperger's Syndrome and Kanner's Autism.' In U. Frith (ed.) *Autism and Asperger Syndrome*. Cambridge: Cambridge University Press.

Wing, L. and Gould, J. (1979) 'Severe impairments of social interaction and associated abnormalities in children: Epidemiology and classification.' *Journal of Autism and Developmental Disorders 9*, 11–29.

World Health Organization (1978) *International Classification of Diseases*, 9th Edition. Geneva: World Health Organization.

World Health Organization (1993) *International Classification of Diseases*, 10th Edition. Geneva: World Health Organization.

Yalom, I.D. (2005) *The Theory and Practice of Group Psychotherapy*, 5th Edition. New York: Basic Books.

Subject Index

affective expression 83–4
anxiety 70
Asperger's Disorder (AD)
   diagnosis of 19, 22
   historical background to 28
   as part of ASD 13
   as part of PDD 16, 17
   prevalence of 16
assessment
   in group interventions
      132–4
   in SCEP 131-2
attention
   assessment of 137, 149
   description of 85–7
   flexible attention 88
   focused attention 87
   and Group adaptations and
      perspective taking 205,
      207
   and Group cohesion 195,
      197
   and Group formation and
      orientation 191, 193
   and Group stability,
      relationships, and
      connections 200, 202
   joint attention 98–91
   selective attention 88
   sustained attention 87
   tasks and activities for 214,
      215, 216, 219, 223,
      238–9, 240–1, 252–3,
      264–5, 276–7, 280–1,
      289–90
   and Terminations, loss, and
      endings 210, 212
Autism Spectrum Disorders
   (ASD)

behavior range in 13–14
definition of 16–17, 21
diagnosis of 29–30
early history in 22–6
as group of disorders 13
historical background to
   22–30
later history in 26–9
as part of PDD 17
prevalence of 16
and social competence
   15–16, 41–2
and social development
   34–6
and social interaction 32–4
stress and anxiety in 69–70,
   71
Autistic Disorder (AuD)
   diagnosis of 17–19, 29
   and High-Functioning
      Autism (HFA) 18–19
   as part of ASD 13
   as part of PDD 16, 17
"Autistic Disturbance of
   Affective Contact"
   (Kanner) 24
"Autistic Psychopathy of
   Childhood" (Asperger) 25
Autogenic Relaxation Training
   (ART) 80–1, 313–15

behavior area 58–60

"cautious contentment" 71–3
change see flexibility
Chapter 5: The end 289–90
child roles within SCEP
   316–23

Childhood Disintegrative
   Disorder (CDD) 16–17
Circles of people we know
   266–7
cognitive/executive function
   area
   assessment of 139–40
   as core area of development
      55–7
communication area
   as core of area of
      development 57–8
   and Group adaptations and
      perspective taking 206,
      208
   and Group cohesion 196–7,
      198
   and Group formation and
      orientation 192, 193
   and Group stability,
      relationships, and
      connections 201, 203
   tasks and activities for 215,
      216, 221, 224, 260–1,
      266–7, 276–7, 278–9,
      282–3, 293–4
   and Terminations, loss, and
      endings 211, 213
core areas of development
   and behavior area 58–60
   and cognitive/executive
      function area 55–7
   and commuication area
      57–8
   and emotion area 52–5
   and motor area 61
   and SCEP 47
   and sensory area 60–1

Author Index

CPI Antony Rowe
Eastbourne, UK
June 20, 2023